Walking Cities: **London**

SECOND EDITION

Walking Cities: London (second edition) brings together a new interdisciplinary field of artists, writers, architects, musicians, human geographers and philosophers to consider how a city walk informs and triggers new processes of making, thinking, researching and communicating. In particular, the book examines how the city contains narratives, knowledge and contested materialities that are best accessed through the act of walking.

The varied contributions take the form of short stories, illustrated essays, personal reflections and accounts of walks both real and fictional. While artist and Royal Collage of Art (RCA) tutor Rut Blees Luxemburg and philosopher Jean-Luc Nancy recount a nocturnal journey from Shoreditch to the City of London; architect Peter St John of the practice Caruso St John offers a detailed and personal reflection on the Holloway Road; and architect and author Douglas Murphy examines what he calls London's 'more politically charged locations' in his account of a solitary walk through an area of South London. Ultimately, *Walking Cities: London* seeks to understand the wider significance of changing geographies to generate critical questions and creative perspectives for navigating the social and political impact of rapid urban change.

Jaspar Joseph-Lester is an artist, Reader in Art and Post-Urbanism and Head of MA Sculpture at the Royal College of Art.

Simon King is co-founder of the Walkative project and Tutor at the Royal College of Art.

Amy Blier-Carruthers is a lecturer at the Royal Academy of Music and King's College London.

Roberto Bottazzi is an architect and Director of MA Urban Design at the Bartlett, University College London (UCL).

Walking Cities:

Contributors
Rosana Antoli, Sean Ashton, Rut Blees Luxemburg, Amy Blier-Carruthers, David Dernie, Duncan Jeffs, Esther Leslie, Jaspar Joseph-Lester, Adam Kaasa, Ahuvia Kahane, Nayan Kulkarni, Sharon Kivland, Douglas Murphy, Jean-Luc Nancy, Laura Oldfield Ford, Steve Pile, Peter Sheppard Skærved, Phil Smith, Tom Spooner,Peter St. John, Jo Stockham and Richard Wentworth.

London

SECOND EDITION

NEW YORK AND LONDON

Second edition published 2020
by Routledge
52 Vanderbilt Avenue, New York, NY 10017

and by Routledge
2 Park Square, Milton Park, Abingdon, Oxon, OX14 4RN

Routledge is an imprint of the Taylor & Francis Group, an informa business

First edition published by Camberwell Press 2016
Second edition published by Routledge 2020

Library of Congress Cataloging-in-Publication Data
A catalogue record has been requested for this book.

ISBN: 9780367407919 (hbk)
ISBN: 9780367407896 (pbk)
ISBN: 9780367809072 (ebk)

Typeset in Sabon and Akzidenz Grotesk
by Samuel Jones

Publisher's Note
This book has been prepared from camera-ready copy provided by the editors.

Contents

Monuments

Music

Dialogue

Introduction

Walking Cities: London explores how the temporal realities revealed through urban walking can act as a method for dialogical, cognitive and empirical mapping. The meandering lines and shapes formed when we walk are traced throughout the pages of this book, in which wandering is directly associated with how we think and feel in an urban context. These walks include both real and fictional accounts of areas in and around London. There are critical interventions into the fabric of the city and along its edges, imagined urban landscapes and night walks through financial zones. Also included are mythogeographical drifts and point-to-point guides, solitary wanderings and dialogical tours. Here walking is situated as art, writing, pilgrimage and protest; walking as constituting boundaries and transgressing boundaries; walking as personal and public; walking as compliance and defiance; walking as wild, mediated and constructed; walking as interpretive, generative and embodied. *Walking Cities: London* speaks of how the city exists as *many* cities, multi-layered, constructed from a myriad of overlapping cultural, social, historical, political and economic paths.

Through bringing together a new interdisciplinary field of artists, writers, architects, musicians, human geographers and philosophers we, the editors of this book, consider how the city walk informs and triggers new processes of making, thinking, researching and communicating, in particular, how the city contains narratives, knowledge and contested materialities that are best accessed through the act of walking. At the core of this enquiry is our shared interest in walking as cognitive method: while the serendipitous and contingent events and encounters that take place during a walk are non-repeatable, it is also the case that walking can function as a tool for activating thought and unlocking knowledge. How then does the act of walking constitute a methodological practice across disciplines? What can we learn from the various ways it is employed by artists, architects, musicians, philosophers and writers? The contributors to this book bring a new range of insights and perspectives to these questions through deploying the city walk as a critical mode of enquiry.

Much of the fallacy of contemporary urbanism – and how it is taught – has to do with its insistence on form, on finished products, and their assumed ability to control the evolution of a city. However, the city – perhaps more than ever – is the result of elusive forces whose presence can only be perceived indirectly or for a limited period of time: the rapid transformations of urban landscapes under the pressure of global capital, climate change, migratory fluxes, etc. Walking through the streets of London is a powerful tool for architects to unearth how physical and immaterial forces are interwoven, a slow, forensic exercise that reveals elements of unnoticed livelihood, traces of profound mutations, and scars that will hardly heal. The mental and physical maps described through walking are pregnant with possibilities seeking broader, lateral tactics that open up unconventional approaches to design. Peter St John takes us through the roads of the North London he experiences daily to show its dynamic and incomplete nature, one that never fails to surprise the walker. He trains our eyes to appreciate London's apparent visual background noise in which he finds a distinctive trait of the capital's urbanism. Douglas Murphy's walk crosses the river stretches from Deptford to Elephant and Castle, via a series of key housing estates. The cross-section he draws through his walk is architectural as much as political: large new developments mark a re-alignment in the ideologies shaping London. The Barbican provides the stage for Adam Kaasa's walk: the infamously meandering network of walkways of this vast housing complex provides a space of resistance for the urban walker. The Barbican's often-frustrating spatial intricacy is here seen as a healthy counterpoint to the prevailing idea that successful public spaces should be flowing and smooth.

In the last two walks of this first section (*Site*), it is the very materiality of the city, its 'deep' and visceral qualities that take centre stage. Roberto Bottazzi's walk takes us to the edges of London, to a fairly innocuous urban artefact–Gravesend-Broadness weather station–whose unusually high temperature readings have found themselves at the centre of the debate on climate change. Tangled up in even bigger and more controversial conversations on the Anthropocene, walking is here a means to survey and familiarize oneself with a strange landscape in which man-made and natural can no longer be distinguished. In the last contribution to this section, David Dernie takes us back to the very centre of London, to Tottenham Court Road. As Dernie repeatedly covers the length of this short and busy London road, he deliberately slows down his pace allowing the complex narratives, objects and materials which give meaning to the urban experience, to surface.

Increasingly produced and encountered outside the gallery, art often takes the form of interventions into urban public space intended to produce immediate and unpredictable public responses. Much of the work in this book is informed by these shifts within contemporary art. The role of walking is often directly connected to the critical and creative engagement that artists have with their changing urban environment. These first-hand encounters with the social and physical geographies of the city provide material in the form of encounter, protest, documentary, spatial narratives, actions, participation, risk, collaboration, fiction, chance and spectacle. It is here that we explore how urban walking connects disciplines and facilitates a range of processes and methods for the production of new critical modes that situate art within the context of our contemporary urban condition.

In section two, *Night*, we consider night walking as key to the way many artists work, think and research. Rut Blees Luxemburg and Jean-Luc Nancy take a nocturnal and circuitous journey from Shoreditch through the City of London to the soundtrack of Hans Zender's interpretation of the first *lied* of Schubert's *Winterreise:* Gute Nacht. The journey starts with a ruin–the ancient columns of an abandoned city–and passes the stone pillars of the Bank of England, the tents of Occupy in Finsbury Square and the construction sites of current corporate development. Nayan Kulkarni takes us on another nocturnal journey, from the heart of global capitalist quasi-public realm spaces in Canary Wharf to private and social housing developments along the pathways to Mile End Park. These architectural episodes are intercut with layers of transport infrastructure, recreational spaces and pedestrian pathways that give an insight into the role played by electric light in determining the economic and social condition of different areas of the city.

In *Writing*, the third section of this book, we focus on how the written word underscores our experience of walking the city. 'Point to Point' is a short story written by Sean Ashton in the form of a walking guide. The walk in the story is mostly underground, encompassing the spiral staircase in Russell Square tube station and the area of nearby Mecklenburgh Square. The story alternates between the literal and the imaginative, culminating in a brief tour of Mecklenburgh Square, the entirety of which – as Jaspar Joseph-Lester's equally fictional Public Notice reminds us – has just been relocated to New Songdo in South Korea. Addressed to local residents, the public notice purports to be from a multinational developer called 'TRANSHERITAGE'. The letter is placed on the residents' noticeboard and gives details of the removal and transportation of Mecklenburgh Square and gardens to the newly built 'smart city' New Songdo. This intervention raises questions regarding new forms of land ownership that determine and restrict the way we navigate and use the city.

In Laura Oldfield Ford's 'The Rotherhithe Caryatids' we move through a traumatized urban landscape undergoing social atomization and the deterritorialization of communal relations. The walk starts in Southwark Park by the statues of the twin Caryatids and ends at the recently demolished Heygate Estate. Through the course of this journey we encounter desolate spaces and the ruins of social networks that have been under assault as a result of the radical reordering of urban space through rapid urban development and the increasing privatization of land.

In *Monuments* we explore how London monuments are encountered through walking and consider what role these fixed landmarks play in helping us navigate the fast-changing social and physical geographies of the city. As Ahuvia Kahane points out while circumnavigating Nelson's Column, 'It [walking] goes around in circles, like all true thought. It lifts the veils of illusion from our purposeful Apollonian actions and our busy metropolitan lives. Walking unconceals.' City monuments, when psychogeographically encountered, can be experienced as a form of this unconcealing. That is, they act as both interrogative and exclamatory punctuation points as well as footnotes to time, place and personal and collective memory. It could be argued that monuments produce modes of participation–that we perform around them both in our minds and with our bodies. They are meeting places, sites of rallies, protests and celebrations. The city monument is sometimes a destination but is often overlooked, ignored, invisible to passers-by, hidden in plain sight.

As a radical experiment in communal living as well as part solution to London's protracted post-war housing crisis, the London squatting movement enjoyed two key 'waves' of influence in Somers Town in the early 1970s and then again in the mid-1980s. In her walk around this part of north London Esther Leslie describes Somers Town as 'a compressed location–a road bounded rectangle of intensity' where housing has always been an 'issue'. The reader is taken on a tour of key sites–the now disappeared, decaying or vestigial monuments that include the mass squatting of the abandoned Brewer's estate houses in North Somers Town in the early 1970s and the large squats in decayed flats deemed 'unfit for human habitation', in South Somers Town in the mid-1980s. The text explores London at a time of change, a city preparing for a whole new level of privatisation and control. We visit Somers Town as a site of lost monuments to communal, anarchistic and creative living. In her illustrated walk through Surrey Quays and Southwark Park Jo Stockham asks '...can a smell be a monument? Are the enveloping tons of particulates poisoning city dwellers an atomised monument to lack of foresight?' This olfactory line of thinking, much like that prompted by Marcel Proust's madeleine in *Swann's Way*, is the trigger for the reverie that follows, an involuntary memory that immerses the writer and reader in time travel to revisit some of the landmarks of this part of Southwark's past and present. The effect of all this is heady, not unlike the writing in Jonathan Raban's *The Soft City* and jump-cut montage in Julien Temple's documentary *London, The Modern Babylon.*

Sharon Kivland and Steve Pile track back over Freud's arrival in London on 6 June 1939, stitching together the fragments of Freud's journey through the city with a series of 1930s postcards of well-known monuments. Freud writes on the back of a postcard of the Queen Eleanor Memorial Cross *These monuments, then, resemble hysterical symptoms in being mnemic symbols.* From Charing Cross the walk continues to Victoria Station, ending at the Victoria Memorial, working back from manifest content through a chain of connections (as in dream analysis).

In the final walk in this section Ahuvia Kahane takes us to Trafalgar Square. Kahane suggests that 'walking leaves us with "nothing to do" but *think*'. Nelson's Column, one of London's most important imperial monuments, replicates a pattern of 'enclosure and shrine' found, on the one hand, in ancient imperial monuments such as Trajan's Column, and, on the other hand, in the monumental architecture of the early Eastern Church, a pattern that deliberately (and, in the case of monumental columns, literally) elevates the person or object at its centre to the level of an 'illegible' divine cipher. Yet modern secularity and politics and the nature and scale of Trafalgar Square as a large 'walking', and thus 'thinking' space, also bear out the ideological 'emptiness' of the cipher of empire and effects an 'erasure' of its ideological claim. This explains Trafalgar Square's paradoxical character as both a space of 'empire' and the prominent site of 'anti-imperial' protest.

The act of walking as a central part of the creative process has been important to many musicians through history. Beethoven used to walk in the countryside around Vienna, carrying a notebook in readiness should he have an idea for a melody that he wanted to jot down.[1] Composers such as Tchaikovsky, Chopin, Britten, Satie, and Mahler all walked as part of their creative practice, thinking of ideas, developing them in their heads, writing them down as their habits dictated, or refreshing their minds for their next session at the piano or composing desk.[2] One might accuse these musicians of being eccentric or idle, pretending that walking was a useful activity rather than an act of procrastination. However, scientific findings have recently started to show that there may be something in this instinct to get up and walk after all. Moments of creativity and flashes of insight are now traceable in the brain, and it would seem that walking is one way of encouraging such 'eureka moments'.[3] Psychologist Jonathan Schooler's research shows that when engaged in a creative piece of work, allowing your mind to wander by breaking off to do a non-demanding task – such as walking – has been shown to allow creative thoughts to surface.[4]

The *Music* section of this book focuses on walking as a source of inspiration and reverie, and on the correlation between walking as a method or process and the discipline of learning to observe the small details of one's life, surroundings and artistic practice. Musicians are often engaged in the act of making and doing, but how might they capture these processes in order to be able to look at them more objectively? In order to look at creative endeavour as a social practice – to capture fleeting processes rather than focusing on an end product (the final performance or the finished composition) – they need different tools. By using a walking methodology to observe the details of their familiar surroundings, musicians and other creative practitioners may be able to discover a new objectivity, a renewed self-awareness, a new view of space, time and self.

As a musicologist and violinist, Amy Blier-Carruthers has developed a research area that focuses on how musicians engage in the act of music-making, both in a live orchestral context and a studio context. Her text elucidates ways in which it is possible to capture and reflect upon artistic processes, using ethnographic techniques such as close observation and the taking of field-notes, as well as by entering into a 'travelling mindset'[5] that tries to see familiar things in a new light. Peter Sheppard Skærved is a violinist whose daily ritual includes walking long distances across city and country. His text offers a link between the act of walking and nightly sessions practising the violin. This dialogue is mapped out on a walk from Hampton Court to his home in Wapping, describing the ways in which various pieces of music are woven in counterpoint with what he sees and thinks along the path.

The post-walk writings in the final section of this book emerge[6] from a series of 'before, during and after' dialogic exchanges and fragments between the writers and Simon King. This methodology requires a way of thinking about urban space–approaching it, *inter alia*, through the prism of time travel, detection, serendipity and artistic and journalistic enquiry. The contributions are thus ordered not by strict chronology but rather by two main tendencies. The first, uniting Phil Smith and Tom Spooner, is of mythogeography–a neologism that, 'emphasises the multiple nature of places and suggests multiple ways of celebrating, expressing and weaving those places and their multiple meanings'[7]. The second, uniting the artists Rosana Antoli and Duncan Jeffs is that of seeing, '[a] multi-faceted city that represents ideological concepts, economic forces, and social spaces that reflect a diversity of cultural, historical and geographical markers.'[8]

Phil Smith's walk 'Curling Up Tight' begins with an invitation: to meet at Paddington Station and explore the mythogeography from there. Along the way, we navigate by foundry insignia on drain covers, boundary markers, a woman with plastic bags and a discussion about a gendered representation of the Holy Spirit.

We move in loops until we find the fulcrum of the walk, with faded views of the City of God, speeding up and closing the noose. Tom Spooner's 'The Sound of Sweetness on the Grand Union Canal' is, in part, inspired by the mythogeography of Phil Smith. The walk is a drift along a section of the Paddington Branch of the Grand Union Canal. During it, we revisit some of the unusually alluring non-spaces encountered much earlier by Spooner as an undergraduate. Driven by a Romantic sense of ruin lust, we attempt to conjure a spirit of place and identify with the poetic in the everyday. The nature of the walk, we agree, feels situated somewhere between the profoundly poetic and a postmodern parody.

'Walkative: A Choreography of Resistance' is a 'rewalking' in which we start at Mile End underground station and walk westwards, via Whitechapel Road, towards Aldgate East. Along the way, we talk about Rosana's performance piece that has inspired this – a chance encounter that resulted in a stranger's 'dance walk' through two bordering but economically and socially very distinct zones. We reflect on the themes that emerged then and seem clear now: choreography, resistance, exclusion, utopia and failure. Duncan Jeffs' title 'The Optimists' alludes both to a long forgotten film by Peter Sellers and the appeal to luxury living – as seen on the corporate hoardings around Nine Elms. The walk, then, traces a circle around two adjacent worlds. Starting on Wandsworth Road, we cross the invisible borders between the labyrinthine estates of Savona and Patmore and the looming developments that are redefining the area of Nine Elms. The conversation on our walk is responsive, raising questions about place, culture, community and the transience or permanence of these things in the distinctive zones covered in our circuit.

On the inside covers of this book are two photographs selected from Richard Wentworth's archive 'Making Do and Getting By'. These temporary assemblages are familiar to anyone that has spent any time walking the streets of London. They are placeholders, temporary fabrications that are precariously balanced. Like the other work included in this book, these images help us to see the city as an inventive, transitory and unsettled landscape. It is with this image that we draw to the end of our journey.

[1] Nicholas Cook, *Music: A Very Short Introduction*, Oxford: Oxford University Press, 1998, p. 65.

[2] Mason Currey, *Daily Rituals: How Great Minds Make Time, Find Inspiration, and Get to Work*, London: Picador, 2013.

[3] 'The Creative Brain: How Insight Works', *Horizon*, BBC 2, 2012–13.

[4] Jonathan Schooler, University of California, Santa Barbara. See Baird, B, Smallwood, J., Mrazek, M.D., Kam, J., Franklin, M.S. and Schooler, J.W., 'Inspired by Distraction: Mind-Wandering Facilitates Creative Incubation'. *Psychological Science*, XX(X), 2012, pp. 1–6.

[5] Alain de Botton, *The Art of Travel*, London: Penguin, 2003, p. 246.

[6] The use of this verb as opposed to, for example, 'result', is deliberate and alludes to Emergence theory. See Steven Johnson, Introduction, 'Here Comes Everybody!' in *Emergence: The Connected Lives of Ants, Brains, Cities and Software*, London: Penguin Books, 2001.

[7] www.mythogeography.com

[8] Allen Siegel quoted in *Screening the City*, ed. M. Shiel and T; Fitzmaurice, London: Verso, 2003, p. 143.

Site

West London Union Workhouse
Upper Holloway Stan
National Schools
Tollington Nursery
Chapel
Grove Ho
Friends Meeting Ho
Manor Ho
Signal Post
Nursery
St Georges Ch
Tufnell Park
ST MARY ISLI
Lower Holloway
3109
Tollington Road
Isledon Road
Citizen Road
Coal Depot
St Lukes Church
Montpelier House
Camden Road

PETER ST JOHN

My Kind of Town

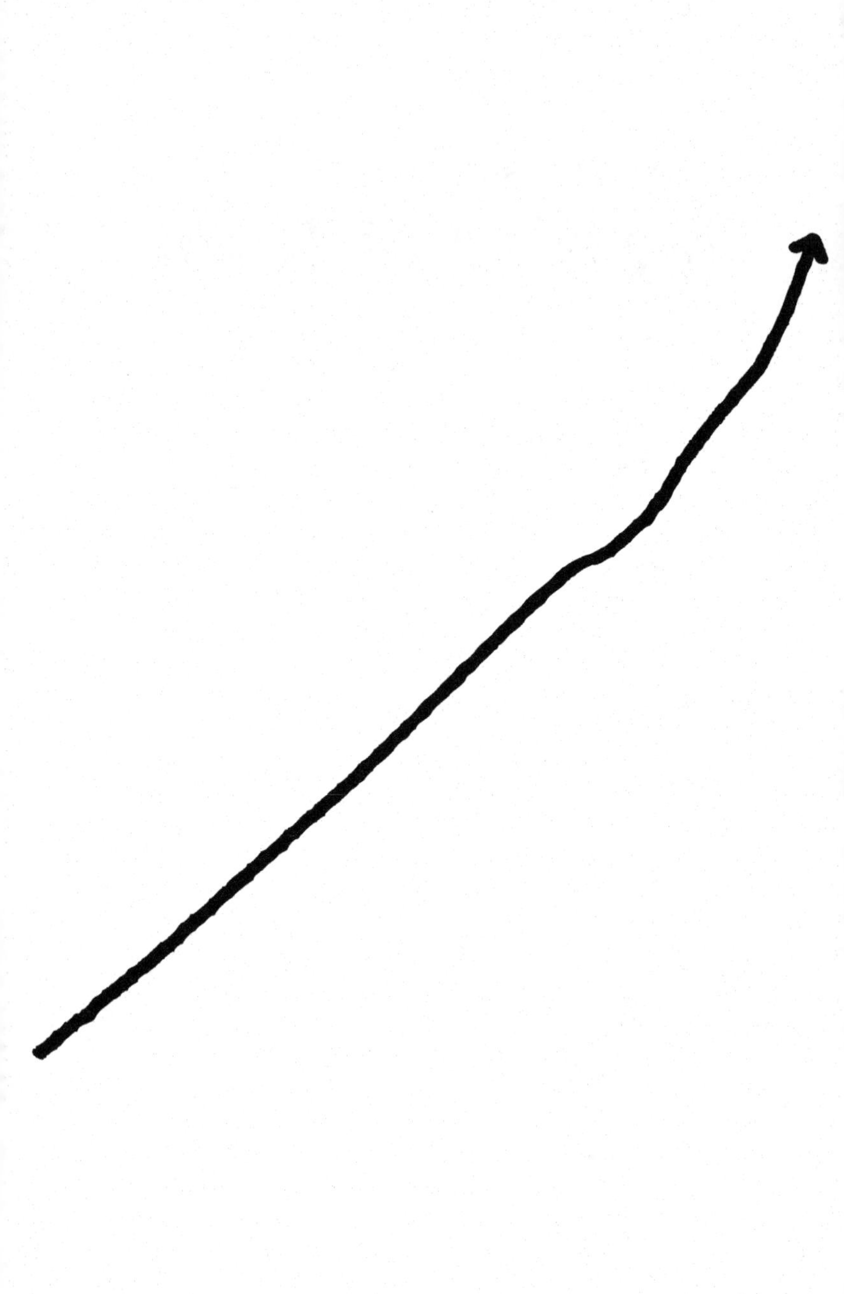

Someone once told me that to look hard and long at what you're doing, it helps to rest and look out of the window occasionally... to a background. I've always liked spending as much time as I can gazing out of windows – whether of houses or offices, cars or trains – and dreaming.

That's what I like about London. It's almost all background. With no grand urban form and no picturesque topographical features, its fabric is the particularity of everyone else's daily life. Every frame of the film from the window is a particular piece of time, without the beginning or the end.

The bulk of London is housing, and in few cities is housing so consistently distributed across the centre and around its institutions. The predominance of speculative terrace housing with gardens has meant that the city is low to the ground and shoulder to shoulder. And yet there is every type of housing. A tower block is like a terrace on end and in both types a home is a repeated piece of a large building the scale of which, when put close to other buildings, is always metropolitan. Everyone sleeps to the sound of fast traffic on a through-route a few blocks away.

To analyse London too much feels unnatural because its urbanism is anti-plan. Its condition reflects complex patterns of ownership and private actions, where neither crown nor state has ever held too strong a sway. Wandering through the city one can imagine a past landscape of fields, streams and tracks whose geography has determined an urban fabric in which you can never see far down a street and the buildings change regularly. In diversity there is tolerance and my favourite pieces of the city are those in which change is visible and the ongoing negotiation between new and old is most extreme. Between The Angel, Islington and London Wall, on my cycle route to work, there is dense public and private housing of every scale from the past 200 years. Sometimes the buildings face the street, sometimes they're free standing, but often you have an unintended, informal view of them. Seen together, the street has an unimaginable formal diversity. In this openness is space for architects to breathe.

Some people would laugh if you described my neighbourhood, Holloway Road in north London, as a university town. Yet it contains most of the faculties of one of London's largest universities interspersed between commercial and public buildings, and a residential population to match that of a small city. There are parks and churches, factories and warehouses. But unusually for a town, they all front on to the main road, stretched out in a jumbled row, with no precedence given to any of them.

The road is wide, too rough and ugly to be described as a high street, but with useful shops. Its width and length give the road an epic quality with fast traffic, broad pavements and a fantastic variety of commercial uses. The dimension of the road and the slightly windy environment gives an air of slackness to many of the shops. Extremely peculiar window displays catch the imagination–some of them haven't changed in the ten years I have known them. Everyone's favourite is the bespoke shoemaker's, which has a single red-sequinned high boot in the window, bending at the knee. Each time you pass it you can speculate on who asked for it to be made.

Although the mood varies, combinations of these crude characteristics give identity to most of London's neighbourhoods, each of them accessible one from the other by Tube. This lack of a single centre is the character of the city. To benefit Londoners rather than tourists, architects of influence should spend more time thinking about London's neighbourhoods and less about cultural centralisation.

I like the humming sound of the double-decker buses on the road and the way they lean impossibly over the pavements at the stops, bringing their front doorsteps right to you. Opposite the Hope workers' cafe, an owner has cut a four-storey reinforced concrete warehouse building in two, taken away half, and is now building a metal facade on the exposed face. Out of the window of the cafe I watch the red buses go by and wonder why architects don't make such extraordinary acts, when the city around them shows such imagination.

RIVER THAMES
SOUTHWARK
SURREY COMMERCIAL DOCKS
WEST INDIA DOCK
POPLAR
ISLE OF DOGS
DEPTFORD
ST. PAUL DEPTFORD

DOUGLAS MURPHY

London Has to Continually Refresh its Offer

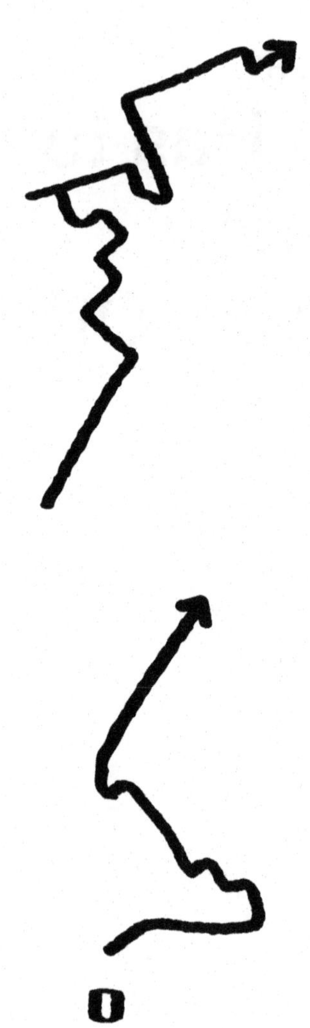

0

1. The Thames at Deptford

This text describes a solitary journey undertaken in February 2016.

I began on a set of waterman's stairs on the Thames at Deptford, in the shadow of the high dock walls of Convoy's Wharf, one of the last empty spaces by the river close to the centre of the city. Convoy's Wharf faces the Isle of Dogs and the financial district of Canary Wharf, still expanding and adding yet more towers to its skyline.

The aim of the walk was to head westwards from the river through South London, gradually turning northwards until I met the Thames again six miles upriver. The intention was not only to explore some areas I had never visited before, but also to experience a slice of the city at a time of rapid change, and to examine some of its more politically charged locations.

The act of walking in order to produce writing and images is clearly related to the way we move around the city in our everyday lives, but it is undertaken with artificially heightened attention. The spaces we pass through are mostly experienced as background, and we often do not notice them at all until something suddenly changes—a new shop opens, or a building is demolished—and the altered city suddenly demands our attention.

But a city is constantly in flux, and a walk like this attempts to see everything as if new, in the hope that it can give a greater sense of the varied social, political, economic and natural forces that have led to a city to being just as it is, that one moment in which it is encountered.

2. Deptford Wharf

Convoy's Wharf was originally a Tudor dockyard, and until recently an unloading dock for products for the newspaper industry, but the Olympia Warehouse with its listed iron structure is one of the only buildings left

standing. Elsewhere, almost all of the previous structures from the 16th to the 20th centuries have been demolished, but various layers of history are etched out in the changing materials across the ground, where docks have been infilled, alms houses demolished, warehouses have come and gone.

3. Just what we need, more homes for the rich

Convoy's Wharf is owned by Hutcheson Whampoa Properties, who recently gained permission for 3,500

houses to be built on the site, after a planning application was 'called in' by Boris Johnson, mayor of London. The local council, Lewisham, had recommended it be rejected, partly on historic grounds, and partly for its massive size–the plans include three 40-storey residential towers. The developer appealed to the mayor to intervene, and as he has done many times over his tenure, he overruled local representatives to give consent.

4. Murals and mattresses

Surrounding the new development is an area mainly made up of post-war housing, in what is a particularly

deprived part of London. Duly, campaigners were concerned that the new development of 'luxury' housing would be a social humiliation, gated away behind the dock wall.

A middle-aged man and elderly woman were out walking. When they saw I was taking photographs of the surroundings, the man offered an exaggerated Marilyn Monroe-esque pose, and they walked past laughing – "I'm ready for my close-up!"

5. Cannons and Bastions

The Pepys Estate, built from 1966 to 1973, borders Convoy's Wharf alongside the river. When built, it was seen as a flagship estate in the Greater London Council portfolio, and consisted of three large tower blocks surrounded by slabs, low-rise housing and a shopping centre, all linked together by a network of elevated walkways. A vast improvement on the slums that its residents had been trapped in previously, it began life as a model of just how successful council housing could be.

That didn't stop the incorrigible snob John Betjeman from snorting, in 1969: "Where can be the heart that sends a family to the twentieth floor in such a slab as this? It can't be right, caged half-way up the sky [...] What is housing, if it's not a home?" Sure enough, by the 1980s the Pepys had become a by-word for trouble. In multi-ethnic Lewisham it was known to be a bastion of the National Front, and was seen as a no-go zone of drug addicts and criminals.

6. Walkways

In 2002, Lewisham Council sold the tower closest to the river to Berkeley Homes, who proceeded to build an extra five storeys on top to create penthouses, and added a new entrance block facing the river, so new private residents could avoid passing through the estate whose building they had taken over.

7. and Crenellations

The architecture of the Pepys Estate is bold, with the

uppermost flats of the slabs seemingly crenellated by the cutting away of large terraces on the top floors. Plastic windows have been installed, as have secure entry points with jolly rounded arches, but the effect is still of powerful, sturdy blocks, plenty of light and space, with nothing to apologise for.

8. Cranes and cul-de-sacs

Even before the riverside tower was sold off, the Pepys Estate had been through a process of being carved up. Most of its walkways are gone, the result of a fever for deck demolition that swept the UK in the 1980s, and much of its housing has been demolished, especially at the more valuable end of the site towards the water. This has been replaced in parts with newer blocks built in

the modest, multi-materialed manner that was popular during the late 90s and early 2000s, while further back, some suburban cul-de-sacs have been incongruously shunted in.

9. Greenland Place

Barratt, best known as a builder of suburban semi-detached homes, are prolifically building modern blocks and towers all over London. Of this development, they say: "Located in an exciting area of south London undergoing a major regeneration, Greenland Place is set to become a vibrant new area to live, shop and relax in."

10. Alloa Road

Leaving the Pepys Estate, crossing Evelyn Street with its heavy construction lorries blasting back and forth between building sites, I walked through small pockets of Victorian speculative housing, hemmed in against the railways that spill out eastwards from London Bridge. Small, with no semi-basement floors, they are salvaged examples of the slum housing that was neither flattened by bombs nor pulled down after the war.

11. Grand Surrey Canal

Further west and these patches of old housing give way to a business park, isolated by a tangle of railway lines crossing this way and that, a stubborn reminder of a previous economic regime, of the docks and factories that once dominated this area by the Thames. This arrow-straight road leads down the former route of the Grand Surrey Canal, filled in as the docks died out.

12. Creative Space

"Creative Space to let" read the sign. The celebrated repurposing of unused industrial space by artists in areas such as Clerkenwell and Shoreditch occurred in an era when the pressure on growth and land prices was less intense. Now, spaces of this type are far more likely to be completely redeveloped as maximised apartment blocks, the slackness of re-used space a memory from cheaper times.

A young man with a beard and carrying an expensive camera walked the other way, and as I turned back a short time later I saw him taking a photograph from the same point I had stood to take mine. Perhaps he was himself looking for creative space.

13. Real Streets

Further west, the housing returns to the neo-vernacular type, dating from the 1980s or 90s, many with crosses of St George hanging from the windows. As I walked, a glowering young man wobbled haphazardly past on a mountain bike, turned abruptly off the pavement into a garden, then dumped the bike behind a wall and ran back off in the direction he'd come.

14. Peace on the streets

The 'midnight bus' belongs to the From Boyhood to Manhood Foundation, a programme that aims to help lost young men from all the communities of Southwark, in danger of falling out of education and employment and becoming involved in gang culture.

15. Bermondsey Works

Along a tight sliver of land between two roads, Bermondsey Works – "A collection of 1, 2 & 3 bedroom luxury apartments, penthouses & villas in South London's newest destination." – is under construction, although the digital renderings designed to entice the viewers were being somewhat undermined by the realities of the site itself.

I turned a corner onto the Old Kent Road, cheapest spot on the Monopoly board, choking with traffic, surrounded by builders' merchants and do-it-yourself stores, anti-urban shopping boxes set in loose car parks.

16. Estate map

17. Estate territory

Like the Pepys, the North Peckham Estate eschewed the prevailing methods of concrete panel construction, instead sticking to a stock brick, in an effort to offer a higher quality of housing to that which had been the case with many of the British panel-built estates. From snaking blocks at its northernmost, North Peckham runs for another kilometre to the south through a grid of housing, originally accessed via decks.

The estate was already notorious when 10-year-old Damilola Taylor was killed there in 2000, stabbed with a broken bottle by a couple of gang boys barely older than he was. The estate was known for its extreme poverty and gang violence, and as in so many other cases the design itself took a lot of the blame. Throughout

the last decade, much of the estate has been demolished and replaced with more conventional housing, but the social and economic problems of the neighbourhood remain.

18. The Aylesbury

Turning north, I crossed Burgess Park, a wide green space that has been progressively formed by demolishing built-up land over the years since WWII, a 20th century park to add to the Victorian municipals.

On a recently laid-out BMX track, a young man – a musician, an actor? – was being photographed, perhaps for the cover of a magazine, as a group of boys on bikes repeatedly cycled past him in formation.

Under a darkening sky, the tall slabs of the Aylesbury Estate loomed sullenly. Another of the vast and notorious South London council estates of the late 1960s, the Aylesbury is said to be the largest housing estate in all of western Europe, and stretches for kilometres in all directions, with long slab blocks ranging from four to fourteen storeys, built from the Jesperson concrete panel system.

19. A fairer future for all

The signs on the hoardings at ground level, topped with anti-climb protection, read: "Building a Fairer Future for all on the Aylesbury", and in smaller print: "We are investing in the Aylesbury in order to provide new homes, jobs, better open spaces and community facilities for local people. Half of all the new homes will be

affordable–higher than any other similar scheme in London, and will include low cost home ownership and social rented homes. We want to provide homes for everyone and are building more three- and four-bedroomed homes for families and extra care homes to help more people live independently in their community."

Why this development billboard would have been written in such a defensive tone was made clear by less official texts that were visible on the building itself: "Public housing not private profit" and "These used to be the offices of Southwark's planning dept. We are occupying them to protest vs the council's plan to demolish this entire estate (almost 3000 homes) and allow developers to make a profit out of public land. Refuse, resist, repopulate, refurbish. It's not too late–fight for the estate!"

20. Public housing not private profit

The messages had been left by a group called Fight for the Aylesbury, made up of a mixture of housing campaigners and local residents, dismayed at Southwark Council's decision to offer the entire estate up for redevelopment. The occupation had occurred a year or so before, and had resulted in the arrest of six campaigners. But it was only one of a number of campaigns that have been raging over recent years as council tenants are told that their homes are to be demolished, to be replaced by private homes for sale, with no real way for them to stay.

In 1997, after winning the landslide general election, Tony Blair made an appearance at the Aylesbury Estate, saying:

> I have chosen this estate to deliver my first speech as Prime Minister for a simple reason. For 18 years, the poorest people in our country have been forgotten by government. They have been left out of growing prosperity, told they were not needed, ignored by the Government except for the purpose of blaming them. I want that to change. There will be no forgotten people in the Britain I want to build.

21. Vanishing territory

Blair was at least correct to identify abandonment and blame. After the 1970s, local government was a target for the new right-wing government, and the ability to spend money on maintenance and upkeep, already hobbled by the financial crises earlier in the decade, was never possible again. Unemployment soared and a drug epidemic erupted across the poorest parts of the UK, and the large inner city estates which had been such a blessing for the residents after their experience of slum living became as stigmatised as anything that had come before.

22. Streets

23. In the sky

But even if it is doomed, the level to which the Aylesbury remains open is surprising. Where many estates have had their walkways demolished, one can still walk most of the way around the Aylesbury at the upper levels.

At one point, this symbolised the latest in sophisticated modern urbanism, but later generations came to venerate the traditional street and believe that 'streets in the sky' were inherently dangerous. Where this world still exists, as here, it is an odd, fascinating way to move around, with new dimensions added to the everyday way of navigating space.

24. Wendover House

25. Harvard Gardens

It was beginning to rain as I walked past what is said to have been at one point the longest single housing block in Europe. It is difficult to be positive about the design: it is the dullest of greys, and its monotony is barely enlivened across its massive facade, but the flats are large, well fenestrated, and all have a substantial outdoor space.

But housing is never simply about shelter, or conveniences. Just beneath the surface of all the bricks, timber or concrete are all manner of aspirations, with housing playing an important role in the quest for human

status. And what could be more blatant, at the northern end of the massive block, than for 'Harvard Gardens' to be under construction? The developer, L&Q, describes the area as "one of the most vibrant and well-serviced new communities in London."

26. The new

27. against the Old

Harvard Gardens is being built on the site of already demolished blocks of the Aylesbury Estate. New streets for the new development and the 'new community' are being named after historic local characters.

But there are already thousands of people here, many of whom have spent their whole lives on the estate. It may be grey, it may be stigmatised, but there are people here and they are part of a community. When the slums of the past were torn down, some lamented at the destruction of traditional community bonds, but at least in those cases people had a brand new home to move into.

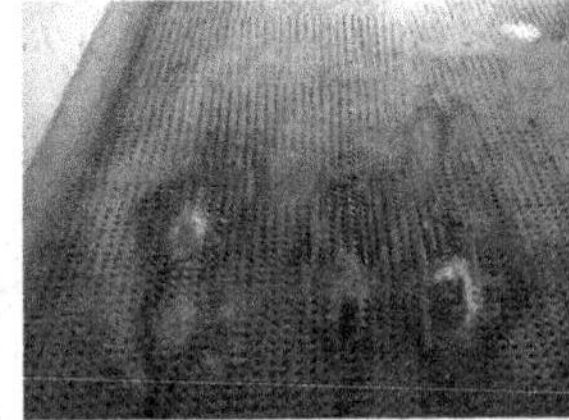

28. Top deck

29. Pop up

On Taplow block, above garages and a doctor's surgery, an open deck runs the whole length of the building, partially under cover, with retail units facing out-

wards. But none of these units remain local shops, whether an off licence or grocers or anything. They are now occupied by a series of artist's studios, galleries and other pop-up retailers. One can only assume that the old leases have been terminated and temporary lets have been given to 'creative' tenants, in anticipation of the forthcoming demolitions.

30. Regeneration

31. Taplow block

The new housing will, it is true, be built to higher standards than were achieved in the 1960s. Regulations for energy efficiency are far better than they were, and construction technology has improved substantially in the past 50 years. But the new properties will be no larger, perhaps even smaller than the council houses of the past, with meaner layouts and less natural light.

32. New London Vernacular

Leaving the Aylesbury Estate behind, and heading north towards Elephant and Castle, I passed a few streets of Victorian housing, before the landscape changed again.

In recent years a significant cosmetic change has occurred to the houses being built in London. Since the crash, a new sobriety has entered housing design, with many new developments reinterpreting the brick architecture of the 19th century. This changed mood has been described as the 'New London Vernacular', and its popularity with developers, planners and architects has even led to severe brick shortages in the construction industry.

In terms of ambition, this new kind of housing for the rich tries very hard–despite its contemporaneity–to be humble, to present itself as part of a continuum. 50 years ago, the mood was different, and the new housing for common people shouted its modernity, its new-ness. It has paid the price for this presumptuousness ever since.

33. A street in the sky

From the early 1970s until 2014, the area to the east of Elephant and Castle was home to another gigantic system-built estate, the Heygate. Extremely long and tall slab blocks occupied the perimeter of the site, facing into the interior, where a number of smaller low-rise blocks were set in landscaped ground. Again, a network of raised access walkways led around and between the blocks. The story of recent history of the Heygate Estate is a depressing one. Like the Aylesbury, it was home to some very poor people, and in the 1980s and 90s had attained a reputation for hostility, helped along by a steady stream of films, television and adverts whose crews flocked to the estate for a quick visual fix of violence and threat.

But at the same time, it was also an oasis of calm in a busy and congested part of London, and over the years the landscaping had matured to create a lush, verdant environment, the low-rise blocks and walkways drifting between the canopies of the trees. The only visible thing that remains from the Heygate Estate is a concrete walkway, still in use as a way for contractors to cross the road. I stood and watched as they climbed a temporary steel ladder, nearly all going the same way, as it came to the end of the contractors' working day.

34. Revitalising

35. Revitalying

Southwark Council entered a Faustian pact over Elephant and Castle, which sits at a major traffic interchange only a few minutes from central London. Interpreting their actions as charitably as possible, it would seem that by offering up the area to property developers, they hoped the money raised could pay for repairs, maintenance and new social housing for the tenants elsewhere in the borough.

But property developers are not humanitarian organisations, and it quickly became clear that Southwark had been stitched up. A redaction mistake revealed that the council had sold the Heygate site to Australian construction behemoth Lend Lease for £50m, after having already spent £44m getting rid of the existing residents. Lend Lease plan to more than double the number of houses on the site, while reducing the number of 'social rented' flats to just 18. People who had bought their family houses on the estate were paid amounts at compulsory purchase that wouldn't cover half the price of

the smallest flat in the new developments, and campaigners drew depressing maps showing the wide dispersal of the former tenants. A number of campaigns were fought: it was shown that the buildings were structurally sound, easily and cheaply refurbished, that the crime rate was lower on the estate than the borough average, that there was a genuinely happy community there, but nothing could be done.

Southwark's guilt shines forth in their reference to "tree lined streets, high quality open spaces and a largely traffic free environment", all of which referred perfectly to the Heygate as it was. Most galling, however, is the reference to 'local', which in regeneration code is a way of euphemising the fact that the existing community are not the beneficiaries of all this 'improvement'.

36. Artwashing

The entrance to the 'Elephant Park' site is tucked in behind a collection of brightly painted shipping contain-

ers full of boutiques, bars and coffee shops. Much like the studios inserted into the Aylesbury, here art and culture are being used to prepare the ground for the 'new community'.

37. Greenwashing

The old joke goes: "What's the definition of chutzpah? The guy convicted of killing his parents asking the judge for mercy because he's an orphan." Another example might be this; where the developer responsible for large-scale class cleansing extols the "established neighbourhood where everybody loves to belong".

38. A newer brutalism

The new housing makes a mockery of many of the criticisms of post-war housing. In so many ways it is larger, more imposing, more 'brutal' even, to use the old cliche. But it is so far not associated with a defeated form of social and economic organisation.

39. Your home next

40. Bear with us while we tear apart your community

Signs of resistance were everywhere, the occupied premises had been Elephant & Castle pub which had been conveniently shut down after a violent incident, and has been earmarked as the location for a branch of the particularly rapacious estate agent Foxtons.

41. Homes, homes

42. and more homes

But there is the sense that the forces being resisted are more tectonic than all that. As I finally began to approach the river again, almost everywhere I looked, housing was going up. That we are at or near the peak of a housing bubble in London seems incontrovertible, with huge amounts of money flying around in all directions, into the sky and under the ground, a true mania. But this is a time when any forces of resistance are historically weak–councils are either austerity-hobbled or climbing on the gravy train themselves, strategies such as squatting have been outlawed, whole parts of the population are having their prospects diminished by speculation and the rentier class.

Today, common sense deems it absurd that poor people might be allowed to live on land that could yield far higher returns in the private sector. For developers it's nothing personal, really, it's just that the estates are centrally located sites of comparatively low density, and are mostly owned by the state and thus easier to purchase. No amount of pleading for the rights of existing residents, or the benefits of a socially mixed society, have any hope when the flow of money is currently so strong.

43. Coin Street Community Builders

In the 1980s, right by the side of the Thames, a community stood up for itself against plans for a mammoth regeneration project of retail, commercial, hotel and

residential space. The Coin Street community made their own plans, and eventually bought the land after the GLC fell behind their vision of the site. Today the area is remarkable for its small scale, as no major development has since occurred, and the community remains in control. But today no such thing would be possible, not least because the municipal authority, led by the Mayor of London, has had no interest in ever going against the wishes of developers.

44. The Thames at South Bank

Instead, the Mayor, who some years ago promised that there would be "no Kosovo-style social cleansing" of the capital, has been more interested in adorning the capital with pointless baubles and white elephants that have done little but gratify his ego and set him up for his long-term goal of leading the country.

Arriving at last by the banks of the Thames, I stood at the point earmarked for the southern landing point of the 'Garden Bridge', a new crossing due to be built later this year. It is controversial–a private attraction, to be paid for with public money, procured in the most murky of circumstances, with no real genuine demand, a sheer frivolity that, with Johnson on the way out, may hopefully never occur. Johnson himself has said "a great city like London has to continually refresh its offer", using the language of property development in his role as an elected politician. The problem is, the part of the population to whom this 'offer' is actually addressed is rapidly shrinking.

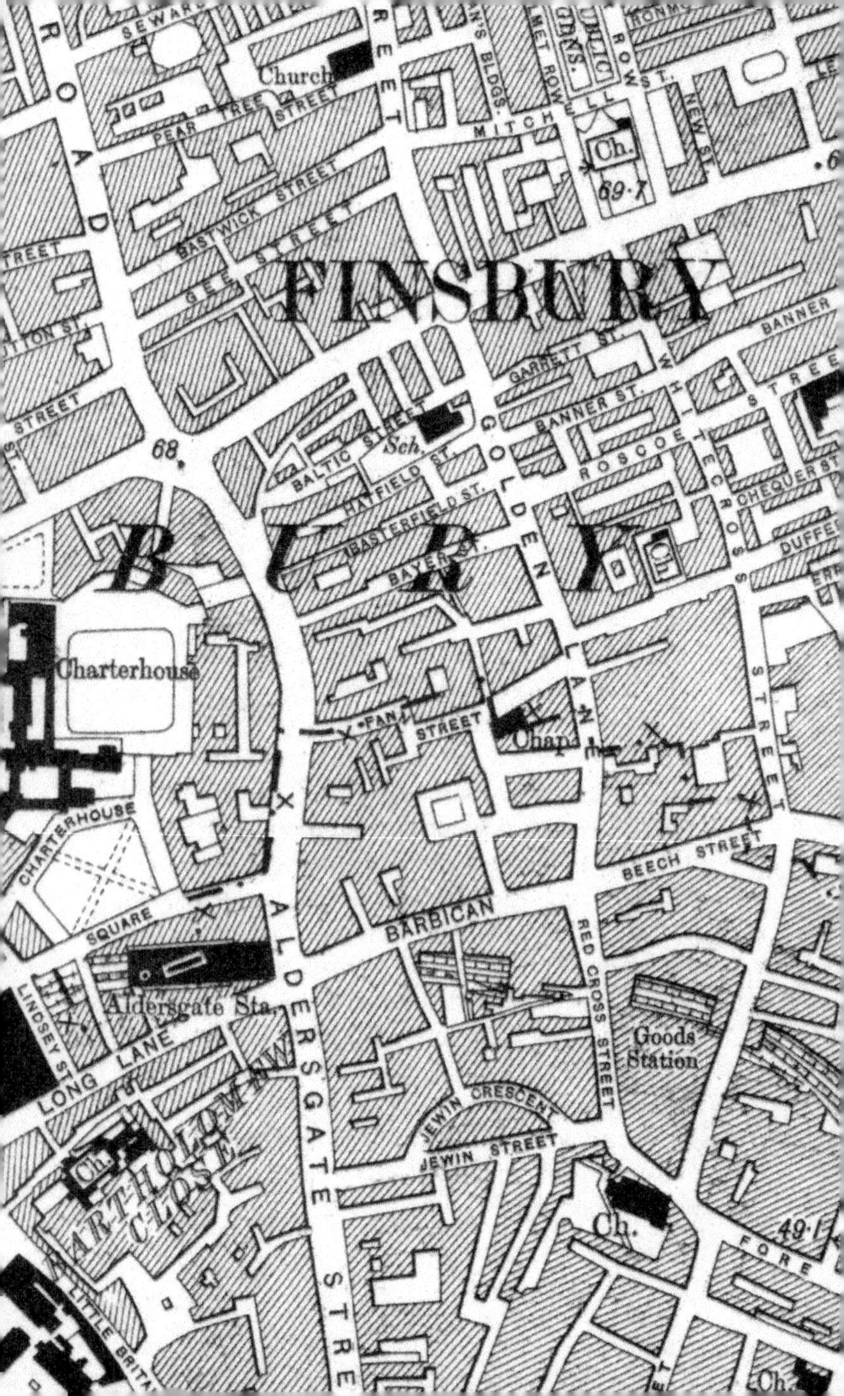
FINSBURY
Church
PEAR TREE STREET
BASTWICK STREET
GEE STREET
MITCHELL
Ch.
69·7
GARRETT ST.
BANNER ST.
BANNER
GOLDEN LANE
ROSCOE
WHITECROSS STREET
CHEQUER ST.
BALTIC ST.
Sch.
HATFIELD ST.
BASTERFIELD ST.
BAYER ST.
68
Charterhouse
CHARTERHOUSE SQUARE
PAN STREET
Chapel
BEECH STREET
BARBICAN
RED CROSS STREET
Goods Station
Aldersgate Sta.
ALDERSGATE STREET
LINDSEY ST.
LONG LANE
JEWIN CRESCENT
JEWIN STREET
Ch.
49·1
FORE
LITTLE BRITAIN

ADAM KAASA

Against Porosity, Against the Crowd: Walking for a Spatial Complex City

All Images by Jane Hall

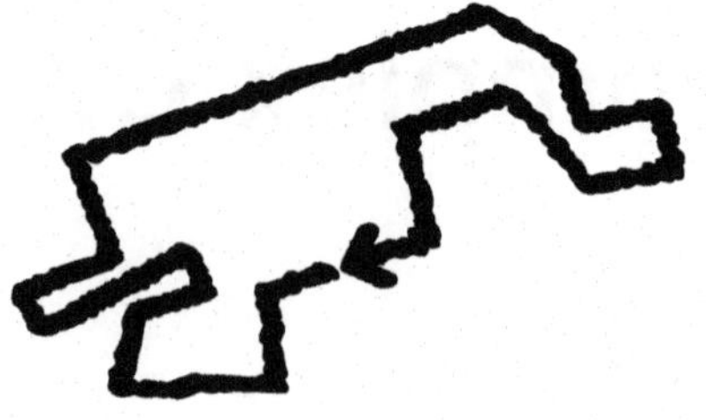

WALKING AS COMPLEXITY

If there is nothing lonelier than being in a crowd, nothing that announces modern urban anomie and spectres of alienation, then perhaps places in the city that are less crowded should be valued. By less crowded, I do not mean to suggest less complex. In those spaces less crowded than others, I want to suggest that walking is a method for valuing spatial complexity. Too often urban scholars, politicians, architects, and city residents have followed the edict that density equals vibrancy. Or that, perhaps, the more people you have in a place, the more chance those people will meet, will share ideas, and will participate in the democratic public sphere. The end point for the privileging of density as a precursor for the civic is that to combat the effects of segregative urbanism, class, race, and other divisions in the city – and even of democratic deficiencies in our modern publics – we need to make cities denser. This density as civic argument suggests that more and more people who are more and more different from each other, through their propinquity, can build up the skills and capabilities necessary to cohabit.

But perhaps simply valuing social density as a signal of urban value, or 'cityness', to borrow a term from the sociologist Saskia Sassen, misses a crucial ingredient in urban politics: spatial complexity. In the aftermath of the summer 2011 disturbances in London, Space Syntax Limited, a company that emerged from University College London, produced a working paper to suggest the corollary that the 'over-complex, under used spaces' of social housing estates in the UK led to riots.[1] Five years later, Prime Minister David Cameron vowed to 'blitz' sink estates (poor social housing blocks), erasing, in Cameron's words, 'the dark alleyways that are a gift to criminals and drug dealers'.[2] The existence of spatial complexity, at least in the UK and particularly in reference to post-war experiments in the production and alignment of civic or social architecture, has led to arguments in favour of straight lines, open spaces, and busy streets. London, then, hails and legally protects the alleyways of the medieval mercantile city, but demolishes the alleyways of the socialist post-war council estate.

Two different imaginaries around complexity and the city emerge. Social complexity privileges ideas of social density, mixture, interaction, even messiness–but can be deeply suspicious of physical gaps, holes, hiccups in the fabric of that space. The other is a kind of spatial complexity concerned with spatial density, with ambiguity, openness, unfinished spaces, occlusions, layers, and even emptiness. When 'over-complex, under used spaces' of a council estate are viewed as dangerous and undesirable by someone like a sitting Prime Minister, the rhetoric becomes about alleys that go 'nowhere,' or at least not anywhere deemed worth going to, or about secret spaces, spaces with ambiguous or no clear commerciable function. A meaning emerges that social diversity and the benefits of social complexity are hindered by spatial complexity. This is what the Space Syntax report about the 2011 London disturbances suggest: riots occur when spaces are complex.

While there seems to be agreement about the value of social complexity, there is a fear of spatial complexity–perhaps a legacy from the clear cut utopic functionalism of modern planning. Spatially complex spaces can be spaces where it's not obvious who owns them, and therefore where it's difficult to know who does and does not belong. Spatial simplicity might suggest readable spaces that foreground the efficient movement from A to B, spaces with clearly defined uses and boundaries, spaces that fall neatly into mutually exclusive categories like 'residential', 'commercial', 'leisure', or 'private' and 'public'. When spaces are simple, the social practices to navigate them are simple too. Whereas a spatially complex space needs to be socially negotiated, and requires the messy frustration of communal contestation and interpretation.

How are we to make sense of spatial complexity in the city? And if I want to argue for it, alongside, or beside the arguments for social complexity through density that remain much more palpable in current urban debates, can walking be a method for, if not making sense of spatial complexity, than allowing spatial complexity to complicate how we make sense in the city? As a way of thinking through these issues, without any promise of a forceful conclusion, I turn to consider a space in central London that tops both the most loved and most hated building in the country; a space of contradiction, evasion, frustration, and joy: the Barbican.

THE BARBICAN SEGREGATES

If cities are claimed to be places where difference is managed by people coming together in everyday life, then why do we insist on building them to segregate us? I ask this question as someone who loves the Barbican, a brutalist concrete city within a city, designed and built between the 1950s and the 1980s, and one that, ostensibly, segregates its temporary and permanent residents

and visitors from the rest of the city. Designed by the architects Chamberlain, Powell and Bon for The City of London, the Barbican is at once emblematic of Le Corbusier's Modernist utopia, and equally a rallying cry against the CIAM model of absolute zoning of functions. Planned as a mixed use residential, education, and arts centre it stands in stark contrast to the offices and banks that surround it in the Square Mile.

The influential planner at the London County Council (LCC) Percy Johnson-Marshall once wrote that the most important contribution of the Barbican was the relatively new principle of pedestrian segregation.[3] That is to say, the removal of pedestrian movement and flow from the space where cars and other motor traffic flow. In the Barbican this primarily happens by lifting the plane of the pedestrian up from the street to elevated walkways, internal courtyards, and protected gardens. While the Barbican can be seen as contradicting purely Modernist ideals about the separation of residential, commercial, and office zones in the city by merging them all within one development, it also represents the zenith of thinking in terms of the absolute separation of various modes of moving. It segregates those that walk from those who drive.

AGAINST EDGES AND CROWDS

The sociologist Richard Sennett asks us to think about the metaphors of borders and boundaries as two edge conditions in today's city.[4] Sennett suggests that boundaries in the city, as in nature, create rigid divisions and lead to segregation, whereas borders (he gives the example of the cell wall, or the shoreline) are able to be both open and closed at once. While both mark a (physical or psycho-social) line in the city, one is a liminal space of mix and gathering, the other a demarcation of unresolvable difference. Sennett's conjecture is valuable for exploring the design implications of thinking the city as a set of border conditions and how, and if, those design possibilities could lead to greater social mixing. But valorising the porosity of a border condition does not help me theorise why I enjoy sitting in the middle of a seemingly abandoned Barbican on a mid-week afternoon.

On quiet days, the vast stretches of brick-laid elevated platforms, walkways and stairwells might be described by casual onlookers as positively 'dead', those same onlookers perhaps opting to cross the river to the ever pre-programmed, always packed, South Bank – a site hailed by most as a contemporary success, and an instance of making space public again, if ever it was. But is the bustle of life on the street, the spectacle of the crowd, the busy edge conditions of the markets where urban life is assumed to manifest, the only city of value? Simmel wrote that 'one nowhere feels as lonely and lost as in the metropolitan crowd', and yet the idea of a vital, vivid cityness remains one tied to the image of the masses, of busy-ness, of many people overlapping, brushing, exchanging in space.[5]

The notion of the border rather than the boundary as a valued condition of public urban life lends us a physical metaphor that goes beyond the human. It is not just the human bodies in spaces that matter in the making of a border or a boundary, but also the physical design of those spaces that can lead them either to connect or to segregate. Ash Amin suggests that 'sociality in urban public space is not a sufficient condition for civic and political citizenship', and that we need to account for 'the total dynamic–human and non-human–of a public setting' in thinking the city and public life. In Amin's terms then, the crowd, bustle, and activity is not enough to renew a democratic ethos to the city.[6] It can't be that the South Bank is cityness and the Barbican dead, based on the presence or absence of people alone. Nor that one privileges the civic more simply by the mass presence of bodies in space. Yet while Amin offers us a way to think of the non-human in an urban context, he also 'traces the "virtues" of urban surplus to public spaces that are open, crowded, diverse, incomplete, improvised, and disorderly or lightly regulated'.[7] That is to say, for Amin, and many others, the open, crowded and diverse parts of the city remain those worth fighting for. If we are to favour the edge condition of the border and the crowd, as much urban theory would have us, the Barbican, then, is not a virtuous space. And yet, I want to suggest that it is.

AGAINST PRODUCTIVE POROSITY

Walking around the edge of the Barbican can feel harrowing. Taking your first few steps from Barbican tube station, you stare across at, and are stared back by, two storeys of brick and concrete wall. Much of the perimeter of the Barbican development leaves the street behind. While there is the odd shop or business (the Barbican Tandoori is about two blocks south), the edge is more boundary than border. If you take the curious, courageous or necessary step and pass through the threshold, within seconds you can feel the result of the boundary. The roaring traffic at the intersection of Beech and Aldersgate Streets seems to hush, the buildings lower themselves against the sky as you rise up the

stairs to an elevated platform, light and air seem abundant, people become anomalies rather than standard fixtures in the landscape, the buildings become present, much more present.

The upper level of the western edge of the Barbican complex closest to Barbican Tube station opens out before you, a huge platform cover over the Beech Street tunnel. Wide, boulevard-esque terraces expand, with planters, fountains, and changes of level. You might notice a yellow-line on the brick-paved ground. This line was introduced as a way-finding device, primarily for theatre, art or concert goers trying to access the Barbican Arts Centre from Barbican Tube station or Moorgate on the east side. But even this attempt to give sense to an otherwise maze-like collection of spaces stumbles. As Jane Northcote writes, 'The Line used to come from Milton Court, for example, so it stops abruptly at a precipice over Silk Street and seems to want to leap into space. The bridge it crossed has been dismantled.'[8] Even systems made to layer on top of, control and command a space, fail, shift, are absorbed and forgotten over time, and this failure alludes to the success of a complex space to ignite the imagination through the necessity to continually negotiate and make sense of an insensible space. There are no yellow lines on the boulevards of Paris.

With half an hour, you can wander, explore, push through, sit, marvel, be lost, be found, be quiet, be loud, see someone, move inside, but find yourself outside, change floors without steps, see water, see rock. If you take Michel de Certeau's 'god's eye' view of the two dimensional map, you might be tempted to break down the walls, open up the inside, to 'activate' the Barbican by populating it through endless design and programme interventions.[9] A contemporary anxiety that fears emptiness, or spaces outside of commercial legibility, wants the Barbican porous, pock marked with holes and connections, and bursting with people, festivals, pop-ups, markets. This is space making sense as spectacle. This is space that performs itself, performs its publicness to the very people who are supposed to *be* the public. Walking uncovers the fact that the Barbican does not make sense. In fact, that might be precisely the point, the challenge, the promise.

WALKING TO AND THROUGH

So why do I enjoy walking through the middle of a seemingly abandoned Barbican on a mid-week afternoon? As a caveat, I inhabit one particular material body that is raced, classed, abled, aged, sexualised, and shaped by histories of coloniality, capital, and desire in particular ways. And material bodies do not all inhabit space, or move and walk in space, the same way I do. The Barbican, its position in central London, its inhabitants and board, the politics of the City, its security, its programming, intersect with distinctions and inequalities of class, ability, gender, race, and geography. I might like walking in the Barbican because of my studies in architecture and the city. It might have to do with the fact that I do not have children, and have a job that allows me, at times, the flexibility to work from various sites across the city, the Barbican included. I might enjoy moving through the Barbican because I can physically move through it without much let or hindrance. Spatial experiences come to matter in reference to multiple bio-socio-historical vectors, so the question of enjoying the emptiness of a spatially complex space like the Barbican begs deeper social and political questions.

But I no longer seek out the South Bank, a post-war experiment that became overwhelmed by the productivity of capital. I continue to be intrigued by the politics of its architecture and its historical moment, and I am drawn to its spatial complexity. But the reaction to its complexity has been to program 'sense' into it. To make its layers flat through legible spaces of consumption. The South Bank is now a destination; that is, something to walk to, rather than walk through.

The difference might be that walking *to* something expecting a readable, and straightforward destination invites an urban temperament of spectacle. What could be more lonely than the crowded spectacle of flattened space that promises the civic possibilities of density and social complexity? If the spectacle of the crowd, if the promise of social density is all the city becomes then the possibility of its political tooling, of learning from the city falls short. We need socially complex cities to learn how to cohabit; we need spatially complex cities to learn how to imagine. Walking *through* something, something complex, is practising the imagination. And we all know our cities could use a little more of that.

ENDNOTES

1 Ed Parham, *2011 London Riots location analysis: Proximity to town centres and large post-war housing estates*, Accessed 5 December, 2015, http://www.spacesyntax.com/project/2011-london-riots/.

2 Caroline Davies, *David Cameron vows to 'blitz' poverty by demolishing UK's worst sink estates*, Accessed 9 January 2016, http://www.theguardian.com/society/2016/jan/09/david-cameron-vows-to-blitz-poverty-by-demolishing-uks-worst-sink-estates#_=_.

3 Percy Johnson-Marshall, *Rebuilding cities*, Edinburgh, The University Press, 1966.

4 Richard Sennett, *The Public Realm*, Accessed 3 December, 2015, http://www.richardsennett.com/site/senn/templates/general2.aspx?page¬id=16&cc=gb.

5 Georg Simmel, (1903) The Metropolis and Mental Life in eds. Malcolm Miles, Tim Hall, and Iain Borden, *The City Cultures Reader*, New York, Routledge, 2004.

6 Ash Amin, Collective Culture and Urban Public Space, City 12(1), 2008, pp. 5–24.

7 Ash Amin, Collective Culture and Urban Public Space, City 12(1), 2008, pp. 5–24.

8 Jane Northcote, *The Yellow Line*, Accessed 9 January 2016, http://blog.barbican.org.uk/2014/11/the-yellow-line/

9 Michel De Certeau, *The Practice of Everyday Life*, Berkeley, University of California Press, 1984.

Broadness Lighthouse
(Flashing White)
Saltings
B.P
Mud
Broadness Salt Marsh
Saltings
Stone
Stone
Saltings
B.S
F.P.
Mud H. W. M.
nscombe Marshes
Manor Way
TRAMWAY
Green Manor Way
Botany Marshes
Gas Wks.
Manor Way Farm
Lower Road
B.S
Parly .Div. Union & U. D. By.
Cement Works
Northfleet Paper Mills
Britannia Cement Works
Pilgrims Road
Chalk Pit
B.M. 75.4
School
Vic
All Saints
mbe Siding

ROBERTO BOTTAZZI

Gravesend - Broadness Weather Station

All drawings by James Smith

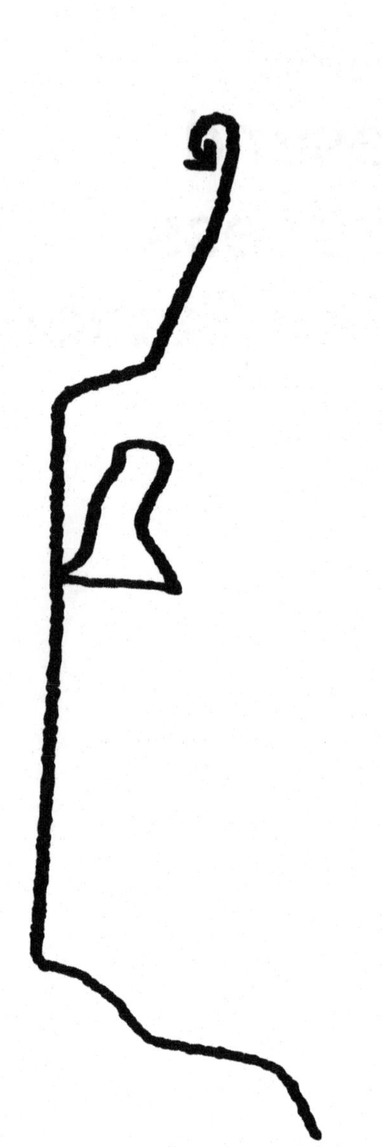

PREAMBLE

Everything moves. Every single element on the planet is in a dynamic state. Be it a natural phenomenon like clouds or a more immaterial one such as your feelings for another person, nothing is stable enough to remain unaltered forever. It may not appear that way to you perhaps because the speed of change might be very slow–think that glass is actually a liquid–or because what you are experiencing could be the result of forces that are invisible to your eyes.

London is no exception as it not only transforms itself at varying speeds but also operates at multiple scales which invariably overwhelm our ability to grasp them. For architects as much as for artists a large part of their personal training involves learning how to see such elusive phenomena in space and time. For a certain period of time, architects thought that in order to see 'more' of the contemporary city they had to zoom out, embrace it through the omnipresent aerial view and give themselves the (false) reassurance of dominating it in one single gaze. Lacking a clear vantage point from which to observe it, the experience of the city is always an incomplete one, negotiating its shifting ground.

The ground–the very element we walk on–is a vibrant element of cities in which–perhaps more than anywhere else–distinctions between natural and artificial blur. It is out of such ground that architecture also morphs from and rests on; in Manuel DeLanda's words built forms can be seen 'as the highest level of geological articulation of the earth's crust'.[1] In the age of the Anthropocene, such a 'geological turn' calls for a different approach in which the vastness of these processes is combined with the intimacy of walking on a landscape; multiple speeds, scales, to abandon traditional disciplinary concerns and embrace the incomplete image of the city and its slow dynamism.

Slow dynamism could also be a good description of walking. The act of walking in cities and landscapes is not only a powerful counterpoint to the once predominant and now obsolete reassuring position of the Modernist architect and urbanist, but it is also a mode to tune into the strange humming of the city in the Anthropocene. Walking allows our perception to appreciate multiple speeds and scales, the slow and continuous flow of matter–'artificial' or 'natural'–which we traditionally attribute to geology, questioning notions of site, linking apparently unrelated facts and myths; thus cutting right at the core of what constructs our cities.

THE WALK

I had never walked to the Gravesend-Broadness weather station. It had caught my attention a while ago as I had read somewhere of talks of its closure in newspapers. Given the current obsessions with measurements and data–which is also my own–that piece of news seemed to be anachronistically odd. The station had been–and still is–consistently reporting the highest temperatures in Britain.[2] Allegedly, its location was excessively subjected to external factors which ultimately were compromising the data coming from the weather station therefore deeming them 'not objective'. Objectivity is a slippery concept which compelled me to walk through this territory; along with other binaries that this site promised to explode–objective/subjective and its mirroring pair, natural/artificial–there is also the most pressing question as to whether Gravesend–technically already located in the county of Kent – can be considered as part of London.

Ebbsfleet Business Park – where this walk starts – is the designated site for the first 'Garden City of the XXIst century' as well as of one of the largest infrastructural projects affecting the near future of London: the Paramount London Theme Park. At present, however, cement factories, steel yards, a small café – Fat Sams – paint a far less idyllic or grandiose image. Flanking our walk along Manor Way – heavily crisscrossed by trucks – is a long escarpment of white chalk. It imposes onto the landscape a long casting shadow but also a visceral material quality with its white, rough texture. It also forms a sort of backdrop for the Gravesend peninsula, both cutting it out from the rest of the area and setting the scene for the walk. From the starting point, the city, in its traditional configuration of institutions, services, and most noticeably housing, has already abandoned us: roads, depots, workshops, packing suppliers, roundabouts, auto part stores, recycling yards, car dealers, factories, metal suppliers, building yards, recording studios, hydroponic equipment suppliers, bridal fabrics, football grounds, petrol stations, taxi service companies, building sites, all incorporated under the omnipresent and yet vague label of the business park. No sign of houses or permanence.

A small gap in a long metal fence marks the entrance to the peninsula. Immediately, the noise of lorries disappears. A line of cement tiles in the ground directs the walk: the vastness of the landscape in which the gaze could move freely has given way to tall grass constraining the range of our gaze. A small stream flanks the walk here, whereas in the distance the silhouette of a water treatment plant begins to appear. However, you realise now that the presence of the plant had already been anticipated by the humming, continuous sound of the pumps filtering water. Without an apparent origin–either in space and time–this deep tone is disorientating and penetrating at the same time; suggestive of larger phenomena, it is 'vast'–vanquishing any thought of how or why it got here. It suggests a scale and depth beyond that of human perception: though artificial is very much part of this landscape, a sustained tone penetrating straight through us; 'connecting an interior to an interior' as Carmelo Bene spoke of the use of electric amplification in his theatre. It is also part of what Timothy Morton calls 'the great humiliations of the human', which have repositioned the human species as 'decentered beings, inhabiting a Universe of processes that happen whether we are aware of them or not' which call for a renewed intimacy with other beings.[3]

Despite its scale–about 1.5km wide–the Gravesend peninsula can only be perceived once the tall grass disappears to reveal a series of gigantic high-voltage pylons traversing the landscape. We stop for a couple of minutes: a large portion of the infrastructures supporting London can be embraced at a single glance. Besides the pylons, barges and ships form the backdrop of our view, dotted by depots and motorways, whereas Tilbury cargo terminal is barely noticeable in the distance. The pylons are amongst the tallest in the country: departing from Stoneness Road Electricity Substation, they morph into a series of sublime metallic sculptures whose presence diminishes as they carry electricity into Kent. The line they form is mirrored underground by the high-speed train coming from the South-East and France.

The rail tracks gradually slope down before disappearing and re-emerging on the other side of the Thames.

Unexpectedly, the walk is gradually revealing the urban nature of this site–a thought difficult to grasp, even after the walk–the constant presence of manmade infrastructures including the natural ones, such as the Thames or air. Beyond the spectrum of what is visible, this site is also electromagnetic fields, ground contaminants, and subterranean infrastructures–also impacting on temperature readings. Below this threshold there is the minimal and yet precious presence of a rare spider. *Sitticus distinguendus*–one of Britain's rarest spiders–inhabits the site in a large colony. It is perhaps telling that this species prefers a dry climate and finds a natural habitat in cement and stony clinker such as pulverised fuel ash. This rare spider is only 6mm long and curiously characterised by having four eyes, dotted on its face like minuscule radars; a fragile presence amidst the heavy infrastructures of the peninsula.

To continue the walk we resort to our mobile phones: there is no sign of the weather station. The familiar silhouette of the weather station–coupled with a much bigger apparatus supporting the radar operated by the London Port Authority–should stand out now. The presence of the monumental pylons has dwarfed its presence in the landscape. We take a right turn towards the east, through a motocross field, to get to the other large body of water in the peninsula. Both ponds are remnants of the heyday of industrial activities on site. The one we are flanking now still bear the traces of its past; its brown shallow waters bear the signs of the metal works that used to occupy the centre of the peninsula and now have drifted to its edges.

Scanning the site on foot returns a rather different, unexpected image: rather than encountering a barren landscape, a void as originally anticipated by the aerial map, the site is best described as full. The sequences of structures, factories, tunnels, invisible fields, fauna, flora, pollution, and processes at work here overlap one another, giving rise to an immersive, saturated landscape: a filled volume rather than the flat surface. The very ground on which we walk is therefore not flat, or inert; rather it is a threshold, an interface mediating between the geological processes at work below it and those unfolding in the air space above.

Once we move past the ponds, the path bifurcates again. This time we can make out the outline of the radar station, adjacent to a little pier. The path is well marked as we are increasingly exposed to the wind blowing towards the Thames estuary. The ground–covered in grass and shrubs–apparently is slightly darker than the surrounding areas–a condition which, again, we absorb without much awareness. This too seems to be one of the contributing factors accounting for the mercurial temperatures captured by the weather station. A scattered group of boat owners are going about their business, repairing boats, barely noticing our presence. Finally, we have reached the weather station. A metal fence doubled up by CCTV cameras protects this rather mundane location. The tall radar tower visually dominates and squeezes the weather station into a corner: it's a standard 4–5 feet tall Stevenson screen, the most common device utilised for temperature readings.

The wandering experience of walking tunes our senses to the low, invisible, strange landscape which both propels and is the result of London. What had first appeared as unimportant or simply generic slowly comes to the foreground; what first looked like 'anomalies' eventually helped us to get accustomed to this landscape, have a feel for it to eventually realise there are no aberrations, this is the very reality we are immersed in: they are the site!

Trapped between the invisible forces only sensed by measuring devices and the unmediated reality of colours, objects and matter of the peninsula, the Gravesend-Broadness weather station speaks of a shifting ground in which traditional coordinates and assumptions must be reconsidered before venturing back to London.

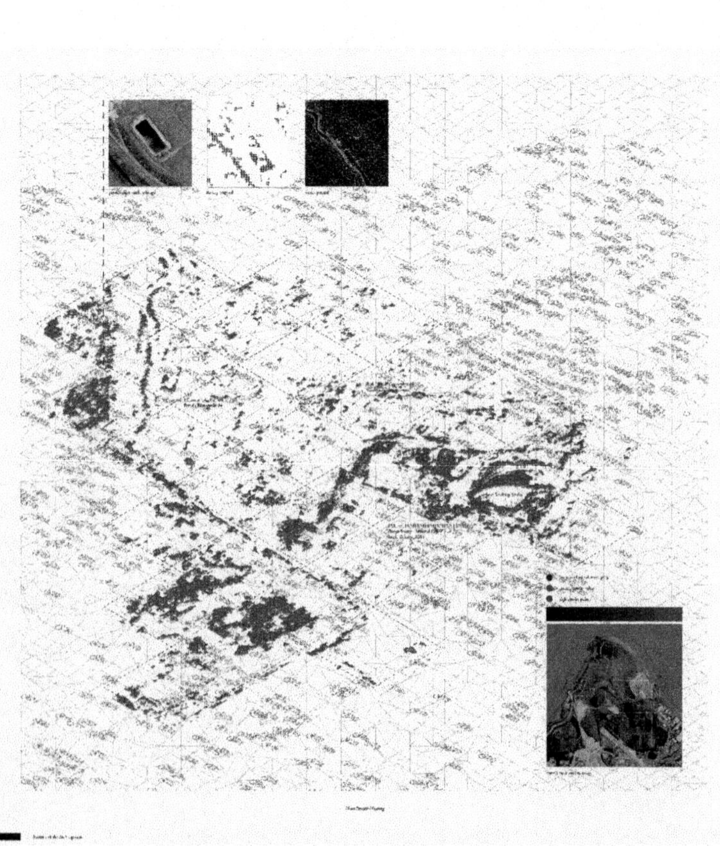

ENDNOTES

[1] Sylvia Lavin, Helen Furjan, and Penelope Dean, eds., *Crib Sheets: Notes on the Contemporary Architectural Conversation*, New York, Monacelli Press, 2005, p. 19.

[2] On 10 August 2003, Gravesend-Broadness registered the highest temperature ever in Britain since official global recordings started at the beginning of the last century. Recording a temperature of 38.1°C did not go unnoticed and rapidly triggered quite a fiery debate on the reliability of the station and its inclusion in national records. Besides sporadic actions, some more serious and organised campaigns involved the likes of Lord Lawson–head of the *Global Warming Policy Foundation*–to question climate data and propose to undertake 'a major inquiry into the integrity of official global surface temperature records'. Soon followed the initiative launched by Anthony Watt–the author of the world's allegedly 'most viewed site on global warming and climate change'–who has also repeatedly questioned the objectivity of such temperature measurements. In the meantime, the station kept featuring as 'hottest spot in Britain': it had the warmest day of 2010 (30.9 and 31.7 degrees), 2011 (33.1 degrees), as well as the highest temperature ever recorded in the UK for October (29.9 degrees).

[3] Timothy Morton, Thinking Ecology: The Mesh, the Strange Stranger, and the Beautiful Soul, *Collapse VI: Geo/Philosophy*, Falmouth, Urbanomic, 2010, pp. 195–96.

UNIVERSITY
WHITFIELD STREET
TOTTENHAM COURT ROAD
HUNTLEY ST
CHENIES MEWS
FRANCIS STREET
RIDGMOUNT GDNS
TORRINGTON PL
TORRINGTON SQUARE
MALET ST
ST. GILES AND ST. GEORG
ALFRED PLACE
STORE STREET
RIDGMOUNT ST
CHITTY ST
CHARLOTTE STREET
TOTTENHAM STREET
PITT ST
GOODGE STREET
WINDMILL ST
PERCY STREET
BAYLEY ST
BEDFORD SQUARE
UPPER RATHBONE PL
RATHBONE PLACE
STEPHEN ST
GRESSE ST
MORWELL ST
CAROLINE ST
BEDFORD
NEWMAN STREET
BERNERS MEWS
BERNERS STREET
SOHO
SUTTON ST
Ch.
Sch.
92·6
86·9

DAVID DERNIE

Walking | Material Conditions of the Street

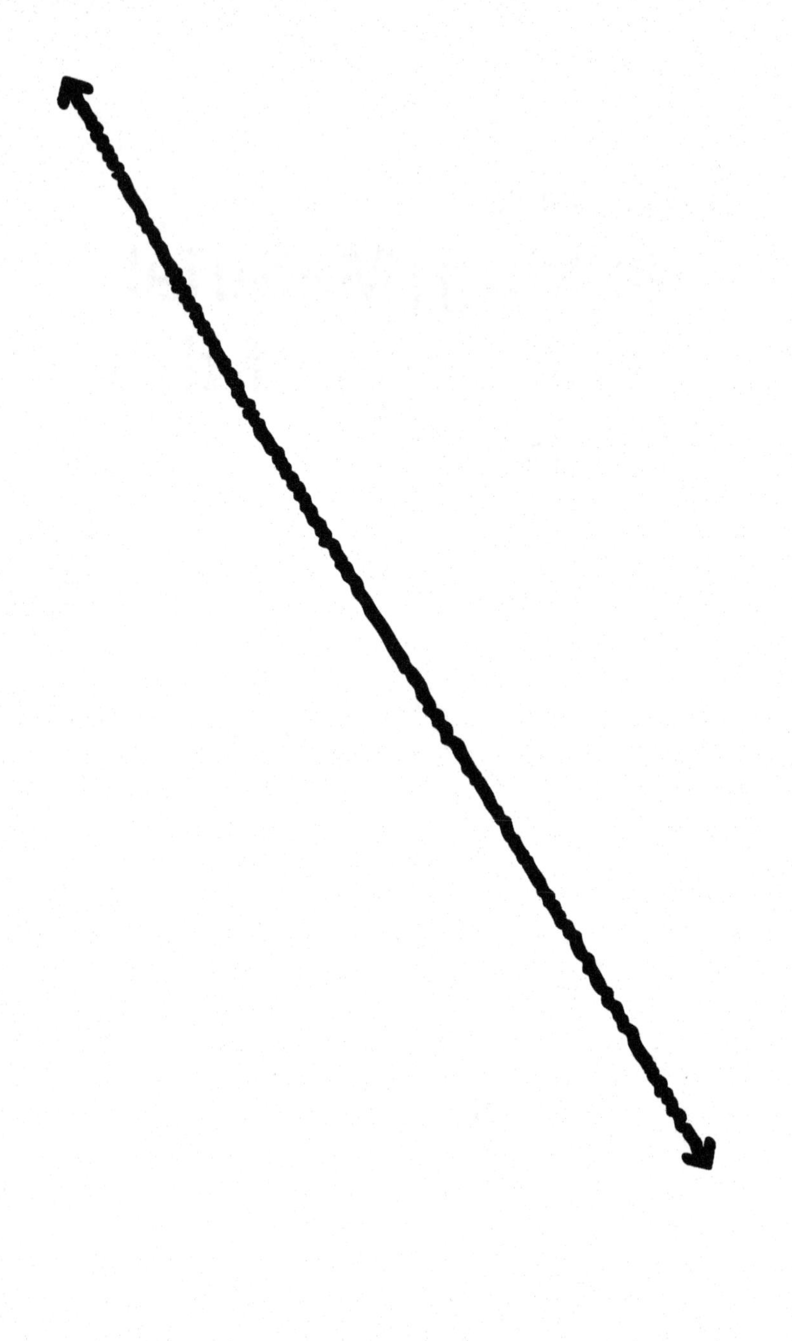

WALK

My walk along Tottenham Court Road is short, slow and iterative. Open to seeing afresh and just being there without particular intention, I meander up and down a short stretch of the crowded street in central London. Virtually rural until the mid eighteenth century, and now still tree-lined, this road north marks the boundaries between Bloomsbury to the east and Fitzrovia to the west. It connects Somers Town with Soho and gathers walkers and traffic from all four directions. Its pavements absorb the rhythms of working days, the ebbs and flows of consumers and travellers.

Its appellation derives from a manor house that once stood at the head of the road, 'Tottenhall', that became known as 'Tottenham Court' in the sixteenth century. Fast forward and the development along Euston Road, with Paddington station to the west and St Pancras and Kings Cross to the east, ignited development southwards: shifting little from its ancient path, Tottenham Court Road grew to become London's principal concentration of furniture stores. Today some of those great stores and public houses are still there, but economics dictate that the street is now overrun with eating places, shops for electronics, offices and supermarkets. Modernist blocks, and more or less distinctive new developments contribute to a fragmented streetscape that as a whole is neither a romantic image of the past, nor without a tangible sense of history and resilience, an identity that is echoed in equal measure by London itself.

Great trees, signage and street lamps line parts the road, interrupting the long view, breaking up the tall facades. Beyond them, the asphalt road is heavily trafficked, with buses, taxis and cyclists for the most part. Its pavements are inhabited mostly by walkers, many plugged in and glued to phones, using the street to get somewhere, as a passageway. But there are also idlers, street vendors, buskers, beggars, people animated by conversation, by romance, by the events of the day. There are even a few pockets of quiet. On the street converge the fast and the slow paces of life. It is a place of performance and display as much as it is a place of solitude amidst its alienating crowds.

The buildings that form the depths of its edges are a backdrop for the extraordinary activity of this ordinary London street: the city's fabric, its density and its block structure, furnish the magical life of this street. As I walk through it, I acknowledge this depth and how much the layers of rooms, houses and blocks that lie behind the facades–the city I can't see–is an integral part of what is on display. The deep structures of the city, the invisible city that lies behind the *scaenae-frons* of the street's facades, weave in and out of the street and feed its metabolism. Along the walk I reflect on the spatiality of the street, how the street gives space for the life of the city to present itself. It is a kind of clearing as much as it is an object or destination. Tottenham Court Road is not an abstract linear space in which things are arranged, but the boundary condition that makes the location of things and the passage of people and transport possible. It appears to me a bricolage-like set of physical conditions that allows things to be connected. The geometry of the Tottenham Court Road appears to be like a transparent, adaptable scaffolding that structures relationships between things, and that facilitates change over time.

Like a *flâneur*, 'the passionate spectator ... amid the ebb and flow of movement, in the midst of the fugitive and the infinite'[1], I set out on the walk to understand better the nature of Street, the ubiquitous urban space of the modern age. I took the flâneur's tool, a hand held camera, and added a sketchbook. My walk wasn't going to be too far, nor systematic, but deliberately slow. I was to make observations about the relationships between things: between scales of experience; between material and immaterial; between the rhythm of walking and the depths of geological time; between the visible and invisible; between the performance of the street and its backgrounds.

The practice of walking was the starting point of the process. I did the same walk several times and took my observations, as a basis for a visual practice of mixed-media/hybrid drawing. I avoided drawings-as-illustrations. Rather the images were a process of discovery–destined to tell me something about the street that I couldn't otherwise have articulated. Walking and drawing informed each other, revealing at times irrational images about the spatiality of the walk, its materiality in relation to the body and of horizons of time and memory. This brief text, which completes the process and articulates its discursive findings, is structured into three registers of the walker's experience–horizon, matter and memory.

HORIZON

De Certeau's well-known framework of urban experience rests on a distinction between the ordinary 'practitioners' of the city, living 'below the thresholds at which visibility begins', and the 'city as an abstract

Horizons (North)

Horizons (South)

concept and map produced and imposed from above by the panoptic eye of the planner or cartographer'.[2] He suggests that the walkers are unable to comprehend the city in the same way as those looking from above can 'read' it, like a text, thus he makes a distinction between the city as lived–on the street–and the city as conceived 'in perspective'.

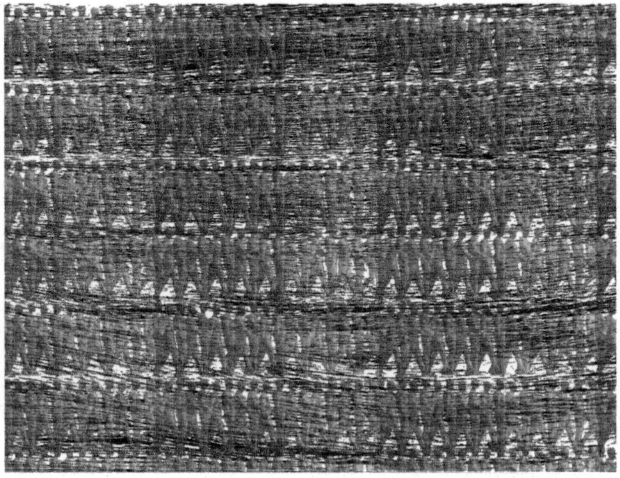

I move the horizon of the street, and the horizon of the street moves with me

In part I find this to be true–and as I walk through the thickness of its crowded pavements, the street-as-object disappears–but not entirely. Although I am immersed in a close-up experience, I retain an abstract idea of the street–a mental map of how it connects me, enables me to imagine where I'm going and what I'm doing. Armature-like, my conceptual image of the street gives me something to hold on to, orientates me and allows me to inhabit the street, to make the street my own.

But the life of the street is always more complex than any one of its abstractions – it is an infinitely richer phenomenon than any one drawing or perspective can articulate: compare for instance the experience of the walker with the plan of the street, to any diagram, section or three-dimensional snap shot. All of these allow a glimpse into one view or geometry of the street, but the walker's experience of the street is only marginally represented by any single view. Our experience of the street is all perspectives together – we comprehend being-on-the-street through multiple senses and as simultaneous perspectives.

De Certeau's aerial view of the street below is in fact not entirely out of sight for the walker. It may not be visible but it is more or less in our mind and helps us orientate and locate ourselves on the street. The walker sees the real street and *at the same time* an imaginary image of the street-as-a-whole, that gives the street a fundamental dimension of stability and comprehension. The conceptual background is not lost on the walker. Rather the opposite is the case: our perception of the street is contingent on our understanding it, at least partially, as an abstract whole.

This far horizon of Tottenham Court Road is marked by towers at both ends, visible like gnomic structures. They give a measure of the street-as-a-whole and the range of my vision, the visual horizon, dominates my walking experience. It stretches from these distant towers to the textures of close-up experience. And as I move along the street, so these horizons move with me, near and far sight overlaid and changing: I move the horizon of the street, and the horizon of the street moves with me. The multiple horizons of the street fuse together and are the primary framing for the place-ness of my walk. My experience of the material life of this street is not limited by one intimate or one distant perspective, but is a simultaneous composite of many different views and experiences.

And as these visible horizons fuse into one, so they are overlaid with non-visible horizons. These are the horizons of my mind and my instincts, my tacit knowledge of the city, cities and histories. I realise that everywhere I look in this street–the heart of a supermodern global city–horizons of history unfold and inform my comprehension of where I am. The experience of these visible and non-visible horizons coming together through walking is also like an opening out of a new horizon of comprehension, a slow unfurling that allows me to make more sense of what could be otherwise an incomprehensible, fragmented urban landscape dominated by the allure of window dressings and bustle of alienating crowds.

The opening and closing of the horizons of the walk in this way is a process that contributes to making this street a place for a tactile appropriation of it and of the city as a whole. The street becomes a familiar to me through an iterative practice of walking and remembering, recalling places and material objects, overlaying invisible horizons of personal experience with visible horizons, near and far, until I make the street's unfamiliar landscape my own.

MEMORY

My short walk back and forth brings the horizons of experience of the street together–the conceptual, the shared, the abstract, the intimate. Through the practice of walking I understand the primary order of the street in its multiplicity of views, and I experience the street as an original condition of the city. As I participate in the street through the performance of walking, through my exchanges with people and interactions with the material objects of the street, so I realise that I am bound to the conditions of the street not only through what I do and see, but also by the experience, memories and associations that I take to the street: the street is receptive to me. In each street resonates all the streets that I have walked: the street we are in is also the streets of our memories, and the streets of which we have dreamt.

This personal memory-exchange with the life and fabric of the street is made possible only by being there, and not just looking: the slow-time of the walk is key. Walking in this way enables us to grasp the street through the range of our senses, and altering the pace of movement enables us to fix our gaze as and when our interest in the street's objects takes hold. We participate in the street and appropriate it by association with our experiences: through the material conditions of the street we bring our memories to the present. As such, walking becomes an act of bridge-making between a conceptual understanding street, our personal memories and intuitions, and experience: it is not an irrational process, but a move from a pre-constituted understanding of the street to a way of constituting the street through walking.

Sometimes we may make explicit comparisons, as a specific memory provokes a reflection on the street we are in, and this is common when we encounter considerable differences or cultures. But for the most part individual memories are assimilated into an implicit background that our experiences collectively contribute to and that underpins our understanding of the everyday. The interchange between what we see, hear and feel in a street, and the experience of the streets we have been in remains unstated, but at the same time it forms a vital body of experience against which we can orientate ourselves and understand the street–almost as though we had seen it–or something like it–before. We re-cognise its streetness and through our pre-understanding we can also anticipate what may or may not lie around the next corner.

In this sense I discover that Tottenham Court Road contains many streets I know and imagine, many stones that are familiar to me. It sits as one layer in a field of my memories of many cities.

Connemara

MATTER

My walk becomes a means of building relationships between my intuitions and memories of the cities that I have walked, my conceptual understanding of the structure of street and its intimate material life. The experience of walking the street offered a slow engagement with the material objects that populated the journey. In other words, I recognise that walking makes me more aware of the relationship between the extraordinary material landscapes of the street and the life that it holds. Through the pace of the walk, I find my gaze intermittently caught by inconsequential details, material surfaces, patinas, in a way that is not intentionally at least, a poetic analysis, as much as it is an instinctive means of adopting the unfamiliar public space as my own, just for a short while.

As I walk through a maze-like bricolage of materials of all kinds, I navigate a spectacle of artificial colours and deep reflections on see-through surfaces, and my gaze is drawn to a spectacle of an altogether different kind: the street's staggering geologies. Pieces of wall, column, pavement and sill, like tableaus of geological time are now suspended, floating on London's muddy earth. They reach out to times beyond the imagination, and to landscapes from all over the world: a fast food outlet clad in some of the world's finest travertine, someone smokes in a side street service entrance, clad in a beautiful Norwegian schist, a former furniture outlet faced in a granite from Quebec that is a billion years old, an age when only bacteria and single-celled organisms existed, long before fossil records.[3]

Such stones capture my imagination and point to a time and a non-human world beyond our comprehension.

left: Serpentinite
right: Theatre of Eternal Wisdom

Stones remain images of stability or permanence, a counterpoint to the intoxicating speed of the modern society. Their mineral figurations signal a natural world in an otherwise highly artificial environment. Stone has lasting value to a modern city and my walk allows me not only to 'see' these details, but to be able to focus my gaze on them. In one movement I close up the distant horizon and open up another, more intimate, but equally complex and at a different scale. Close up I realize vast horizons of geological time embodied in the stones' imaginary landscapes. As my gaze allows me to inhabit the rich figurations of the street's stone, I momentarily lose myself. I discover its powerful, primordial geological space, the unravelling threads of a geological narrative. And I reflect on how ordinary life is played out against these extra-ordinary minerals, now they are precariously fixed onto structures that float between the street's towering structures above and depths of infrastructure and tunnels in London's muddy geology.

My examination of the surfaces and depths of the street's materials is deliberately free from the trappings of cultural associations, liberated, as Yve-Alain Bois suggests, 'from all ontological prisons.' Rather, these surfaces are there for my direct interpretation, as 'raw phenomena'.[4] The stones speak to the aqueous surfaces of glass and mirror, the glazes of terra cotta, faience, cast iron, bronze, the shape of roots, tree bark and London's skies. Replayed and reassembled in my imagination, I realise that the elemental diversity of this super-modern street is ultimately rooted in and animated by the timeless surfaces of the natural world.

ENDNOTES

1 See Charles Baudelaire, *The Painter of Modern Life*, New York, Da Capo Press, 1964. Originally published in *Le Figaro*, in 1863.

2 Michel De Certeau, *The Practice of Everyday Life*, Berkeley, University of California Press, 1984, p. 93.

3 All geologic information taken from the excellent resources published in various forms by Ruth Siddall. See for instance 'A Walking Tour of Building Stones on Tottenham Court Road and Adjacent Streets in Fitzrovia and Bloomsbury', UCL Earth Sciences 2012, https:// www.ucl.ac.uk/earth-sciences/impact/geology/walks/Building_Bloomsbury-TCR.pdf; and the website resource at http://londonpavementgeology.co.uk.

4 'The time has come' declares Bataille, 'when employing the word materialism, to assign to it the meaning of a direct interpretation, excluding all idealism, of raw phenomena, and not of a system founded on the fragmentary elements of an ideological analysis.' Georges Bataille, *Materialism* in Documents no. 3 (1929), quoted in Yve-Alain Bois and Rosalind Krauss, *Formless: A user's guide* Zone Books, 1997, p. 53. See also Jane Bennett, *Vibrant Matter: A political ecology of Things*, Durham and London, Duke University Press, 2010.

Night

FINSBURY CIRCUS
FINSBURY PAVEMENT
MOORGATE STREET
SOUTH PL.
ELDON ST.
W. ST.
E. ST.
BLOMFIELD ST.
N. BROAD ST.
BROAD ST.
DRAPERS GARDENS
OLD BROAD ST.
BISHOPSGATE STR. WITHIN
St. HELENS PL.
LOTHBURY
THREADNEEDLE
BANK OF ENGLAND
Royal Exchange
Statue
CORNHILL
LEADENHALL
LOMBARD
KING WILLIAM ST.
GRACECHURCH STR.
FENCHURCH ST.
EASTCHEAP
Statue

RUT BLEES LUXEMBURG
& JEAN-LUC NANCY

London Winterreise

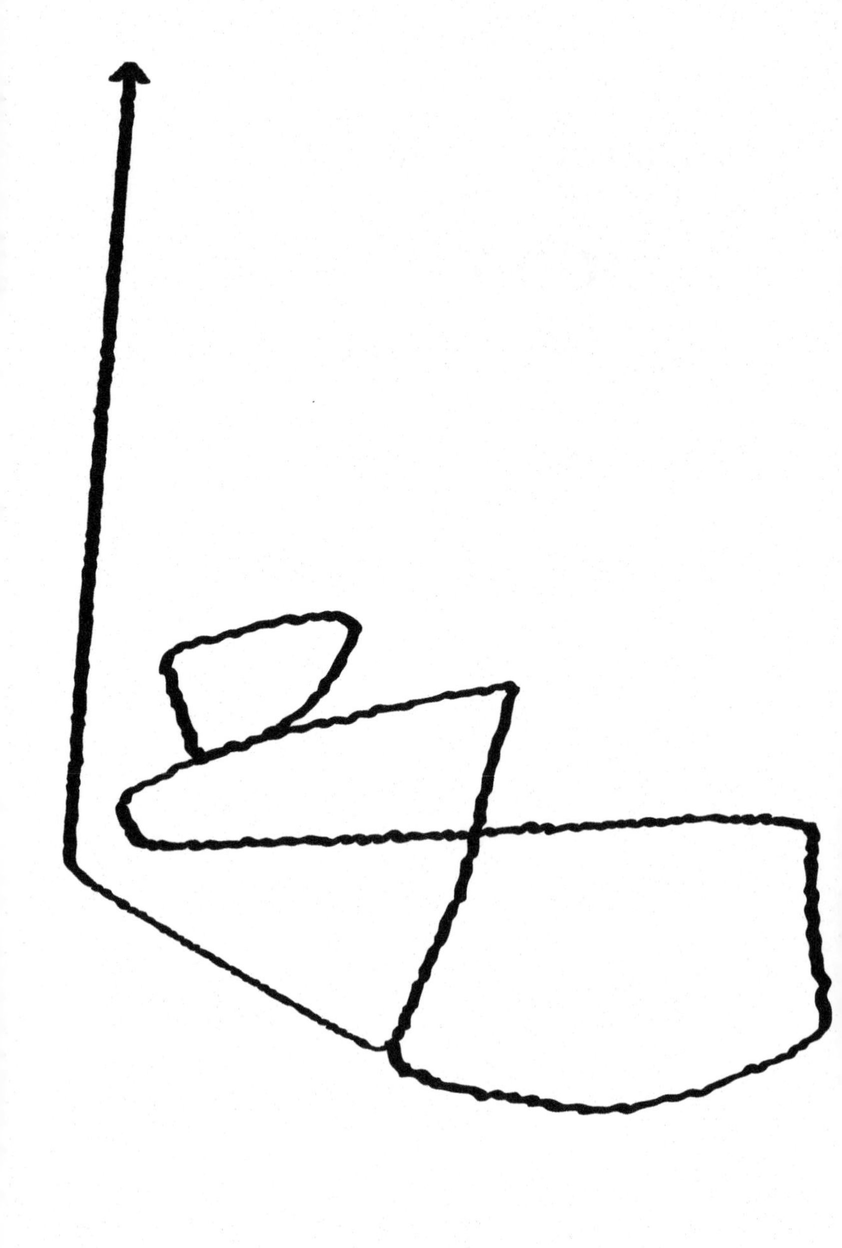

London Winterreise

The tracking shot wrests itself from the frozen image of a Greek colonnade. It travels, it journeys across the city in winter along with Schubert's bittersweet melody, in which the voyager sings that he came and will also leave a stranger.

The journey goes nowhere. Having wrested itself from the photographed Greek colonnade, from a ludicrous advertising poster with a troop of recycling containers lined up in front of it, the journey ends after several stops or stations, several meditative or puzzled halts. It has reached a miserable and grey, hostile and futureless obstruction. The world is so 'trüb', the voyager sings, so grey, so drab, so murky, so disenchanted.

The world is 'a much bigger mess', a mess much bigger than the mess of the camp, he may read as he comes across the tents set up by outraged protesters. And only a few steps further it says 'love is the answer', an echo of words sung by the voyager, 'das Mädchen sprach von Liebe'. The young girl has been glimpsed as she went by with her friend right in front of the recycling containers, while the poster of the Greek temple moved away into the background. Later the fluted and massive columns of the city's monuments will parade at the speed of a walk quickened by restlessness, just before we are led to dirty walls, nocturnal passers-by who are intrigued by the camera, and then on to the big shambles, a plastic bag next to a neo-Roman gate, a group of people waiting for a bus, and once again the lower parts of supposedly Doric or Ionic columns, shown repeatedly as if the repetition were the beat of the ambition to create a polis. The whole city becomes its own temple, lifted up by other and mimetic columns into the cathedral sky, by a spiral or a heavy cone or shell, by signs that gesture towards a sky overloaded with dusty steam and yellowish or blueish pollution. Only one image cuts through it all with its straightforward colours. It is the image of a blue arch with a frieze made of bricks. All that can be seen through its wide gape is an intense blackness into which the beige floor disappears as it turns greenish. Why should I stay on if I am going to be expelled, the voyager asks, and he begins to look elsewhere, in darker places. The high fronts of buildings and the glimmering partition-walls of the construction sites are shot through with lights that shimmer excessively, as if they were trying to emit a radiance that no longer does any good since all that may be left inside is emptiness. Perhaps the polis and its temples no longer have an inside, just like the ruins of the Greek temple on the poster, and all we can do on the construction site is walk from ruin to ruin, while a tired worker wearing a boiler suit as orange as the surrounding lights leans on something. What is he thinking of? He may see the passing voyager, or he may not. Love loves to gallivant, the voyager sings, to turn itself into a ballad, it loves to go from one to another. It passes in front of wire fences, in front of 140 LONDON WALL written in big antique-style letters, and then continues to heavy concrete blocks that are not topped by columns. Good night, my gentle darling, the voyager says before he vanishes. He does not wish to disturb her, he simply wants to let her know that he has thought of her in the night of the city, in the vicinity of the columns and the shambles, the Greek skyscrapers, the colourless dome, and the torn sails displayed along the construction sites, tinted the colour of mimosas or periwinkles. The photo captures all these

Brookfield
BM

140 LONDON WALL

nuances, these streams of dirty beige, of grey, of rancid butter, of greyish-brown and bistre, of bitumen and cobalt, of steel, silver and putty, it captures all the vestiges and pulverescences, all the flakes on a hat, all the fluorescent flashes on a protective net, and also the dense chocolate of the river that features a gliding boat, a boat that is not used by voyagers but by tourists who are in town and want to gaze at the Greek ruins, tomorrow or way back, before or after the big city. Writing of lights, photography, rain of bright photons that emanate from the sullied marble and from the lemony attire of a black night watchman whose cigarette lights up suddenly with a magenta sparkle. There is misery, abandonment, and yet there is also the voyager's song, the pausing of the camera, a patient waiting for each image to lay itself down, a note or a touch placed like tender mist.

MILL MEADS
TOWER HAMLETS CEMETERY
BROMLEY St. LEONARD
REGENT'S CANAL DOCK
RIVER
THAMES
WEST INDIA DOCK
WEST INDIA DOCK
SOUTH DOCK
UNION DOCKS
DRY DOCK
GLOBE POND
LAVENDER POND
ACORN POND
STAVE DOCK
THWARK
ARY ROTHERHITHE
CENTRE POND
LADY DOCK
COMMERCIAL DOCKS
QUEBEC POND
CANADA POND
NORWAY DOCK
GREENLAND DOCK
SOUTH DOCK
DEPTFORD WHARF
MILLWALL DOCK
ISLE of DOGS
BLACKWALL BASIN
EAST INDIA DOCK
Ordnance Wharf
CUBITT TOWN

NAYAN KULKARNI

Night Moves

PROLOGUE

Urban lighting can be understood as a political technology. It is subject to regulatory control, deployed through state legislative authority and managed through tiers of international, national, regional and local policy. This is a politics of technology that affects the citizen through spatial ubiquity and, through disparate forms of technocratic mediation, excludes them from an effective agency in its deployment and distribution.[1] Furthermore, in an urban context the manifestation of public realm lighting is almost always seen in relation to the more contingent proclivities of the private development. The photon does not recognise the transition from the public realm to the private realm and so bleeds from one into the other. The nocturnal urban mise-en-scene is then comprised of both state light and private light, both appearing to us as a totality; a simultaneity of light in space.

RED LIGHTS

On a clear evening the City of London and Canary Wharf dominate the eastern view from Waterloo Bridge. Many things change when the sun goes down. Seemingly immutable surfaces that contain, frame and regulate the city take on very different qualities. It is as if the natural order of things shifts into a different register, a register that might have something in common with imagination. Or perhaps the rendering of space in artificial light is also a form of imagination.[2] Nevertheless, many of the light systems in the city appear to have been installed with more prosaic and practical uses in mind. They demand something of the pedestrian; to do, or not do, something. Simple lit instructions cascade through history from the port and starboard (red and green) of the maritime system and the red flag waved in front of Robert Stevenson's Rocket, both warn and mark edges and masses. They are instructions, the first preventing a possible death and the other fluttering in advance of a certain but avoidable death. These light and colour systems speak of movement and attempt to regulate it.

Powerful red lamps order the architecture in relation to the capital's flight paths; the aviator's gaze is inscribed into the pedestrian's field of view.[3] From this position at the centre of London the river affords sight lines that allow us to follow these flight paths and recognise the function of the lamps. The modern airport constitutes a terrain of absolute regulation. From both sides of the terminal (airside and landside) arrival is marked by an ever-reducing set of possible physical movements. An examination of *Annex 14 to the Convention on International Civil Aviation Volume 1 Aerodrome*

Design and Operations[4] reveals the extent to which artificial light can be regulated to the point that it functions as a set of signifiers that, for the pilot, should each have only one possible reading.[5] The purpose of these standards is to produce and maintain a completely transparent system that through visual means prohibits unsanctioned movements. Furthermore, this language is required to function anywhere in the world. It seeks to be a universal language of light and colour.[6] The hierarchy of illumination and the accompanying performance and installation tolerances speak of a closed system that seeks to negate uncertainty. A passenger on a stormy night is safe in the knowledge that the pilots will read the signs and not respond discursively. They may well gaze across the airfield, gaining some optical pleasure from the sparkling display of colour, but this is not their point, it is simply a pleasant by-product, an excess.[7] Shortly after disembarking at London City Airport[8] the traveller is already very close to the heart of Canary Wharf. They are likely to have flown over it (particularly if the wind is from the east) and then on exiting the terminal building they have to confront it as a dominant figure in the landscape.

Returning to the landing. The pilot has to contend with a double reading of this language of light that cannot, should not, be allowed to coincide. It is crucial to bear in mind that a discursive reading in this moment could produce multiple mortalities, or as an architect remarked, ‘it most certainly results in having to write a lot of reports at the very least, and probably also some not inconsiderable costs to argue about’. However well trained the pilot might be, these lights are also the mark of: port, arrival, an orientation, a beacon, home; the pilot sits in the preferred seat, is the preferred reader.[9] Touch down, normal gravitation applies, the pilot can hand over, 'Welcome to earth'.[10]

In these advanced aerodromes we are given a precise diagram, or in Norman Klein's terms a 'script'[11] of landside.[12] These spaces are not exceptions to the rule of the 'global city'[13] they are its symbiotic intensifications. An aerodrome points us towards a functional space that breaks down the organisational necessity of getting into the air into ever more precise operational elements. The modern airport in no way breaks this logic. Instead, successive layers have been added to both sides of the entree/exit portals reproducing the city and exposing the portals as a fictive necessity. We are regulated on both sides; there is no transition, no (space).[14]

From this bridge the ensemble of red lights, on tall buildings, is complemented by another group of lamps. The aerial linear composition is completed by a field of tower cranes which together produce a network of red relationships in the night sky. Some of these lights are blinking. They are here in advance of the new buildings that they mark. Perched high in the skyline they are harbingers of a future where all that is air will congeal into a solid, they mark the spaces and warn. When the cranes leave the city these red markers will remain, placed high and so visible they become difficult to see, appearing to be able to hide in their own brightness and ubiquity.

Down at pavement level brake lights amplify the lines of rear warning lights on buses, vans, cars and motorbikes as they retreat from view. Each single, twin and multiple pairing informing us at once, that 'I am here', and 'I am now slowing down'. Red lights indicate a presence and then a deceleration, they are either receding or advancing. Traffic lights suture the street and bear the mark of regulations that relate this one light sign (stop, go and caution) to a network. The seasoned driver, or nascent traffic engineer, holds a tacit knowledge that these sign systems' staccato connect this junction to every other mainland road junction in the UK, they are all related to the same flows. Professional traffic engineers are beholden to what these lights mean for movement, they know their flows and understand the dynamics.

Following a slow panning gaze on the bridge it is impossible to miss a massive source of red light in the city. For whatever reason, the London Eye's illumination appears to have been paused. Normally, this installation of overbearing colour changing linear lights shifts through seemingly arbitrary colour cycles. But now a subjective choice appears to have been made, and it is simply glowing red.[15] We could anticipate that this colour has a meaning, a connection to a narrative, a relationship to an event that could be local, or even international. It could simply be that the lighting control system has failed on red. Nevertheless, the 'Eye' is red and it might mean something, to someone, at some time. This now fixed dynamic lighting is presumed to have a meaning; that is to point itself out, to make the structure clear in the scene of the city. The site is emphatically positioned through a kind of structural abstraction in colour and light. The sources of the architecture's illumination are tied to the structure in such a way that at night, the lamps, not the steel structure, are seen first and in this way the wheel can be observed.

This image of structured moving light comes into being as an event that reproduces a self-propelling logic, maintaining the wheel in the visual consciousness of the city. It persists because the lit image is calibrated to advance the object in space. Functioning as 'a this' rather than 'a that', duplicating the totemic at the level of an image, re-inscribing the iconic object with 'iconic lighting'. The problem we encounter in this city now is the invariability of this approach to aesthetic light. Seemingly every facade, structure, pilaster, canopy, can also be a support and a surface for bright and often saturated coloured lighting. The ability to emphasise an object in space is sequentially diminished as neighbouring structures adopt lighting as aesthetic signage. Consequently the nocturnal image is increasingly a totality of light. Each element bright, colourful and even dynamic. Following this additive logic, darkness then must be the remaining addition that could *point something out.*

The 'Eye' is a form of architecture that seeks to offer the wheel rider the city as a moving image. Moving, in so far as the city changes as the occupants of the viewing pods advance through the single cycle of the wheel. In contrast to this slow physical movement through space, the pattern of lights can cycle at the refresh rate of the control technology, changes in colour and intensity can occur at the speed of electronics, shy of the speed of light. Pulsing light is connected etymologically to the spinning of the body and points towards a perceptual imbalance. From the Greek strobos, an act of whirling, strobing light is experienced in rhythmic flashes, a regulated spinning, a form of voluntary action, a ritual even. This visual assault will never be seen by us because these frequencies of light modulation and excessive physical changes produce sensory bombardments that could have both physiological effects and other unpredictable affects. Through this illumination, the 'Eye' itself becomes the image that prohibits a seeing.[16] The 'Eye' sees itself within the blind spot of its own offered image, it sees itself within the image that it forms in the city rather than the images it provides to the paying guest. The wheel rider cannot see what the 'Eye' produces within what the 'Eye' offers.

Turning back towards Canary Wharf, a bright white light sparkles at the apex of the stainless steel pyramid that is grounded as a building but positioned in the sky.[17] Our eyes are drawn from these many red lights towards one luminous white centre: a pharotic[18] moment within an arrangement of tall buildings all of which, in one way or another, use façadism to link the architecture to a conservative order.[19] These building technologies can be skinned, dressed if you like, in any manner, in a style. The pyramid, above and at once at the centre of it all, is a device to speak of and towards a cosmological exteriority: a structure in stainless steel, resistant to corrosion, an alloy whose surface seeks an atemporal status, not permanent but persistent. The roof has been formed as a symbolic gesture that anchors this island of commerce both to this city and to the cosmos. The white light is a beacon and also a warning.[20]

ARRIVAL

At Canary Wharf Jubilee Line Station every possible movement from the doors of the underground carriage to the mechanical barriers at the top of the escalator appears to be accompanied by light. The vaulted space itself combines numerous approaches to ambient and task lighting, some concealed, others hung more conventionally. When the uniformity of ground plane illumination is looked at more closely we find much higher levels of light at the thresholds and potential conflict zones. Light sources are installed in all planes and at all levels: from beneath the ground, ankle, knee, handrail, eye, just above head, ceiling. The final ascent to Middle Dock is covered by a glass canopy which supports an array of bright white lamps. This arch of light causes the more calmly lit external spaces opposite and adjacent to the entrance to appear to be much darker than they are. Retinal perception is extremely sensitive, children are warned not to stare at the sun, and when they do stop (voluntarily or otherwise) the world around them slowly fades back to light.

On completing the ascension and exit from the station moving light divides the building to the right. Installed on 30 South Colonnade is a moving horizontal ribbon constructed in a grid of orange lamps. This sign is showing stock values. Thomas Edison's Universal Stock Ticker (1869) disgorged its tape, printing in a delicate analogue line a constant record of an information stream. Now digital light proceeds along this façade, constantly updated ephemeral values are marked in flickering diodes. This perpetual cycle of movement and erasure is attached to the architecture, planted in the eyes through amber illumination: it is another caution. In this horizontal movement, temporal spiralling values pertain to a loop that is both a noose and an escape as it spins around the architecture. It appears to be understood in this neighbourhood as nothing more than a moving conveyor of value. In this installation, value and ephemerality are explicitly rendered in light;

there is no distance between what is being conveyed and how it is conveyed, providing this place with a totally transparent light sign. Then without a pause it suddenly changes into a Reuters' news feed, displaying fragments of texts, bold headlines, the news.

RESTAURANT

The Henry Addington seeks to extend its terrain to the outside. These lights are simply here to illuminate the pavement adjacent to the doors. Understood from the inside, they afford a soft landing as a patron exits and simple task lighting for the plain air patrons. These are later additions to the façade, demonstrating clearly that the lamp cannot be disassociated from its effects. A simple luminaire is generally comprised of three elements: the lamp, the housing and the electronics. The housing may or may not have some form of optical system that regulates and controls the light as it moves outwards from its source. The electronics can be as simple as a basic logic gate: an 'on' or 'off'. The source transforms energy into both heat and light (generally more heat than light). Heat is a problem of efficiency and efficacy. A direct view of the lamp can produce mild discomfort to permanent retinal damage.

Every type of lamp, from the candle flame to the OLED (organic light emitting diode), delivers photons in specific wavelengths. The combinations of these factors determine how artificial light comes into contact with our bodies, both via the eye and skin. These luminaires, mounted not far above eye level, have the following characteristics: narrow band wavelength, medium to poor colour rendering index, direct view of lamp from close range. To put it another way, cold and harsh, or another way, cheap and not so cheerful. This light installation is in the order of the aggressive police interview.

As we turn away from the door towards the docks, the water acts as a welcome retinal analgesia. A gentle breeze causes the dark surface to undulate and ripple, breaking up the grids of light, turning points within architecture into technological jalarka.[21] Across this surface sources of light are broken up and woven into a new kind of material; a new image is formed in these reflections. This turbid screen is reflecting more red and blue, than green. Skittering from side to side, white and red light blurs; it is also reflecting light from the trains crossing the bridge above.

SQUARING UP

John Cabot may well have discovered parts of North America in 1497 but we can encounter him here, over 500 years later, in the form of a square bounded by commercial office space. Jeff Bell's *Cast Glass Panels* (1992) order Cabot Square by deploying lead crystal glass and fluorescent light at its cardinal points. They are also shields to protect the viewer from seeing the ventilation service arrangements from the mall below. Here the artwork functions as a cover to the more prosaic requirements of the subterranean shops and services. These spaces need to breathe and the holes provide a spatial opportunity for an aesthetic gestural addition to the square. A hole becomes a pattern, a scaled up lampshade. Peering through the gaps in the glass structure we can glimpse a rather less decorative, even industrial, installation of grilles and lights attached to steel structure.

Ventilation ducts can also be the sites for a kind of art in architecture.[22] The technical necessity of having pipes, grilles and passages from below to above produces a formal dilemma: to celebrate or cover. These are screens that protect us from an unpleasant view. Here expediency provides a space with an opportunity. Cabot Square is mounted on a plinth of granite and so speaks of being planted, rooted into the earth. If visible, the grilles would reveal that what appears to be terra firma is in reality a stone deck, and that the ground that you are standing on is a roof. Bell's artwork is covering up much more than four holes.

It can be observed that these bespoke lanterns fulfil a multiple function, they exude the special, the organic, the honest craft master plying their trade. They also glow, revealing the particularity of the material, this is the real thing, it has quality. The authentic moment of craft in these panels is so much to do with the blemishes, for it is the blemishes that signify the handmade. 'The sheer magnificence of cast glass–light and airy, and at the same time sturdy and immensely strong–is perfect for display in open, public spaces'[23]. They illuminate, or rather, they intercept the source of light and filter it. This filtering and dispersal of industrial light is transformed by the cast glass and refers to the visceral; light seen through skin. The panels are situated between us and the source of light and because of this we are spared the retinal discomfort of a direct view into a lamp. But then these lamps are only installed to reveal the qualities of the materials and to add a softer, more pleasant ambiance to the square's illumination. We cannot be certain which light effect is primary because both are working in the space; they are products of each other.

This vertical arrangement of light occupies the same plane as the pedestrian, it is a screen positioned at body level in space. Bell's artwork contains much of what we can see in more contemporary manifestations of wall as light source in built space. In the decades since this installation, technological developments in solid state lighting now mean that the animation of surface light through materiality can take the form of actual screens in the form of scaled up flat displays, and material animation is replaced with digital movement. In both instances the surface mediates the light source. In Bell's glass screens the mediation and resultant animation is a simple product of industrial illumination meeting an organic filter. In the emerging paradigm of wall as screen (both as mask and display) the light source becomes the movement, materiality is replaced by digitality, substance by technological effect. Sensual changes created in the play of bodily movements of eyes in space are replaced with the (impossible) stable view point inscribed in the screen: the unmoving body.

To see a manifestation of this new mode of urban lighting we need to move both through time and space. In Speirs & Major's *Kings Cross Tunnel LED Concept* (The Light Lab, 2014) we can experience the celebration of a double movement: the actual movement (a necessity) of the people through transport infrastructure and the optical movement of light and colour on the walls of a particular pedestrian tunnel. In Argent PLC's Kings Cross Development we find a situation of technological material (screen) covering an engineering necessity (tunnel) providing an enhanced optical experience within a space of transit. In both cases, spanning over twenty years of art in architecture, abstraction underpins a logic of space. In this tunnel, an architectural surface simply moves through illuminated animation, it is the fact of change and movement in the abstract mode of coloured light that counts. It is both stable, in so far as it illuminates the space, and unstable, in so far as its lit effects are animated. However, this is a very safe kind of instability as darkness is not included in its programme.

Both artworks communicate a value granted to space above the value of a concrete structural wall, which is also a structural necessity. They then function as a gift to space, an addition, a gain.[24] So between these two installations we can see actual material value (cast lead crystal glass) produced in an abstract language (non-figurative) shifting to the value of a digital moving surface, a kind of pure abstraction. In both situations the surfaces are covering something up, concealing in a play of light: in Cabot Square a play of light and material, and in the Kings Cross Underpass simply in light. They are both skins, at a level that can be touched not just seen, inhabiting the same plane as the body.

HARD LIGHT

A short distance beyond Canary Wharf's freehold, into a more complex layering of public street and private development, routes lead to a zone where the streets congeal into a complex of private and social housing. Just off the Thames Path, the pavements track through less dramatic territories where light is more commonly a form of social and domestic utility; a tool for seeing. However practical it might be, does it still show us more than it lights?

Here in the courtyard bounded by Bethlehem House and Padstow House, a series of floodlights[25] have been mounted onto the walls, each luminaire installed so that the car park, is powerfully illuminated from all directions. It is as if the gazes from the flats above are represented by this radiant energy. Relying on the orientation of the domestic circulation, the residents' points of view are aligned to this illumination of the enclosed external space. The panopticon, the all-seeing eye at the centre of things, is reversed in this triangular yard bounded by three blocks. The power of these lights means that a double function is performed. The primary is that of utility, we can see and can be seen. In addition the visitor can see but not comfortably, this happens through an effective blinding constructed in the dramatic contrasts experienced in the deployment so much luminal power accidentally aimed at the eye.

This is an order of illumination where each balcony position becomes an optical centre. Does this mean that a resident can only be truly safe when completely illuminated? We are minded to think of defensive encampments, this liminal space is off the street, yet not the front door. At a perfect range for viewing from above, the space is lit to enable easy visual recognition of those who belong here, the familiar, the neighbour. In this simple application of a secure-by-design method the stranger, visitor and itinerant can be quickly and effectively surveilled.

TUNNEL

A few strides away from the estate there is at last the possibility of darkness. Here the canal eases its way under Commercial Road. It is a wide road, so the arch is just long enough to make it feel like a tunnel. Beyond this, leading us to the southern edge of Mile End Park, the path continues into a narrow embankment containing the water. At present this canal towpath enjoys a very low level of Illumination, so in turning right at Basin Approach, successive lights between us and the tunnel create what appears to our eyes as a dark void.

At a predefined distance from the tunnel's threshold some type of switch is triggered by proximity and what was seen as a dark void is filled with white linear light. This movement, physical and electronic, banishes the shadows revealing the empty passage; if there was already an occupant they too would have tripped the switch. If we pause and remain still for long enough, will this problem of light resolve itself and allow us to inhabit the shadows again? Tick tock, an 'on' is an 'off', the lights on means that sight is off; seeing through the tunnel is negated by enabling this seeing within. Now that the interior of the tunnel is illuminated, it effectively obscures the view through. Rapid shifts in illumination change the experienced retinal contrast and this plays games with space.

The towpath north of the bridge remains unlit but is not totally dark. Here illumination is contingent upon the spill from other places. The canal glints in this stolen light. For a few hundred metres shadow reasserts its place in the night. Evanescent images appear in the coincidences of light and water. Here space can be seen in a different register to that which determines Cabot Square, material in this place is gifted an evocative subjective force.

PARK

I'm strolling from the canal towards a tarmac path through Mile End Park when a lit corridor appears, which signs and supports pedestrian movement through the now dark glades. The park has been made more accessible through this deployment of artificial light. Here a conventional street scene seeks to maintain spaces' uses into the night. White lamps carve a channel making the connection, or rather keeping the connection from north to south. So mobility is linked to civility and technology extends its temporal utility. This light makes night time more useful, more productive; a path through the park produces more effective use through an idea of safety inscribed into illumination. Fear may well still lurk in the shadows. In the light we are available to and absorbed by the technocratic panopticon economy of monitoring cameras. It is the very ubiquity of this kind of lighting that invites us to use space and wander through its distributed eye without caution.

In planning a future city, surface infrastructure seeks to constitute new realms of free movement.[26] Through 'enhancing' the street lighting are we ready for these emancipated territories? It is in this insistence on a logic of space, an orientation that also produces a centre, that we can find the approved versions of here: where we are, where we were, where we should be. Because we can see clearly where we are going, we can also be observed from the forced shade at the edges of the beams, the light is shared and has a double purpose. We should be aware that we are being watched. We are revealed from positions within the now unlit fringes, after all we are lit. The parkland is not. But this light envelopes the walker in a safe blanket of electromagnetism and, as with the extended life of the irradiated fruit, the moment of inner corruption is deferred, the entropic powers of germs suspended.

NAKTAM[27]

Technological illumination is a planned intervention in and upon the dark, it is a deliberate act rather than a response to what is given to us by the sun. One of the effects of this illumination is to heighten darkness, accentuating what remains unlit, and through this process it dramatises the presence of what is illuminated. And so as artificial light illuminates certain spaces, it also makes them into images: images rendered with force. This is a force that imposes an alternative order to space. Light creates images by surrendering a form of flat ubiquity, a kind of honesty, into a theatre of chiaroscuro. This rendering privileges and excludes. In one place it might cover up, and in others dispense with the imperfections that can be seen in the sun. It does this through masking them in contrast.

Joachim Schlör writes of the nocturnal city at the turning on of the streetlights, as a series of images that 'condensing into solid metaphors, [bring] the imagination closer to practical knowledge, experience and everyday life'.[28] Here we find a possible bond; the adhesion of the idea of the city to our experiences within it. Like an epoxy, this adhesive operates in a process through which a body is acted upon by a catalyst. Initially the body is fluid, sticky, almost ephemeral (almost because it tends to leave a stain on whatever it comes into contact with). In this state, things can move about and be reconfigured, even get replaced. The catalyst then acts upon this body and does two things, and this action is deliberate. Firstly, it secures the adhesive properties. Secondly, in this securing moment it transforms the fluid into a solid. This is an irrevocable molecular level event. In this new state, the body has been transformed into a stable condition; a permanent bond. Like a formal contract between the metaphor and its image, the catalyst acts as both agent and witness. We have moved from a bond as action to bond as noun, and now that this bond has been made it can only be unmade through another force.

Solid-state lighting combined with advanced networked control systems means that digital image effects, once contained within theatrical and cinematic production, have begun to infiltrate the built spaces that we occupy. Furthermore, it can be seen that complex arrangements of functional and aesthetic lighting are increasingly deployed to intensify the exploitation of the city at night. In the coincidence of the deliberate act to light with the contingencies of time and built space, its effects play out on the body and the eye. However complex these deployments of light might be, their language remains constrained by the binary oppositions of welcome and warning, beacon and path marker; even as they act as instructions, chaperones, they perform like showmen and take on the role of the guard.

The intensity and complexity of street, architectural and feature lighting are combining into stable forms of lit city image. Although seeking to be specific solutions to particular places they are instead merging into a unified (globalised) static set of normalities. The paradox is this: technological development means that light and image projection could coalesce into prolific forms of image making embedded in the city's infrastructure, the authorships distributed and only partially controlled. Instead, this possibility is ossifying into a set of conventions that turns us towards the stable, familiar, entertaining, and ultimately clinical.

ENDNOTES

1 In Andrew Barry's (UCL) short paper at the Lighting Futures Seminar (Configuring Light, 2015) urban lighting was framed through describing a number of modalities. It should suffice to note that standardisation plays directly into the delivery capabilities of large, often multinational, corporations. As a political technology it can only be fully accessed as a phenomenon by the technical specialist. As a manifestation within a broader urban infrastructure it is nested in regulation and is controlled by another community of specialists. Additionally, it is produced in the public sphere through layers of planning and strategic policy through the agency of yet another configuration of specialists. Through these processes it establishes its own socio-technological world.

2 Latin lumen 'light' (rendering phen-, from Greek phaino- 'shining').

3 All buildings in the UK, when extending above a legally defined height, have to be marked.

4 International Standards and Recommended Practices, ICAO, Fifth Edition, July 2009.

5 Dominant Code.

6 Totalising.

7 This excess follows Zizek's radical subjectivisation in so far as the delight, or imaginative projection/refraction, turns the scene inside out. I am making a parallel here with the distancing effect of being above the aerodrome at night and its immanent subjectivisation.

8 A very modest aerodrome indeed.

9 This formulation of light situates the pilot within a space of a double reading developed form Stuart Hall's framework. http://visual-memory.co.uk/daniel/Documents/S4B/sem-gloss.html#negotiated_code. That is, in the position of the 'ideal reader' both making a 'preferred reading' and an 'aberrant reading'. This is simply an attempt to situate narrativity and imaginative projection as being folded into (within and between), not coincident to,

the 'dominant code'. In this sense imagination is not a separable, rather, imagination is structured, contained, within the rules of these lights. Imagination, here, is not free but constituted.

[10] Dean Devlin and Emmerich Roland, *Independence Day*, Twentieth Century Fox, 1996. This is the statement accompanying Capt. Steven Hiller's (Will Smith) punching into insensibility an alien pilot. Not only does this scene provide us with a stark critique of US immigration policy, it also marks landing as a radical departure.

[11] Norman Klein, *The Vatican to Vegas: A History of Special Effects*, New York: The New Press, 2004, pp. 327–29.

[12] Airport architects refer to 'landside' as uncontrolled zone and 'airside' as controlled zone.

[13] Term that Saskia Sassen coined to mark the radical shift in how we should understand the city in the late capitalist period.

[14] The parenthesising of space follows Henri Lefebvre's challenge in *Towards an Architecture of Enjoyment*. In order to propose a space of freedom in architecture he argued that it was necessary to imagine a kind of architecture that was outside, perhaps defended from, analytical or productive disciplines.

[15] This deep orange red colour is probably linked to the new partnership of the London Eye. The *Coca-Cola* London Eye. https://www.londoneye.com

[16] This is a result of the bright light partially obscuring the views outwards from within the pods.

[17] According to aviation law, as the light is white it has to pulse, red can stay in a steady state.

[18] Pharos, the lighthouse erected by Ptolemy II (308–246 bc) in c.280 on the island of Pharos, off the coast of Alexandria. Cited variously as one of the Seven Wonders of the World.

[19] The first iteration of the Canary Wharf development deployed building technologies on whose structural frameworks could be hung (bonded and bolted) materials and compositions that form the important rain screen and insulation package. These panels and the detailing have the potential to conform to an idea of a building style. It is clear that this first generation of Canary Wharf towers allude to the permanence and values associated with marble, granite and stainless steel, referring to buildings constructed in solid stone, a lineage.

[20] As the turbines spun down at Battersea Power Station Thatcher's government were spinning up, liberalising, and deregulating land for other kinds of motive power. One year after the steam abated and the air cleared, The City of London's resistance to Credit

Suisse First Boston's (CSFB) development plans produced proposals for a new office that could unlocked the other potentials of the Isle of Dogs. After the initial consortium, CSFB and Morgan Stanley, pulled out of the development Canadian developers Olympia and York developed the initial phase; they in turn went bust. (information from Wikipedia). Canary Wharf continues to grow from the docks and the reclaimed land.

[21] जलार्क, jalArka n.image of the sun reflected in the water (Sanskrit).

[22] Examples and short narrative to follow.

[23] http://www.glasscasts.co.uk/public.html

[24] A planning gain in the case of Kings Cross and an element of the environmental offer that is Canary Wharf.

[25] Flood Light is a powerful combination of verb and noun; the specification warns you of its proclivities.

[26] At least since the European shift towards pedestrianisation of high streets, the legible cities movements, the access for all agendas…'The general consensus was that municipalities (smart cities) will be in control in future when it comes to lighting design, media architecture and even energy supply. Right now a lot needs to be learnt. The market is in relative turmoil, the situation complex, the software revolution ongoing. Media architecture will continue to have a huge impact, hopefully in a more controlled, conscious way to be able to curate and choreograph activities and engage the community in the city they inhabit. 'Media Architecture Biennale 2014', Professional Lighting Design, 2015, 63.

[27] Sanskrit, naktam, at night, by night.

[28] Joachim Schlör, *Nights in the Big City*, London: Reaktion, 1989.

Writing

British Museum
Bloomsbury
Foundling Hospital
Regent St. Peter's
RUSSELL SQUARE
BLOOMSBURY SQUARE
RED LION SQUARE
QUEEN SQUARE
BRUNSWICK SQUARE
MECKLENBURGH SQUARE
TAVISTOCK PLACE
GREAT CORAM STR.
BERNARD STREET
GUILFORD STREET
GREAT ORMOND ST.
COMPTON ST.
HARRISON STREET
SIDMOUTH STR.
LEIGH STR.
BURTON CRESCENT
WOBURN PLACE
UPPER BEDFORD PLACE
BEDFORD PLACE
MONTAGUE PLACE
MONTAGUE STREET
SOUTHAMPTON ROW
GREAT RUSSELL ST.
HART STREET
NEW OXFORD ST.
BLOOMSBURY STR.
CONDUIT STREET
LAMB'S CONDUIT ST.
NEW ORMOND ST.
CHAPEL ST.
ORMOND YARD
THEOBALD'S RD.
HENRIETTA ST.
TAVISTOCK
Ch.

SEAN ASHTON

Point to Point

A Circular Walk through Bloomsbury Incorporating Mecklenburgh Square

START POINT: Russell Square tube station
END POINT: Russell Square tube station
GRID REF: TQ3022682125
DIFFICULTY: Moderate

1.

On leaving the train at Russell Square, ignore arrows to the lift and proceed along the platform to the spiral staircase. At the bottom of the staircase is a Transport for London sign: 'This staircase has 175 steps, do not use except in an emergency'. Ignoring the sign, plant one foot firmly on the first step and bring your other foot up onto the second step. Then bring your trailing foot up past your lead foot onto the third step. And repeat. There's an option to put your hand on the inner or outer rail of the staircase for support, but the recommended route is down the centre.

2.

With the central shaft of the staircase on your right and the wall of Victorian tiles on your left, proceed upwards, bearing first north, then east, then south, then west; north, east, south and west again, and so on, completing a full revolution every twenty-six steps. Though classified as 'circular', the walk would be more accurately described as 'helical', given the continuous ascent. In fact, several circles are completed throughout.

3.

Continue on your north-east-south-west-north-east-south-west bearing, breathing at regular intervals. Though the early stages of the walk are not difficult, the steps taper towards the central spine of the staircase all the way up due to its natural geometry, leaving less room for the foot and making progress along the inner rail hazardous. The going is easiest on the outer rail, but those coming down tend to favour this line, and it's wiser to keep to the middle.

4.

Step 40 is the first recommended stop. The scenery here isn't substantially different to Step 19 or Step 34: the Victorian tiling is impressive, but the central shaft of the staircase is concealed behind steel cladding, and the fluorescent light doesn't really do justice to the interior of Leslie Green's Grade II listed building. However, if you turn to the wall and close your eyes *there is a spectacular view of the Chilterns rising up over the picturesque town of Wendover, with the Red Lion Hotel, a half-timbered building of brick noggin dating from the 17th Century, visible at the bottom of the valley.*

5.

A little further on is a convex mirror bolted to the wall, allowing those going up to see those coming down and those coming down to see those going up before they appear in person, so that those coming down find it difficult to ambush those going up, while those going up find it equally difficult to ambush those coming down: a security measure.

6.

A further 20 steps brings you to another a point of local interest. On a ceramic tile close to the skirting, in faded capital letters, is a piece of racist graffiti: *SOMEONE PLEASE PUT US ALL OUT OF OUR MISERY NOW BEFORE THIS COUNTRY TURNS INTO A NATION OF HALF-BREEDS.* Above this, on an adjacent tile, someone else has added: *LAST MAN TO LEAVE UK TURN OUT THE LIGHTS.* The words are barely legible but you can just make them out.

7.

Leaving the racist graffiti behind, follow the same route until you reach a small rectangular air vent. Opposite this is a small opening in the cladding around the staircase's central shaft, through which can be seen the wiring that runs from the ground floor of the station to the platforms below. The opening isn't wide enough to see more than a few feet of the plunging interior, but the restricted view of the cables zip-tied to the aluminium trunking, bunched together with different kinds of electrician's tape, everything thrown into soft-focus by several generations of dust, spiders' webs and interstitial crud, is impressive in its own way.

8.

A few more steps brings you to the final stage of the walk. Gone now is the musty smell that seemed so persistent when you set out on your journey. Absent too is the trepidation you felt on taking the first of your 175 steps, 130 of which you have already completed. At step 142, turn to the wall, close your eyes, put your coat over your head and take in *the stunning views of the Darent Valley in Kent. A small tributary of the Thames, the River Darent powered several water mills in its day, but riverside ecosystems are now threatened by reduced flow in the area.*

9.

Leaving the stunning views of the Darent Valley behind, keep to your north-east-south-west-north-east-south-west bearing until the terrain changes, the steps now unfolding not spirally but as two straight flights separated by a landing – a transition not indicated in advance by any kind of signage. The risers of these steps are slightly higher than those of the spiral staircase, adding difficulty to the final stage of the walk. The second flight brings you past the lift, where you bear diagonally into the ticket hall.

10.

The ticket hall itself is something of a disappointment: people jostling impatiently, uniformed staff with their hands behind their backs, rocking absent-mindedly on their heels. However, by closing your eyes, putting your coat over your head and wadding up your ears with toilet paper, you can easily imagine *stepping out onto the concourse of Grand Central Station in New York, with just enough time for a cocktail before boarding your train to the conference in Philadelphia.* Spend as long as you like in Grand Central, then place your Oystercard on the yellow circular pad of the ticket barrier. The gate should open automatically, giving access to the ticket hall and the street beyond.

11.

Emerging onto the pavement, you see that it's only quarter past twelve. However, the walk can be extended at this point if you turn right out of the station and go past the Brunswick Shopping Centre towards nearby Mecklenburgh Square. *A Georgian residential development, Mecklenbugh Square has recently been dismantled in its entirety and relocated to New Songdo in South Korea. An impressive, rectilinear void now marks the site of its period architecture and gardens. A substantial amount of soil has been removed, and some of the rubble is still visible at the bottom of the excavation.* A circuit of the square brings you to the lower end of Lamb's Conduit Street. The recommended pub here is the Lamb, which has an excellent selection of cask ales. The recommended lunch stop is the Star of Bengal, an Indian restaurant just round the corner.

Bloomsbury
British Museum
Foundling Hospital
RUSSELL SQUARE
QUEEN SQUARE
RED LION SQUARE
BLOOMSBURY SQUARE
BRUNSWICK SQUARE
MECKLENBURGH SQUARE
REGENT SQUARE
HARRISON STREET
SIDMOUTH STR.
LEIGH STR.
COMPTON ST.
HUNTER STREET
MARCHMONT ST.
HENRIETTA ST.
GREAT CORAM STR.
WILMOT ST.
BERNARD STREET
GUILFORD STREET
GREAT ORMOND ST.
GREAT ORMOND YARD
TAVISTOCK PLACE
WOBURN PLACE
UPPER BEDFORD PLACE
BEDFORD PLACE
MONTAGUE PLACE
MONTAGUE STREET
SOUTHAMPTON ROW
THEOBALDS RD.
LAMBS CONDUIT STREET
MILLMAN STREET
HART STREET
GREAT RUSSELL ST.
NEW OXFORD ST.
BLOOMSBURY STR.
Ch.

JASPAR JOSEPH-LESTER

Public Notice

Relocation Services
1 Central Park
New Songdo
South Korea

05.09.2015

Dear Resident,

Closure of Mecklenburgh Square Gardens (MSG / 1476)

Stage 1 of relocation work to the gardens will commence on **01.10.2015.** The TRANSHERITAGE relocation project will begin with the excavation and transportation of the London plane trees located at the center of the gardens. Roads surrounding the gardens will be closed at regular intervals from **01.10.2015 - 01.10.2016** for crane and transportation vehicles (see timetable of Mecklenburgh Square road closures).

The excavation and transportation of the London planes to New Songdo will be followed with excavation work to the remaining trees, plants and large shrubs. The grass, paths, railings, benches, BBQ's, tennis court and drain covers will be removed and transported as part of Stage 2 relocation in November 2015.

Work to prepare Mecklenburgh Square houses for removal will commence on the east side of the square from 01.02.2016. Numbers 11 – 20 will be first to be removed and transported for re-construction. Further details regarding the removal of the houses, pavements, streetlights and roads will be circulated shortly.

We apologize for any disruption over the period of relocation work.

Hamilton Lake
Head of Marketing and Communications
TRANSHERITAGE

DOCK
SOUTH QUAY
Upper Pool
Parliamentary Boundary (Southwark)
Thames Tunnel
Station
High Water Mark of Ordinary
St James Ch
Rotherhithe Union Workhouse
All Saints Ch
PARK
Cricket Ground
SOUTHWAR
Patent Rope Manufactory
Electric Telegraph
SOUTH EASTERN RAILWAY
Glue Works
Patent Manure Manufactory
(BRICKLAYERS ARMS EXTENSION)
Parliamentary Bound
Southwark
Lambeth

LAURA OLDFIELD FORD

The Rotherhithe Caryatids

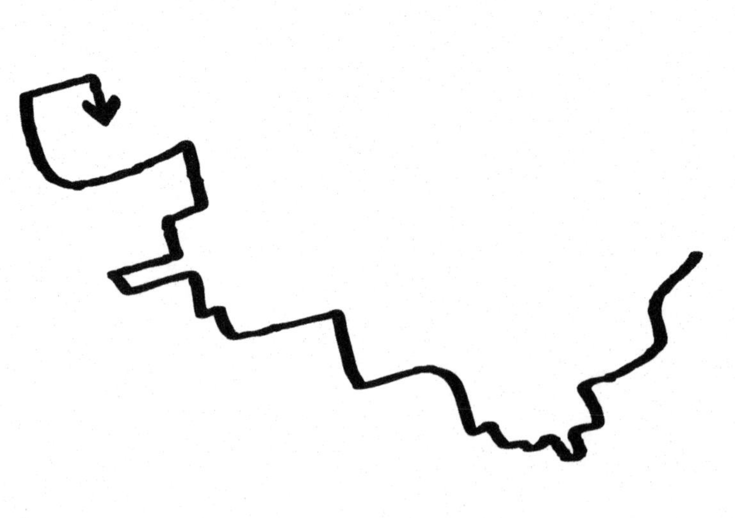

A caryatid (/kæri'ætɪd/; Greek: Καρυάτις, plural: Καρυάτιδες) is a sculpted female figure serving as an architectural support, taking the place of a column or a pillar, supporting an entablature on her head. The Greek term karyatides literally means 'maidens of Karyai', an ancient town of the Peloponnese. Karyai had a famous temple dedicated to the goddess Artemis in her aspect of Artemis Karyatis: 'As Karyatis she rejoiced in the dances of the nut-tree village of Karyai, those Karyatides who, in their ecstatic round-dance, carried on their heads baskets of live reeds, as if they were dancing plants'. (Kerenyi, 1980, p. 149).

THE ROTHERHITHE CARYATIDS

Paradise Gate, Southwark Park.

You walk through avenues of oak and cypress, gems of light swarming like heatstroke–obelisks, circles, paths veering into sepulchral groves. Twin caryatids casting pale light.

You remember them from the Heygate Estate, that sunken garden on Deacon Way. Their presence here is disorientating, it shocks you, a sharp point of return. The thought of them had surged prismatically when you heard the estate was being demolished, you imagined them stolen by antique dealers, left in a shed somewhere, dusty and broken. Now, after years in exile they are here again. You are stunned by their serenity, their totemic strangeness; you realise this encounter signifies the unspooling and repositioning of time. They emerged bearing wreaths of laurel and oak at Rotherhithe Town Hall in 1897 flanking the entrance with mournful ceremony. In 1974 they were moved to the Elephant and Castle where the first plattenbau blocks were forming in the rubble of slum clearances and bomb damage. The statues, in their solemnity, took possession of a hidden garden, a crypt-like zone of roses, maples and walnut trees.

You edge the boundary of Abbeyfield Estate, gardens leaching out onto parched avenues of Southwark Park – a lost church – *Rotherhithe the Epiphany* – concrete shell silently transmitting Scotland, austerity, endurance – you are repelled by the exhalation of damp – the powdery blooms of mildew. You remember those houses in ruins – Aspinden Street, Dilston Grove – doors opening onto cascades of masonry; orange curtains, a pale blue sitting room. You look for traces amidst the point blocks and maisonettes, sift through the dust for the handfuls of pebbles flecked with blue emulsion that you know are there. Thaxted Court, Damory House, a network of a exuberant gardens, a profusion of roses, damask pink, the sherbet scent of floribunda – The day's heat is stored in the concrete, the interwoven paths, walls keeling beneath arcs of jasmine. You feel the potential teeming in every surface – of course you think of him, in these moments he is near.

Rotherhithe New Road. A narrow path between a closed 60s precinct and a span of railway arches. You remember it from 2001, coming down to confront the NF, fragments coming back – police cordons, walking from the Elephant, blokes forming up in the Ancient Foresters. The path lets you brush the skin of the railway arches, the bricked-up shells of doorways, the oil slick iridescence of steel panels. You emerge in a CGI vista of cruel angles, brick avenues of 12-storey flats. You're not sure whether they're inhabited or not. These empty landscaped zones cause a loss of bearings. You think of the Silwood Estate, those flats stranded like a bomb blast for years. Hollow rooms, exposed walls, regimented squares of peach, coral, duck egg blue. You remember how the black text erupted like ground elder, bindweed, the swarming colonisation of forsaken land–*Tox, Fanta, Zombi*–

Silwood street. Azure sky, bleached pavements, rippling mediterranean heat. You feel the tension, the quiet conflict on this new estate. The will to impose order always a struggle with the damp, the shifting tides, the ceaseless overturning of populations. You come to a desolate vista of pale meadow grass and ferroconcrete, acres of shingle surrounding the power station. Walk under the railway bridge, vistas of rubble replicating in chalky arches like a collapsing empire.

The path is bone dry, engulfed at either side by banks of coiling briars. You walk through the muscat scent of elderflower, potent boughs reaching over you. This is the interstices, the border between Lewisham and Southwark; jurisdictive disputes leave neglected parcels of ground. You understand them as zones of wilderness, moments of rupture in the expanse of accelerated development. You step through drifts of ash, heaps of aggregate, a million twitching movements–convolvulus, knapweed, hogweed–

Beyond the wire fence the Millwall ground reminding you of that trigger–April 2001, shock heat of spring; you were on the platform of a stranded station, think now it must have been South Bermondsey. You saw a load of lads you knew from the North Peckham estate, said they'd squatted a row of shops in New Cross and asked you to go with them. You all jumped the train to Queens Road, crushed up together in the doorway, cans of cider, adrenaline surging from the violence in Bermondsey. You walked past dilapidated houses, blackened paintwork cracked like parched riverbeds. You remember the motel and the Montague Arms and the headache stink of traffic. The place was an old kitchen appliance shop opposite the Goldsmiths Tavern; they were harbouring stuff for the big Mayday demo—military flares, tyres, plastic sheeting. You disappeared through a door concealed beneath a dense strata of club flyers and squeezed into a room stinking of cordite. There were grilles at the windows and blackout curtains, you had to stand still a moment to let your eyes adjust. You climbed through a jagged aperture into the adjoining house and groped towards a stark rectangle of light. There was a back yard, an amethyst jungle of lilac and cherry; settees and office furniture, strings of light webbing the branches. You remember having to listen hard to the accents, Darndale, that estate with horses on the edge of Dublin. That day was the cataclysm, triggering a sequence that would break the seal on your life in the Heygate, forcing the door you could push through.

You carry on past the New Den, Surrey Canal Road– the spectral conduit is there in the straightness, the embanked verges.

The recalling of it makes sense of the dilapidated warehouses, the yard with caravans and portakabins. You're sure you've been here before, splinters of memory resilient in the derelict hoardings, the rigid layers of posters.

You pass beneath a railway bridge–brick spandrels punctured by the grasping pleas of property developers–*big fees paid for intros to landowners–social clubs, religious sites, scaffolds yards–*

A crossroads, banks of parched grass and a stone marker. You recognise the herma and think of him again, the mediator, escorting souls across the threshold–

Ilderton Road.
A millennial estate–Varcoe Road, Verney road–ochre terraces, pitched roofs, an evocation of middle England swathed in George Crosses. Walls are cracking down the middle, sections completely out of alignment.

An incongruous Victorian pub, the Bramcote, opening up time before the Blitz, before the slum clearances. You touch the plywood boards, the fractured blue paint and remember the pavements crushing blue and white with Millwall skins, the nihilistic roar–*we hate humans–no one likes us we don't care–*

That was the night the truck was set on fire, fruit machines smashed off the wall–you remember the plaster curlicues, the chipped cornices glowing with eroticism, and you think of his face, his hands on your waist–

The estate sprawls on, territory demarcated with beer garden furniture–drop down to a yard behind Selco, that massive builders merchants. Stop to talk to someone you haven't seen since you lived down here, one of your old neighbours on the Heygate. She's smoking in a doorway having a break from the refunds counter. The car park is encircled by black hoardings and a speckled tide of cigarette ends. Colombian flags, Ecuadorian snack stands, blokes sitting on kerbs in the sweltering heat.

You remember the buzzing anticipation, working through your shift on a hot day; standing in front of the mirror on every break, orange lipstick, black mascara, more and more until you walked out in a haze of perfume. She says you should come out later, Windsor first then Afrikiko, that club that used to be the Canterbury Arms. You remember how they boarded it up on match days, open as usual scrawled on the wooden hoardings and lines of riot police outside.

Massive new housing development on Rotherhithe New Road, that point where the Surrey Canal intersected the Old Kent Road. Telford Homes re-branding the zone *Bermondsey Works*. Feel the yearning undertow of the spectral canal.

Currys–PC World. Stop in McDonald's for a coke, sparkling cold in the car park with blokes from the construction site, luminous vests and the stink of blueberry kush–walk past the new Asda, the African churches encased in office blocks and industrial units. Burgess Park, the dusky edge of it–thickets of crab apple, walnut and sycamore. You get flashes of that party on Ossory Road–*Reclaim the Future*–a dark warehouse, cold breath of mildew in the loading bay where the crew sat taking the money. You remember conjoined yards then cerise light and the tropical heat of a vast room. You climbed metal stairs to an elevated platform–must have been the overseer's office, and looked out across a vast hangar, hundreds coming in wrecked on k. It was too much, you wanted to get out, broke through the nesting shells of the building and walked down the Old Kent Road.

You follow paths, subtle veins tracing the burrows of Burgess Park and come to the ornamental lake–huge circles drinking together, barbeques and merengue music. The Aylesbury is suddenly there, brutalist slabs radiant in the heat.

You walk through a plantation of silver birches, lad running through the maze of tracks like a rabbit, bags of *white and brown, seeds in his hands*–

The topography has altered since you left, new hills and woods have emerged. In 2002 it was a flat expanse of coarse grass, you could find the relics of the old Surrey canal and the ghost streets that branched from it.

Albany road, boundary of the Aylesbury Estate–trusses of roses, clematis clinging to satellite dishes–

This is the occupied zone–razor wire and security guards; new fences constructed to enclose the estate, purple gloss reminding you of the 70s, permeations of psychedelia, the seeping militancy of counterculture.

You find traces of graff from the protests, *down with the fences* and the ghostly strains of confrontations with police–

You pull yourself up into the twisting branches of a lilac, squeeze through a gap in a metal gate and drop down into a space between two walls. A narrow track unfolds between plywood panels and steel mesh. You press metal grids with your palms until you find one that unhooks, wrenches out of joint and prises off. You slink through, reminded then that walls have perforations, not always visible, fleeting moments when the threshold is gauzy. At that point of crossing there is peace.

Inside the zone it is paradisiac; the heat is intense, the birdsong exuberant, roses blooming for *no one but themselves.*

You have tapped into an ecstatic seam, a rush of euphoria like LSD stored in your spine unlocked after two decades–

The estate is suffused with chlorophyll light, colour saturated like a 70s photograph. You follow paths through stately conifers, squares of sitexed maisonettes–

A figure emerges from a concrete staircase, IFSEC logo–Brixton accent, asks if you're visiting someone–

Visiting someone–you are stunned that people are still here–must only be a scattering in this abandoned zone where zinc covers windows and
lines of displacement stretch out to Thamesmead, Woolwich, Bexley–he turns unconcerned back to his van–

A *visitation*–they are still here–in these melancholy gardens, saplings they planted break walls and fences, patio palms become giants–

You walk through a span of shimmering gardens, sweet canopies of elderflower, quatrefoil petals dusting your hair. You find tiled vestibules, frozen lifts, a network of aerial walkways riven by thistle, red campion, unexpected bursts of ornamental lilies–

You remember the paths you navigated, different routes every day, to the Heygate, the Aylesbury's twin. You look now across a private citadel, Elephant Park. It means nothing to you, a glossy shield around it, the unfurling of ironic platitudes–*an established neighbourhood where everyone loves to belong*–

The Heygate, a place indelibly etched. You knew how it all connected, prized your knowledge of the brutalist blocks, the bridges over breezeblock yards. You remember the olive green paint and the pale outlines of 80s graffiti. And all those nights, fierce moments of bonding in that sullen, airless room. They've obliterated the estate but you can still conjure it, it never goes away.

The sunken garden occupied a different temporality; its emptiness, the strangeness of the statues reminded you of a De Chirico painting. It seemed unreachable as you looked down from your 10th-floor window, an enclosed woodland responding to the cyclical time of the seasons. The looming slab blocks sheltered it from the frantic diurnal rhythm of the shopping centre, the market, the Charlie Chaplin pub.

The carved symbolism of the caryatids was lost to you then but feels poignant now in the moment of decoding–oak for resilience, laurel for triumph.

You scan the hoardings depicting an Elephant and Castle you don't recognise–a cleansed zone, an affluent white population. It is sanitised, porosity of the rookery sealed. You wonder if the caryatids might transmit something of the Heygate in their glade in Southwark Park. In their circling worship of Artemis, they signal a return to wilderness.

You look through the perimeter fence at the new development, the 30-storey towers with their *diverse brickwork and asymmetrical balconies*. You want to locate the garden but the coordinates are shifting.

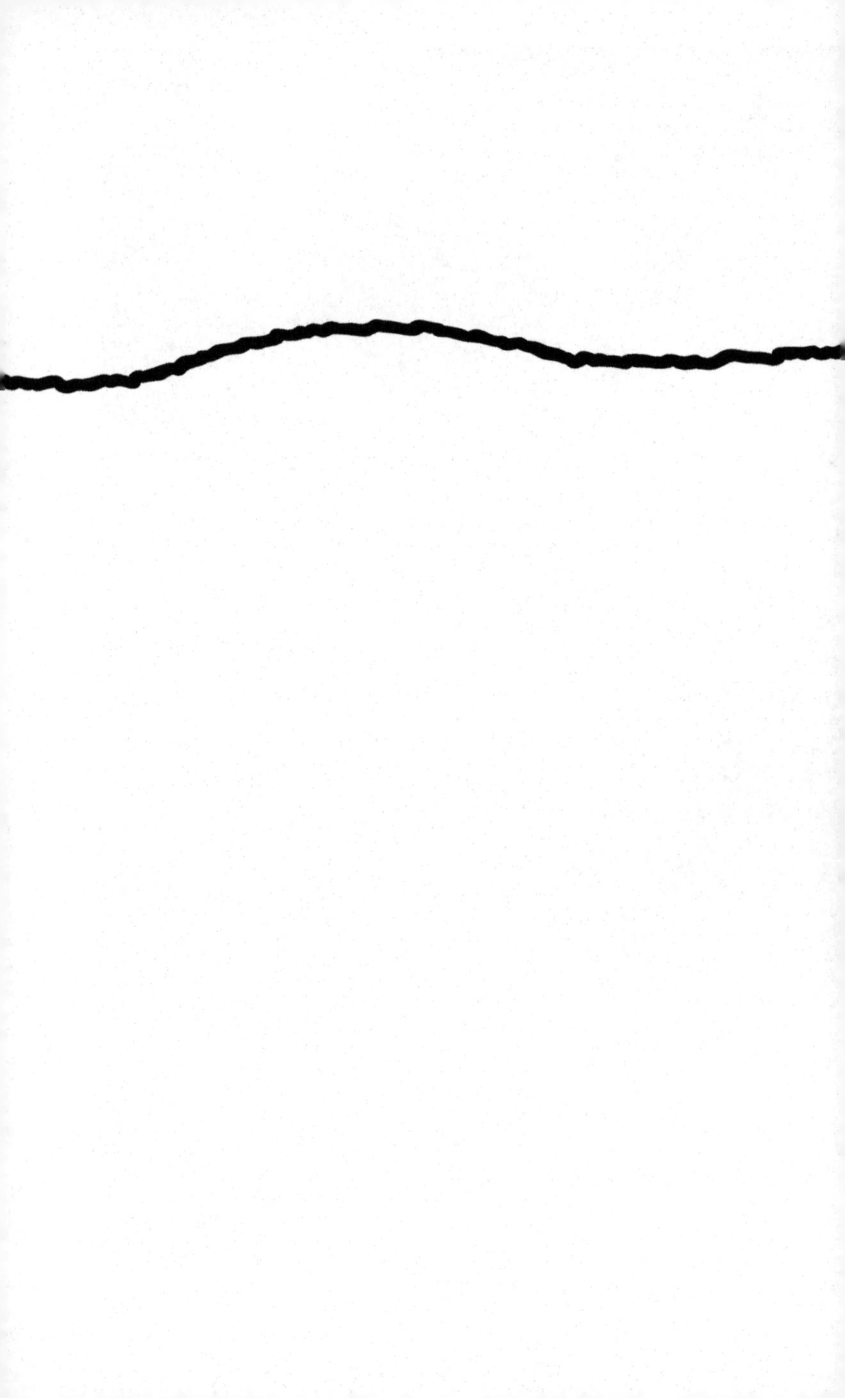

Monuments

Stores
ROYAL VET. COLLEGE
St. Pancras House
Locks
Ch.
Coroner's Court
Town Hall
Infirmary (South)
ST. PANCRAS GARDENS
Old Ch.
CAMDEN STREET
COLLEGE PLACE
Schs.
CROWNDALE ROAD
GOLDINGTON CRES.
PANCRAS ROAD
CAMBRIDGE STREET
Coal Sheds
OAKLEY SQUARE
L.B.
WERRINGTON ST.
HARRINGTON ST.
MEDBURN ST.
PENRYN ST.
GOLDINGTON ST.
PLATT STREET
STIBBINGTON STREET
BARCLAY STREET
JOHNSON ST.
BRIDGEWATER ST.
CLARENDON STREET
SIDNEY ST.
PURCHESE STREET
Coal Depot
HAMPDEN ST.
PHOENIX STREET
SOMERS TOWN
SEYMOUR STREET
OSSULSTON STREET
CLARENDON SQUARE
BARNBY ST.
GEE ST.
CHARLES ST.
CHALTON STREET
CHAPEL ST.
Goods Shed
MIDLAND ROAD
Terminus
DRUMMOND CRES.
Euston Station (Terminus)
Euston Sta. (Elec. Ry.)
LANCING ST.
CHURCHWAY
Hospl.
EUSTON PLACE
Hotl.
GRAFTON PL.
DRUMMOND STREET
MELTON STREET
EUSTON GROVE
EUSTON SQUARE
B.M. 78·6
B.M. 70·0
Lodges
80·2
UPPER WOBURN
DUKE'S RD.
FLAXMAN TERRACE
MABLEDON PL.
CARTWRIGHT GDNS.
BURTON
SIDBOROUGH
EUSTON ROAD
COBURG
GARDENS
84
64
56

ESTHER LESLIE

Squatted Somers Town

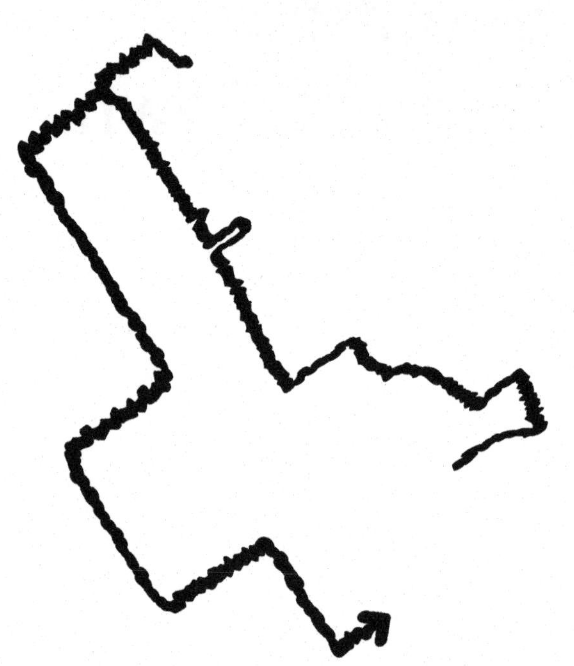

Somers Town is a compressed location – a road-bounded rectangle of intensity. It has been cut through by large building projects, such as the railways, the British Library and the Francis Crick Institute. There are institutions, but it has also long been a place dense with housing. These homes came in waves. Some developments are now disappeared, such as the Polygon that housed William Godwin and Mary Wollstonecraft or the 1820s terrace on Platt Street where Robin Farquharson died in a fire. Some are decaying: the council flats of the Ossulston estate of the 1920s, modelled on Karl Marx Hof in Red Vienna. Some have been through the up-and-down cycles of old stock Victorian London housing over 200 years – built for the middle-classes, only to become slums, bought by the council, divided laterally into flats, turned hard-to-let, sold off on the private market for large sums of money. Some housing is yet to come: the massive 'luxury' 25-storey tower blocks planned to eliminate Purchese Street Park. This is not council or so-called affordable housing, but more than 50 flats for high-price private sale. The Community Investment Programme – which promises the rebuilding of a primary school and a youth club – is financed by the attraction of private wealth. The cost to the local community is space, air and sky. Not that the air has been good, given the proximity to three mainline railway stations, nearby busy roads and massive building sites, but at least it was air. The muck produced by the building of HS2 is to be mitigated by deafening ventilation units and pollution filters. This, combined with the noise of construction work (75 decibels of banging and humming), means that authorities recommend 17 years of closed windows in the area.[1] No air at all.

Housing has always been an issue here. Until the wreckers of HS2, Crossrail and property speculators came, it was a living museum of social housing from the last century, beginning with the efforts of the St Pancras House Improvement Society in the 1920s to clear slums and bugs and build anew.[2] Somers Town also attracted two waves of mass squatting, or, in other words, radical experiments in living in recent history: In North Somers Town, in the early 1970s, squatters occupied the abandoned Brewers Estate houses. In the early-1980s, large squats existed amidst decayed flats, 'unfit for human habitation', in the South.

In London, in August 1946, squatters, tens of thousands of people, mainly ex-servicemen and their families, moved into empty military camps around Britain. By early September the squattings had spread to hotels and flats. The episode peaked in the 'Great Sunday Squat' on 8 September, organised by the Communist Party, when around 1,500 people took over flats in Kensington, Pimlico and St John's Wood. The legitimacy of the homeless squatters case was recognised by the authorities and efforts were made to provide substitute accommodation. Local authorities promised not to penalise squatters by putting them at the bottom of the housing list and the police promised not to use force against the squatters, which would increase sympathy for them.

Squatting took off again in outer London areas, such as Redbridge, in the late 1960s, where activists, most notably Ron Bailey, rescued homeless families from squalid hostels.[3] In Redbridge, the council had bought and boarded up 1,000 houses. They were waiting for a time to pull them down and develop the area. Activists began to squat empty and derelict buildings, citing a law from 1381, devised by the Barons, against 'forcible entry'. No person could force entry into a property and evict occupiers without a court order and the name of the occupant.

Need for housing in the London boroughs was enormous, while there were also were 100,000 empty homes in Greater London. Squatting activists in London developed a campaigning and advice organisation: the Family Squatting Advisory Service. This helped squatters to occupy homes as short life housing, on a No Rent, No Repairs basis. Rates, water and electricity bills were paid. But some councils did not cooperate with such a policy, preferring emptiness and decay.

1960s Camden had many boarded-up houses. Developers purchased chunks of Georgian and late Regency terraces, in order to demolish them for new private estates. The council had plans for new social housing too. Some were compulsorily purchased as part of schemes to widen roads. But the dwellings festered – as, for example, the houses in North Somers Town, on Charrington Street, Penryn Street and Medburn Street. These were old unmodernised stock without inside toilets or bathrooms. Camden Council proposed to start renovating properties in the area in 1968, but nothing much happened. The buildings hung in a half-life, between renovation and demolition. In August 1972, squatters moved in, occupying a derelict corner shop and claiming squatters rights.

The BBC made a film – Somers Town Squatters – which was broadcast at 22.15 on 7 November 1973. The *Radio Times* described it:

> The first of a series of six programmes about six different groups of young people who are dissatisfied with the society in which they live and are trying, in their own way, to change it. The Somers Town Squatters are a loosely knit group of 200-300 young people who have taken over a block of old houses in London and made their homes there.[4]

The squatters had their own channels: a newsletter for one, *Summerstown Community News and Culture.*[5] Its editorial addresses were 24 Charrington St and the Great Joint Happiness Commune, 54 Charrington St. The latter was the renamed grocers, which functioned as a community trading centre selling 'health food', dispensing ideas and legal advice. Inside one issue, the first to be printed by the Islington Free Press on offset litho, with a price rise to 5p, a critical review of Ron Bailey's *The Squatters* reveals the differences between the family squat movement of 1968 and this one. It gave praise: 'We need fear no more council "heavies"; we can make demands on the council…'. But it also noted that Bailey worked with councils. Camden and Islington squatters in contrast followed the lead set by the London Street Commune at 144 Piccadilly. They were Communards 'rejecting the work syndrome, compartmentalized conditions of straight society'. They were practical too, engaged in organising, repairing, restoring houses. All this was done without 'chairmen'. They had their reasons to distrust the council. For example, Camden Council denied squatters the use of library facilities. A directive was issued to staff instructing that squatters were not classed as 'residents' and were not entitled to borrow books. Attempts were made to prevent squatters obtaining advice from council-aided advice groups.

Another item mentioned in the newsletter detailed a battle between 24/26 Charrington St and the London Electricity Board. The Greater London Council, which shared responsibility with the borough councils for housing, had asked the LEB to refuse to connect electricity supplies. The squatters were, therefore, in the midst of a court case. They were not alone in this – squatters organisations were working to establish the principle that electricity should be supplied to anyone who was in a house and willing to pay a deposit. The minutes of the All London Squatters (ALS) Meeting, held at The Roebuck, Tottenham Court Road, London W1 on Sunday 6 January 1974, at which approximately 95 people were present, records this theme and the success at Charrington street:

> The GLC councillors are scared about their public image. Labour are still not sure of themselves, and therefore they are willing to meet us and discuss things. The GLC backed down in the case of Charrington Street. We are going to go ahead at all levels, but we must start immediately.[6]

Elsewhere in the *Summerstown* newsletter, a march on the Ideal Homes exhibition is announced.[7] The display of domestic indulgences was, it noted, an outrage, while 50,000 London people had no homes. The newsletter also announces a Spring Festival in Charrington Street, with fertility rites, and the establishment of the Somers Town Claimants Union at a meeting in 9 Penryn Street.

Other traces of this community can be gathered from the corners of the Bishopsgate Institute archives or low-ranked searches online. Various reports relate that one morning in 1973 almost all of the circa 60 squatted houses were raided by the Bomb Squad. The police were looking for SAM missiles that could bring down jumbo jets bound for Heathrow airport. Out of this experience, which provoked anger at police heavy-handedness, an ad hoc committee was formed. There is evidence of it in a notice in the *New Statesman* in 1973:

> DEFENCE OF CIVIL LIBERTIES MARCH Assemble 2 p.m. SATURDAY 6 OCTOBER at Charrington St. NW1. March to New Scotland Yard. Org. by London Ad Hoc Committee for the Defence of Civil Liberties

The demonstrators carried a papier mache bomb, which was confiscated by police.

Mick Brown's article, in July 1973, titled 'Be It Ever So Humble, There's No Place Like Home' on the Charrington Street squatters, outlined the autonomy at stake.

> 'People who've never had the time or opportunity to create their own environment can now influence the way they live' said a squatter. Tools are swapped around. Lead piping is swapped for nuts and bolts. Camden council leaves them alone. Police cars patrol the area but without intervention.
>
> Several empty houses on the block had their toilets smashed and lead pipes pulled out. They were 'tinned', boarded up with corrugated iron. But they get liberated once the van has left.
>
> 'The few remaining council tenants living in the block don't seem to mind either'. They realise we're utilising the empty properties. They've said they feel safer with us here than with homes empty, anyway, because of the vandals who were always breaking into places.[8]

The implication is that there is more community in these houses than in the new tower blocks. Brown also reveals that the average weekly income of a squatter was only £7. Not everyone was poor though – a report in 1973 in the local newspaper, the *Camden Journal*, mentions Aidan Quin, a mechanic operating from there who had massive car repair and import business.

A darker story concerns Robin Farquharson, who lived for some time in Charrington Street. He was one of the mentally disturbed, as well as being an extraordinary mathematician who had written about game theory. Once an academic, he dropped out, as his book called it: He was also the founder of the Mental Patients Union, a self-organised grouping for mental health patients, which met in Charrington Street, as the MPU notes state:

> Robin Farquharson offered accommodation in Charrington St. N.W.1 for the MPU in a house that has been procured by squatting and needs a certain amount of repair. Offer accepted.[9]

In April 1973, Farquharson was living in a squat on Platt Street. A fire in the house led to his death – the fire was the result of arson and two men living in the squat with him were convicted of unlawful killing.

Madmen, poets, teachers, students, doctors all crammed together in this smaller spot of a small spot, living differently in the early 1970s. The BBC film portrays the back gardens of the houses of the Brewers' Estate made into one and it filmed a musical evening of ecstatic hippy dancing.

Such larks irked the MP Norman Tebbit, as recorded in the *Hansard* minutes of a Housing Committee Debate on 20 November 1973:

> We would do ourselves a good service if we stopped the great game of inflating council waiting lists by taking on to lists as homeless

> everyone who turns up at Euston or King's Cross from wherever they come. Of course local government is spending a great deal of money on accommodation—local authorities are giving it away to all comers. If one opened a banana stall at King's Cross station and gave away bananas, there would be a very high bill at the end of the day for bananas. Therefore, local authorities which give away accommodation will also have a great bill. ... Perhaps I should draw (to his) attention (to) a complaint made about the number of squatters in Somers Town: Few were really homeless and most were mixed-up kiddies acting out their middle-class guilt. Council tenants have suffered a barrage of intense noise, music, nudity, fires, vermin and more defiant behaviour than anyone could legally publish a book on. This was described by the speaker concerned as 'intense provocation' and also as a 'violent street confrontation'. That was not said by some diehard; it was said by a gentleman called Mr. Kazantzis, a Labour GLC member from Somers Town, who believed that those squatters were not homeless at all but were troublemakers.[10] This is what will happen all the time if local authorities open up their housing lists to all comers.[11]

In contrast, P. Goulstone–who polled just 60 votes in an election against Kazantzis–stood for the Great Joint Happiness Homes for All (GJHH) party, emanating out of Charrington Street.

A poet was nearby. Andrew Aidan Dun conceived his epic poem Vale Royal there and then. As he put it in an interview:

> 'It was around February of 1973, on the roof of the largest squat in the history of squattocracy, in Charrington Street,' remembers Mr Dun. 'I look up from the page of Rimbaud's Illuminations and I see the text in the landscape. I look back from the landscape to the poem and I see the landscape in it. And I look over my shoulder and Arthur Rimbaud is there, like Virgil talking to Dante, saying: "Yes, I noticed this too." I apprehended immediately the significance of it, but I didn't know what to do with it.'[12]

Dun evokes an earlier radical history of a Somers Town on whose fringes Rimbaud lived. It also housed an extraordinary building called the Polygon, built in 1784, amid fields, brick works and market gardens. This was a housing estate, with fifteen sides and three storeys holding 32 houses. William Godwin lived here, who, in 1780, encountered the teachings of French enlightenment philosophers while being, like his father, a nonconformist minister. His passion for Republicanism developed. He came to London in 1782 with the aim of using his ministerial office and capacity to persuade others to overthrow and redevelop all of the institutions that govern life – church, parliament, educational. In the 1790s, Godwin wrote a bold and significant work, a critique of the state and a vision of how a minimal or stateless society would look. In *Enquiry concerning*

Political Justice, and its Influence on General Virtue and Happiness, he argues that government corrupts, produces dependency and promotes ignorance. Godwin wants the expansion of private virtue and morality – law, private property, marriage locks us into rule-based rather than rational behaviour and he rejects them. He read a travel book that Mary Wollstonecraft wrote in 1796: 'If ever there was a book calculated to make a man in love with its author, this appears to me to be the book. She speaks of her sorrows, in a way that fills us with melancholy, and dissolves us in tenderness, at the same time that she displays a genius which commands all our admiration.'[13] In 1790, Mary Wollstonecraft had written *A Vindication of the Rights of Men*, an attack on Edmund Burke and a salvo in a pamphlet war over the meaning of the French Revolution. She followed this in 1792 with *A Vindication of the Rights of Woman*, in which she argues that women are not naturally inferior to men, but made so socially and make themselves so, by being what she calls 'spaniels' and 'toys'. On 30 August 1797, her daughter Mary, who would later imagine Frankenstein, was born, but puerperal fever led to the mother's death.

Somers Town was now home to radicals and new ways of living. It suffered though as industrial capitalism developed and utopian energies dried up. Charles Dickens lodged there as a boy, and included the Polygon in *Bleak House* in 1852, as the home of the down-at-heel eccentric, Mr Skimpole, who existed amongst 'poor Spanish refugees'[14], loose knockers, missing bell-handles and dirty footprints:

Slums arise. But some are made. Somers Town became slums. Amidst these slums, the squatters of the 1970s enjoyed certain victories. Camden Council allowed squatters to stay in what it defined as short-life properties. The GLC negotiated substitute homes.15 But the council also smashed up buildings to make squatting impossible. They sent in the wreckers and some areas were demolished totally.

Through the 1970s, the All London Squatting movement faded, but the need for homes, especially for working class youth, young people who had fallen out with their families, refugees did not go away. New legislation made squatting harder. A criminal law act of 1977 repealed the forcible entry acts and made squatting more difficult. Owners could obtain an eviction order and bailiffs break into empty houses and move possessions, so squatters needed to have permanent possession of a building to protect things.

In the south of Somers Town the quality of what had once been flagship social housing was deteriorating. The local newspapers, the *Camden Journal* and the *St Pancras Chronicle*, reveal story after story about tenants' dissatisfaction with the state of homes on the council estates. The *Camden Journal* of 17 October 1980 reports drainage problems at Levita House. Chalton Street is losing its small shops and becoming derelict. In Walker House, half of the flats are empty and boarded up.

On 23 October 1981, the *St Pancras Chronicle* reported that the go ahead had been given by the GLC to begin rehabilitation, but the works do not start. In the *Camden New Journal*, on 30 September 1982, there is a report of 40 angry residents marching to the town hall with a jar of cockroaches from the

PLATT ST
T.H.JONES & SON LTD
SCRAP METAL MERCHANTS
Est. 1908
387-2074
I FEEL
RANDY

Ossulston Estate. Squatters moved into empty flats in what had once been model estates. The inevitable eviction orders came, once the funds for renovation were received in 1984 from the GLC. But the battle to remove squatters was protracted. *City Limits* magazine of 8–14 June 1984 reported the following:

> 200 squatters in Somers Town have been told to get out or face eviction. They are mostly young and single. Squatters say there are nearly 2000 empty properties in the borough. The flats in Chamberlain house are not amongst those considered fit for habitation. "But as Jeremy [Hardy], a stand up comic, points out: 'We don't have any emotional clout like people with kids, so they just push us around. But we've been here a year and stopped this place falling apart'.

An interview with squatters Una Sapietis and Catherine Campbell, in the *St Pancras Chronicle* in June 1984, makes a similar point–they were single homeless people and there was no provision otherwise.

There were violent battles. The squatters pleaded their case with labour leader Neil Kinnock when he visited shiny new Tolmers Square, post-squats and battles. They took direct action to stay–or be rehoused. The *St Pancras Chronicle*, on 22 June 1984, reports on how squatters threw petrol bombs at the police. Riot police moved in on the Wednesday night, as squatters set fire to two flats and heaped furniture in the courtyard. On 15 July 1984, newspapers report that eviction is delayed. The £1 million renovation programme was not ready to begin. Eviction notes were sent out to squatters in Levita House on 5 February 1985, including to the 48 squatters and caravan dwellers in the courtyard. By mistake, they were sent to all tenants, and this caused panic. In May 1985 there was a huge fire in Chamberlain House. 70 short life tenants and squatters were made homeless. As the buildings emptied, the wreckers arrived. For example, at Goldington Buildings, according to the *St Pancras Chronicle*, council workers smashed up flats and bricked them up with squatters' furniture still inside.

In 1985, the Advisory Service for Squatters estimated that there were 30,000–35,000 squatters in London, more than in the 1970s, and equal to the squatting boom of 1946. The Board and Lodging regulation was reintroduced on 23 November 1985, meaning that people under the age of 26 could only get rent-paying benefits for 8 weeks.

The money came in for renovations. By the early 1990s, these blocks in South Somers Town were refurbished and reopened. 25 years later they are rotting again and about to be overshadowed by more major building projects to follow the Francis Crick and the British Library. The once squatted houses in the North of Somers Town are now mostly in private hands and sell for more than a million.

ENDNOTES

[1] Tom Foot, HS2 residents warned to keep their windows shut... for 17 years, *Camden New Journal*, 20 July 2017.

[2] There are many studies of this. One is Kenneth Ingram, *Basil Jellicoe*, London, Centenary Press, 1936.

[3] Ron Bailey, *The Squatters*, Harmondsworth, Penguin, 1973.

[4] Radio Times, *Issue 2608*, p. 59. 1 November 1973.

[5] One copy exists in the Bishopsgate Institute Archive of Squatting materials.

[6] Squatting Archive–ALS Meeting (6 January 74), http://www.wussu.com

[7] See Terry Collins' reminiscences at http://jakartass.net for more on this.

[8] Excerpted pages in Bishopsgate Institute Archive of Squatting materials; name of magazine not evident.

[9] Cited at *Mental Health and Survivors' Movements and Contexts*, http://studymore.org.uk/mpu

[10] Tebbit was referring to Alexander or Alec John Kazantzis, who stood for election to the GLC in 1973.

[11] Findable at http://hansard.millbanksystems.com/commons/1973/nov/20/london-public-services#S5CV0864P0_19731120_HOC_333

[12] http://thelondonnobodyknows.tumblr.com/post/8511883724/the-voice-of-kings-cross

[13] This is quoted in an appendix to the book, Mary Wollstonecraft, *Letters Written during a Short Residence in Sweden, Norway, and Denmark*, Broadview Press, Toronto, p. 254. 2013.

[14] Chares Dickens, *Bleak House*, Bradbury and Evans, London, 1853, p. 419

[15] Confirmed in an email to author from former squatter Terry Collins on 21 September 2016, 'our politics were not one of confrontation. Which is to say that the brother of Jeremy Corbyn, Piers, preferred to live behind barricades in Elgin Avenue (?), where as we were 'creative', satirical even, in making our 'protests' about leaving habitable properties empty when all we wanted to do was live decent lives, in tune with our neighbours. That we were able to negotiate with the GLC for new premises to move into when they were ready to renovate the ones we were occupying–yes, we were given a licence to remain–suggests that we all benefitted.'

LONDON DOCKS
WESTERN DOCK
Shadwell
SHADWELL NEW BASIN
Wapping
Parliamentary Boundary (Southwark)
Parliamentary Boundary (Tower Hamlets)
Thames Tunnel
Clarence Wharf
Baltic
9
Albion Yard
MAIN DOCK
Centre Yard
Rotherhithe
Whitbread, Sulphur & Saltpetre Works
All Saints Ch.
ALBION POND
CANADA POND
Cricket Ground
SOUTHWARK
Patent Rope Manufactory
Electric Telegraph
St. Anne's Ch.
Patent Manure Manufactory
SOUTH EASTERN RAILWAY
(BRICKLAYERS ARMS EXTENSION)
Animal Charcoal Works
Parliamentary Bound.
Southwark
Lambeth

JO STOCKHAM

Docked and Parked

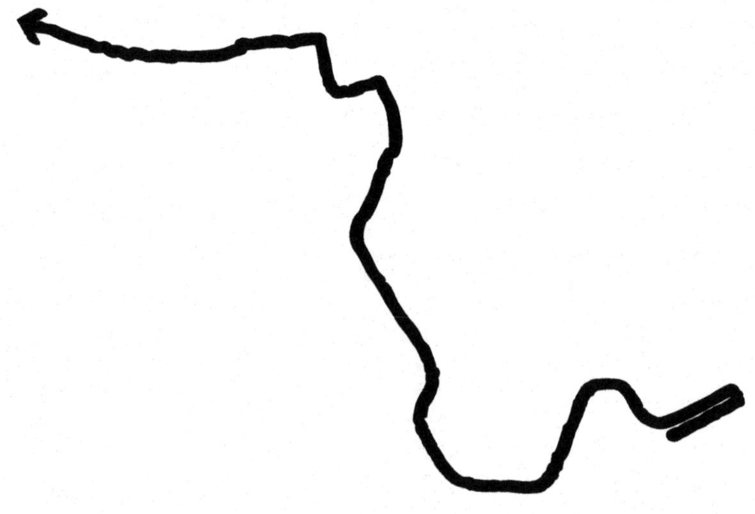

Jo Stockham, Lithograph, 2011.

Can a smell be a monument? Are the enveloping tons of particulates poisoning city dwellers an atomised monument to lack of foresight? When the air is so thick with dust you can taste it, is this a cloud monument parallel to the concrete poured and the rubble pounded? To walk is to be naked to the surfaces of the world, the holes of the body invaded, sound, sight, taste, smell, all without the filter of screen, of glass. An exercise in space-time travel, exposure to the elements, changeability of weather, movements of others. People, animals, goods, channelled by patterns of work, histories of construction and demolition, persisting traces of worlds gone forever or moved out of sight.

To walk is to be intimate with the matter of things, weight of body on foot, pressure of foot on shoe, step of shoe on cobbles, on tarmac, on concrete, on stone kerb, on grass. See traces of a medieval gate post, spaces where words were: PEEK FREANS. Bermondsey, once a hub of making: Pottery Street, Weavers Lane, Mill Street, Tanner Street.

Wharfs suffused with rich spices, cinnamon and coriander. Days scented by sugared air: ginger nuts, bourbons, coconut creams: time marked in biscuits. Hartley's chimney spews smells of sweet berry jam, Sarson's vinegar sours days with fermenting malt. The very air tastes of manufacturing. Time marked by rhythms of conveyor belts, die stamps, and trucks. Baking, boxing, brewing, dispatching, a choreography of bodies united in time and motion.

A stone seal marks Alaska Furs, huge wooden drums where urine washed seal skins, turned into hats, sheepskins into RAF flying suits for animal clad fighters. Now luxury living, warehouses, accumulating capital

by sitting still, people work elsewhere juggling money not wood, information not skins.

Surrey Quays station; index of regeneration, working landscape leisured, Docks become Quays (1989). Outcry: local history erased, working life hidden, a process of denial? Docks become: retail parks, marinas, a city farm, libraries, leisure centres, a multiplex cinema, wildlife parks and housing. About turn, every work trace becomes a marketing tool (2015): authentic warehouses and mock dock boutique developments, in warehouse architectural style, co-mingle.

River-time: corner of lower road, cross onto Deal Porters Way, monument to the men who walked planks, juggled battens and boards, shifted and stacked sliced units of tree.

Deal Porter, Surrey Docks in 1933, A.G Linney.

The steamers bringing softwood from the Baltic or Northern Russia have lately embraced all flags: these vessels arrive with high stacked deck cargoes and they often have tall thin funnels. In Greenland Dock, in contrast, one sees large, modern steamers with labour saving gear and great, deep holds. Some bring a number of passengers cross the Atlantic. This harbours a different type of vessel from the rest of the Docks in Rotherhithe, for here come the Cunarders, Furness Withys, C.P.R and United States Line Traders, all of a large size.[1]

Shiploads of new canned tastes: American peaches, tropical fruits, Canadian salmon, corned beef. Move through Jamaica Road, Quebec Way, Russia Dock, Norway Dock, Canada Dock, an atlas of names, a live streaming of people and goods from all over the globe.

Busy dock becomes flat pond, still wheezing with a tidal swell and drop, grimy water, cold slurry, eddying in manic swirls by jetties and steps. The snake of Thames with its capacity for loads, for work, for communication, winks with disco-boats and tourist cruises, puts on a firework display once a year and drifts, underemployed. Clock on, clock off or stand at the call on shelter, waiting time, waiting to work time. Unproductive once-factories clock up capital, click, click, click, accumulators for future trading, money generators with a river view. What is the time of work or no work, call centre not call on shelter, how does the day get measured? The hinterland fractures, gallons of white emulsion, container loads of plasterboard, patch up dilapidated real estate, held together for future demolition.

Salter Road, after Ada Salter, first woman Mayor of Southwark, who formed the Beautification Committee (1920). Shrubs and trees in local streets; the Tree of Heaven (Ailanthus), a favourite, drops its branches without warning. Legacy: parks, gardens, playgrounds, the open-air lido (1923, closed 1989).

> The drab sordidness of old Bermondsey will be gone forever and the district will be illuminated with touches of colour and beauty never known before. We shall have available to all the inhabitants many of the benefits of civilisation previously obtainable only by the

> favoured classes who could afford to live in the most desirable residential areas.[2]

Salter Road, after Alfred Salter, independent Labour MP, GP, who established pioneering health services (1924). Mobile cinema, converted disinfectant van tours the borough plugging into street lamps for power. Huge bugs on screen, a man points to a giant tooth: crown, neck, root, as children look on.[3] Kids without sunlight, equals rickets, give them space to swim, to play, send them to Switzerland to sit on a mountain, the GPs–they have cared for years. Bermondsey, a socialist arcadia of cottages and parks, an inner city-garden city, utopia, here on earth, Quakered.[4]

Ack-Ack, anti-aircraft guns in the park, as the docks burn (1939–45). Park-time: pace shifts, draw in lungfuls of leaf breath, time of sap and photosynthesis, clam damp, pine smell. How much grass makes a park? All of us outlived by arboreal growth, time laid down in rings, bark protected. Varieties of vegetation: girth of plane, of maple, of oak, of swamp cypress. The lungs of London: trees breathe into us, cleaning, filtering, absorbing. Walk in the park to be oxygenated, hydrated, inaugurated into the company of trees.

Early morning lake squall, bobbing things, two swans, six cygnets, gulls, pigeons, mallards, crows, clamour, caw, flock, squabble, gabble, swoop, waddle, splash. Rowdy bird-crowd. Human mammals move through, skaters skate, joggers jog, scoot, roll, wheel, step, jump, run and walk dogs, energies in furred form.

Weather, whether rain, mist, hail, sun, moonlit frost, breeze, through autumn, winter, spring, summer, the park indexes flux in the shape of stem, structure of trunk, flaccidity of leaf. Cloud, fog, dew, drought, flood, haze, lightning, shower, sleet, smog, snow, in a park, are atmospheres. To walk is to be immersed, drenched in the present condition, amongst the elements. Park edge; Clare College Mission Church (1883) aims to spiritualise a destitute district. Becomes Dilston Grove, poured ferro-concrete church, first of its kind in the country, replaces original church (1911). Spiritual bunker, Italianate, deconsecrated, artist's studio (1962) then empty for 20 years, rank with dead pigeons and broken windows.

As the 20th century ends, in the cold gloom, on a huge screen, flicker projected traces of people now dead, building for the future present, places for local people to live in. Digitised double from a Soho editing room, where on a reel-to-reel deck, seconds of film were copied and coloured, slowed and looped. A line of men push over walls, demolishing slums, rocking and swaying in perfect unison. With ropes and muscle, they topple slabs of brick and disappear into clouds of dust. A celluloid monument performs a preserved, fragile document of hopeful propaganda.[5] Another generation, another re-generation, a space transformed (2010): performance space, meeting space, container for the rituals of art. Cross the park towards Rotherhithe, exit at the mouth of a road-tunnel. Brunel Road, Marc and Isambard Kingdom, Thames Tunnel (1825–1843). 18 years of dug mud, dug for the first time in the world, a tunnel under a river, an under-water monument. Norwegian and Finnish churches, sailors (lost) at sea. Hope (Sufferance) Wharf, the Watch-house (1821) keeps the grave robbers away. Let's go down the local: The Mayflower, The Ship.

Dilston Grove in 2000.

Step off Tooley Street onto Paradise Street, walk along Bermondsey Wall towards Tower Bridge. Butlers Wharf, tea trading area, temporary artists' studios, burnt in a suspected arson attack (1978), forces occupying artists to move on, to make way. Design Museum (1989), Shad Thames, derelict banana ripening warehouse, continues the cultural quarter but now moves west.

The city is choking; try not to breathe, the air is making us sick, particulates replace TB. Walk but dodge the main roads, sidle through small parks, appreciating flower boxes, and green walls. Slip past small artisan bakers, coffee roasters, cheese merchants, brewers, inhabiting the railway arches, smells return repackaged. This neighbourhood has upped and come, for whoever can afford to stay. A supermarket on every corner, and estate agents marketing smaller and smaller spaces, bijou, boutique, studio flat. Buildings grow higher and higher, and glass reflects our hurrying selves. Avoiding eye contact, streams of walkers tune into small electronic receiving devices, heads in the cloud.

Only the river, an ever-changing monument, resists the recalibration of time and space. Watch it, breathe it, walk it, dwarfed by its surges and swells. The water in all bodies pulled and swayed by tides, the small homeostasis of each one of us, sucked and subsumed by hardcore and asphalt, released by the pull of the sea.

Still from 'Some Activities of Bermondsey Borough Council'. Dir H.W.Bush, 1931.

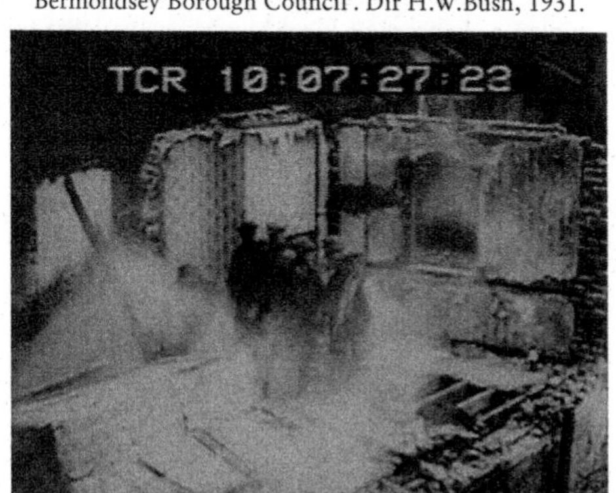

ENDNOTES

[1] A.G. Linney, *Pocket Guide to the Docks of London*, London: Newton & Company Publishers, 1933, pp. 38–39.

[2] Elizabeth Lebas, 'The Making of a Socialist Arcadia: Arboriculture and Horticulture in Bermondsey after the First World War', in *Garden History*, Vol. 27, No. 2 (Winter, 1999), pp. 219–237 contains quote from *Twelve Years of Labour Rule* 1922–34, (1934) London: Labour.

[3] Information taken from Elizabeth Lebas, 'When Every Street Becomes a Cinema: The Film Work of Bermondsey Borough Council's Public Health Department 1923–1953', in *History Workshop Journal*, Issue 39, 1995, pp. 42–66.

[4] For more information read Fenner Brockway, *Bermondsey Story: The life of Alfred Salter.* New South Wales, Australia: George Allen and Unwin, 1949. Republished by Independent Labour Publications, 1995.

[5] The exhibition *If Not Now When* took place in Dilston Grove, 3rd November–5th December 1999. A catalogue of the exhibition which explores elements of local history is available from CGP London http://cgplondon.org.

Belsize Park
MARYLEBONE
REGENT'S PARK
Camden Town
Paddington
HYDE PARK
KENSINGTON GARDENS
ST. MARGARET
WESTMINSTER
LIBERTY OF THE CITY OF WESTMINSTER
South Kensington
Brompton

SHARON KIVLAND & STEVE PILE

Freud in London

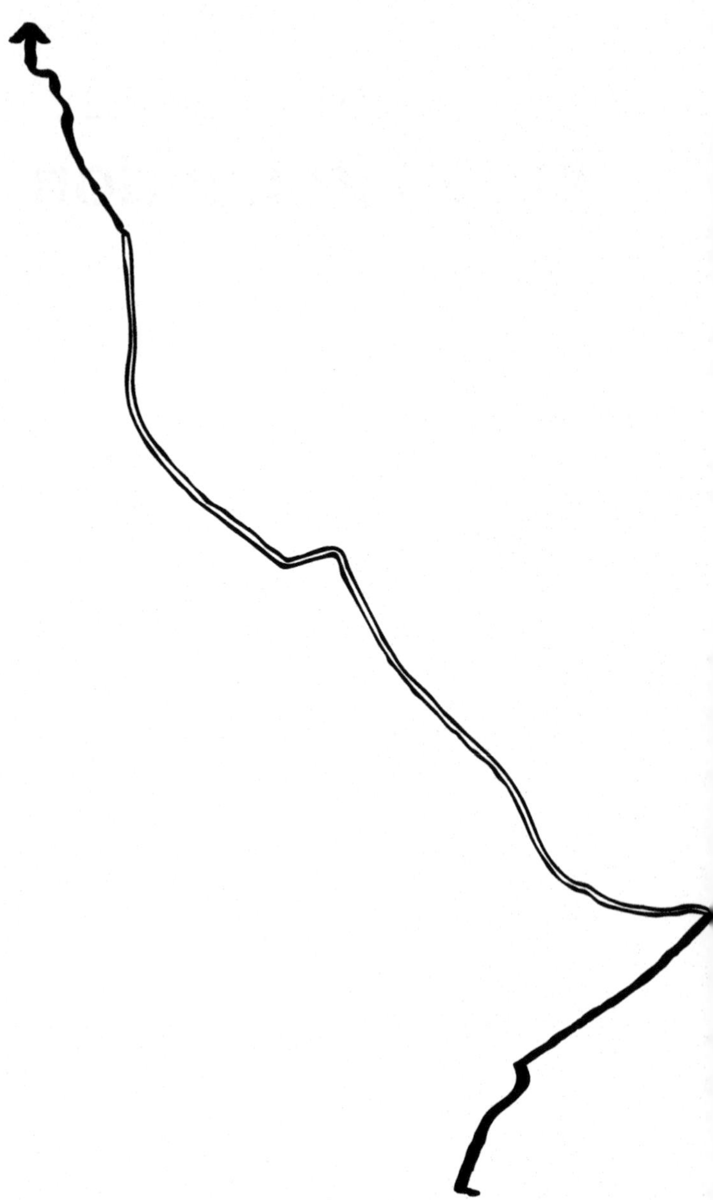

Sigmund Freud arrived in London on 6 June, 1938. He and his entourage left Vienna on Saturday 4 June at 3 o'clock in the morning, by train, the Orient Express. There is a photograph showing Anna, his daughter, and Freud in a train compartment. His last short letter dated 4 June, written in Vienna, is addressed to Arnold Zweig: 'Leaving today for 39, Elsworthy Road, London N. W. 3. Affect. greetings Freud.' In Paris, they rested at the home of Marie Bonaparte for twelve hours. They crossed to England by night on the ferry-boat to Dover. The Lord Privy Seal, Lord De La Warr, had arranged diplomatic privileges for their luggage and with the railway authorities, that the train should come into an unusual platform at Victoria Station, to avoid any crowd or press. Freud's escape from the Nazis had been widely publicised and there was enthusiastic public interest in his arrival. Frail and exhausted, Freud stepped down from the train early on the morning of Monday 6 June.

The Superintendent of the Southern Railway and the Station Master of Victoria welcomed Freud and his family, who then departed quickly in Ernest Jones' car, leaving his son Ernst and Anna to collect the large amount of luggage. Jones describes driving past Buckingham Palace, Burlington House, to Piccadilly Circus and up Regent Street, 'Freud eagerly identifying each landmark and pointing it out to his wife'. He first stayed at 39 Elsworthy Road, Hampstead, a house with a garden rented by Ernst while looking for a more permanent home. Martha Freud and the maid Paula Fichtl moved into 20 Maresfield Gardens on 16 September, and Freud, who had been admitted to hospital for several weeks, joined them on 27 September.

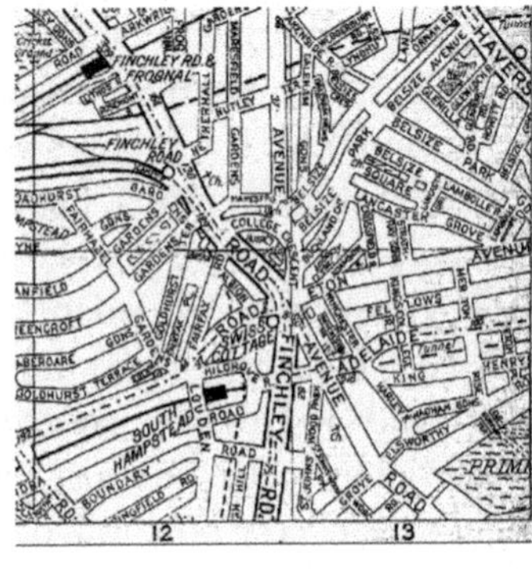

S.K. and S.P. have tracked back over Freud's arrival, stitch-ing together the fragments of Freud's London. Our group met at Maresfield Gardens, now the Freud Museum, where we watched some archive films of Freud in London. Using a facsimile of the 1939 London A–Z as a guide, we then walked to Elsworthy Road. Following trains of thought, we took the Tube to Charing Cross, using the city as a model for psycho-analysis, as Freud so famously did himself; with Rome of course, but also with London, in *Five Lectures on Psycho-Analysis* (1909), wherein he compares the monuments of Charing Cross and the Monument with hysterical symptoms, as mnemonic symbols. We were like the unpractical Londoners he describes, for 'not only do they remember painful experiences of the remote past, but they still cling to them emotionally; they cannot get free of the past and for its sake they neglect what is real and immediate'. As the unpractical Londoners that we are, we wished to hold on to experiences of the past.

Freud was a refugee and his arrival is worth remembering. Yet, as we followed Freud through London, we also wanted to dwell on the fragments that comprise the unconscious of the city.

From Charing Cross we walked to Victoria Station, pointing out the views enjoyed by Freud on his arrival, stopping at the Victoria Memorial, going back through Freud's London, albeit in the pouring rain… working back from the manifest content through a chain of connections (as in dream analysis). Our small group assembled for a final reading near the platform where (our best guess told us) the Freud family alighted from the Dover–Victoria boat-train. The information office was closed, so we were unable to confirm at what platform Freud had arrived. At each resting-place, a 'secondary' correspondence of postcards between Freud and S.K. was read aloud, one she invented. Owing to the difficulty in reading Freud's handwriting, S.K. transcribed the notes she received from the past, from S.F., Sigm.: she added nothing, the words are his and his alone, although she may have held back some information for the sake of discretion. The postcards, reproduced here, are contemporaneous with Freud's time in London, but do not always correspond to the place in which they were written, while it is a pleasure when they do.

At the Freud Museum, Emilia Raczkowska told us a story that resonated strongly with our walk. Apparently, after Freud had settled into Maresfield Gardens, people would write their dreams on pieces of paper, bind them to stones, and then throw them into the garden. For S.P., this resembles the way that cities are littered with the fragments of dreams. Like the dreams found in Freud's garden, it is only through acts of imagination and interpretation that we might discern the underlying desires and fears that comprise the unconscious of the city. The first step is to pay attention to the fragments, without leaping to judgement about their meaning. S.P. read out dream fragments at each of the places that S.K. and he had identified as having Freudian significance. We start at the end of Freud's journey, Maresfield Gardens.

I

20, Maresfield Gardens, London, N.W.3

What an unexpected and welcome letter. Not everything I could tell you about myself would coincide with your wishes. But I am more than 83 years old, thus actually overdue, and there is really nothing left for me but to follow your poem's advice: Wait, wait.

Yours very sincerely,

Sigm.

Thames Embankment and Cleopatra's Needle, London

20, Maresfield Gardens, London, N.W.3

I haven't written to you for a long time, while you have been bathing in the blue sea. I assume you know why, can even recognise it in my handwriting. (Even the pen is no longer the same; like my doctor and other external organs, it has left me.) I am not well; my illness and the aftermath of the treatment are responsible for this condition, but in what proportion I don't know. People are trying to lull me into an atmosphere of optimism by saying the carcinoma is shrinking and the symptoms of reaction to the treatment are temporary. I don't believe it and don't like being deceived. Some kind of intervention that would cut short this cruel process would be very welcome. Should I look forward to seeing you at the beginning of May? And herewith I greet you warmly, my thoughts are often with you.

Yours,

Sigm.

The Freud Museum, 20 Maresfield Gardens: Anna's bedroom, S.F.'s bedroom, the entrance hall, S.F.'s consulting-room, with a view to the garden through the French windows, where dreams, dogs, a burglary (some silver, a watch), another burglary (ashes), and death were discussed.

Walter Benjamin tells of a popular German tradition that cautions against recounting dreams on an empty stomach. Before breakfast, the thinking goes, the person is still in thrall to the world of dreams, despite seeming to be awake. Benjamin observes that washing only acts on the surface of the body and serves only to stir the body to wakefulness. The mind, however, is not so easily awoken: 'the grey penumbra of dream persists and, indeed, in the solitude of the first waking hour, consolidates itself [...] The narration of dreams brings calamity, because a person still half in league with the dream world betrays it in his own words and must incur its revenge' (*One-Way Street*, p. 46). The dream reveals too much of the dreamer's inner desires–and the revelation of desire must have a price. No longer is the dreamer unconscious and consequently innocent of the dream's content. Now, the dreamer is aware of what they are saying and this self-awareness makes them accountable for their desires and fears. Only after eating can the dreamer gain sufficient distance on their dreams to be able to retell them. Only at a remove can dreams be safely revealed. Like the body, only when dreams are washed clean can they go out in public.

Freud, of course, needed unwashed dreams and converted a room at Maresfield Gardens to entertain those dreams and their revelations–as if the dreamer had not had breakfast.

II

20, Maresfield Gardens, London, N.W.3

Your mysterious and beautiful book has pleased me to an extent that makes me unsure of my judgement. I haven't read anything so substantial and poetically accomplished for a long time. Won't you give me the pleasure of paying me a visit? I have time in the mornings.

Yours very sincerely,

Sigm.

TRAFALGAR SQUARE, LONDON

20, Maresfield Gardens, London, N.W.3

I can hardly write, no better than I can speak or smoke. This operation was the worst since 1923 and has taken a great deal out of me. I am dreadfully tired and feel weak when I move. I have actually started work with three patients, but it isn't easy. The house is very beautiful. There is only one great drawback, no spare bedroom. Everything here is rather strange, difficult and often bewildering, but all the same it is the only country we can live in, France being impossible on account of the language. During the days when war seemed imminent the behaviour on all sides was exemplary, and it is wonderful to see how, now that the intoxication of peace has subsided, people as well as parliament are coming back to their senses and facing the painful truth. We too of course are thankful for the bit of peace but cannot take any pleasure in it. The views of the beautiful castle in Brittany were the last sign I had from you. I trust that I shall hear from you soon.

With warm greetings,

Sigm.

We assembled at Oscar Nemon's bronze statue of Freud, sited on the junction of Belsize Lane and Fitzjohn's Avenue, originally hidden in an alcove behind Swiss Cottage Library, and moved to its present location in 1998.

Freud recounts many dreams in *The Interpretation of Dreams* (1899; translation, 2006). Many are his, some are anecdotal; others are those of his patients. One is described as lovely (p. 301).

He is driving with a large party along X-street, where there is a modest inn (there is not, in fact). A play is being performed on the premises; at one moment he is in the audience, at another an actor. At the end there is a question of people having to change to get out again. Part of the staff is shown to the stalls areas, another part to the first floor. Then there is an argument. The ones up above are irritated that those downstairs are not yet ready, thus preventing them from descending [...] Then he is walking along up the hill that X Street forms towards the city, and his gait is slow, so laboured, that he makes no progress whatsoever. An elderly gentleman joins him, complaining about the King of Italy. At the end of the rise, the going gets much easier.

III

39, Elsworthy Road, London, N.W.3

This England is in spite of everything that strikes one as foreign, peculiar and difficult, and of this there is quite enough, a blessed, a happy country inhabited by well-meaning hospitable people. At least this is the impression of the first weeks. Our reception was cordial beyond words. We were wafted up on the wings of a mass psychosis. After the third day the post delivered letters correctly to 'Dr Freud, London' or 'Overlooking Regent's Park'; a taxi driver bringing Anna home exclaimed on seeing the number of the house, 'Oh, it's Dr Freud's place.' The newspapers have made us popular. We have been inundated with flowers and could easily have suffered serious indigestion from fruit and sweets. There were letters from friends, a surprising number from complete strangers who simply wanted to express their delight at our having escaped to safety and who expect nothing in return. For the first time and late in life I have experienced what it is to be famous.

Affectionate greetings,

Sigm.

We stood on the pavement outside 39 Elsworthy Road, now the home of David and Cindy Sofar, a pleasant prospect, a pond with goldfish, and great happiness. Although Freud struggled to adapt to life in a house with more than one floor, he nonetheless found it charming. He found refuge, 'under the protection of Athene', and expressed the intense wish, unfulfilled, to become an Englishman. Here Freud met Salvador Dalí (at Dalí's third attempt, having pursued Freud from Paris) on 19 July 1938. Dalí's sketch of Freud makes his head resemble a snail's shell. Freud, for his part, wondered if Dalí's fanaticism might explain the Spanish Civil War. In some ways, both Freud and Dalí are refugees in the house of dreams.

We have long forgotten the ritual by which the house of our life was erected. But when it is under assault and enemy bombs are already taking their toll, what enervated, perverse antiquities do they not lay bare in the foundations. What things were interred and sacrificed amid magic incantations, what horrible cabinet of curiosities lies there below, where the deepest shafts are reserved for what is most commonplace. In a night of despair I dreamed I was with my first friend from my school days, whom I had not seen for decades and had scarcely ever remembered in that time, tempestuously renewing our friendship and brotherhood. But when I awoke it became clear that what despair had brought to light like a detonation was the corpse of that boy, who had been immured as a warning: that whoever one day lives here may in no respect resemble him (Walter Benjamin, *One-Way Street*, pp. 46–7).

IV

CHARING CROSS, LONDON.

39, Elsworthy Road, London, N.W.3

If you take a walk through the streets of London, you will find, in front of one of the great railway termini, a richly carved Gothic Column – Charing Cross. At another point in the same town, you will find a towering, and more modern column, which is simply known as 'The Monument'. These monuments, then, resemble hysterical symptoms in being mnemic symbols. What should we think of a Londoner who paused today in deep melancholy before the memorial of Queen Eleanor's funeral instead of going about his business? Or again, what should we think of a Londoner who shed tears before the Monument that commemorates the reduction of his beloved metropolis to ashes, although it has long since risen again in far greater brilliance? Yet every single hysteric and neurotic behaves like these two unpractical Londoners. Not only do they remember painful experiences of the remote past, but they still cling to them emotionally; they cannot get free of the past and for its sake they neglect what is real and immediate. I wish I had arrived in London in a better condition.

Affectionately yours,

Sigm.

We gathered again at Charing Cross, the Queen Eleanor Memorial Cross – a Victorian replica, commissioned by the South Eastern Railway Company, built in the forecourt of a railway station in 1854–55, no longer in its original position at the top of Whitehall where it marked the centre of London. The original Eleanor Cross was destroyed during the English Civil war in 1647. The Monument, almost two miles to the East, commemorates the Great Fire of London of 1666; two painful periods of English history, either end of London's Strand. Eleanor, Queen of Castile, was married to Edward I, known as the hammer of the Scots: another painful memory in the British constitution. Yet, at this point, the past seems remote; the angry fires of London's history turned to gently crumbling grey stone, while the engines of taxis choke the air and commuters threaten to overwhelm the station of the cross.

The most heterogeneous temporal elements thus coexist in the city. If we step from the eighteenth-century house into one from the sixteenth century, we tumble down the slope of time. Right next door stands a Gothic Church, and we sink to the depths. A few steps farther, we are in a street from out of the early years of Bismarck's rule [...], and once again climbing the mountain of time. Whoever sets foot in a city feels caught up as in a web of dreams, where the most remote past is linked to the events of today. One house allies with another, no matter what period they came from, and a street is born. [...] The climactic points of a city are its squares: here, from every direction, converge not only numerous streets but all the streams of their history [...] Things which find no expression in political events, or find only minimal expression, unfold in the cities: they are a superfine instrument, responsive as an Aeolian harp–despite their specific gravity–to the living historic vibrations of the air (Swiss journalist Ferdinand Leon (1935), cited by Walter Benjamin, *The Arcades Project*, p. 435).

V

39, Elsworthy Road, London, N.W.3

Jones met us at Victoria and drove us back through the beautiful city of London to our new house. It is quite far north, beyond Regents Park at the foot of Primrose Hill. From my window I can see nothing but greenery which begins with a charming little garden surrounded by trees. So it is just as if we were living in Grinzing. The house itself is elegantly furnished. The rooms upstairs, which I cannot reach without a sedan chair, are said to be particularly beautiful; on the ground floor a bedroom, a study and dining-room have been arranged for us, quite beautiful and comfortable enough. We can't stay here for more than a few months and will have to rent another house, to be ready for the arrival of our furniture. I have remained so matter-of-fact up to now. The emotional climate of these days is hard to grasp, almost indescribable. The feeling of triumph on being liberated is too strongly mixed with sorrow, for in spite of everything, I still love the prison from which I have been released. The enchantment of the new surroundings (which makes one want to shout 'Heil Hitler!') *is blended with discontent caused by little peculiarities of the strange environment; the happy anticipations of a new life are dampened by the question: how long will a fatigued heart be able to accomplish any work? Now you may write again – and whatever you like. Letters are not opened.*

Affectionate regards,

Sigm.

There followed a brisk walk to the Queen Victoria Memorial and the Mall. Ernst Jones drove the Freuds past Buckingham Palace to Piccadilly Circus and Regent Street. S.F. pointed out each landmark to Martha, eagerly identifying it.

The streams of history converge upon a city's circles and circuses. The Queen Victoria Memorial was unveiled on 16 May 1911; designed by the sculptor Sir Thomas Brock, this his most famous work. At the dedication, two of Victoria's most senior grandsons stood together: George V (taking Victoria's titles) and Wilhelm II (of Germany). Near enough three years and three months later, these two Kings would be at war. Also in attendance was Winston Churchill, as Home Secretary. The female figure that tops the memorial is Winged Victory, perhaps offering encouragement to those contemplating a war. In one hand, she carries a globe, clearly indicating the stake of wars to come.

The Memorial is an elaborate iconographic scheme. Beneath Winged Victory are figures embodying the qualities that made Queen Victoria great: Constancy, Courage, Motherhood, Justice and Truth – and Victoria herself. Had Freud not been rushed past, he might have considered the sheer number of painful pasts that this structure also embodied. Funding for the memorial came from the corners of the British Empire (notably donations from Australia and New Zealand and the sale of goods from Africa in Liverpool) as well as donations by the British public. It symbolised less Victoria than the values and reach of her Empire. At the corners of the memorial space are large bronze figures with lions. There is Peace, Progress, Agriculture (represented by a peasant), and Manufacture (in the form of a blacksmith). South Africa, Australia and New Zealand, in particular, are present in these figures. Hypographs, meanwhile, are suggestive of British sea power. The Memorial overtly celebrates the achievement of Empire, but covertly casts up its basis in military domination and economic exploitation.

Freud has entered a city that has produced more refugees than it has saved. The map of London's monuments is also a map of its traumatic pasts. In this, London is like any other city. Monuments preserve the different histories of a city, saving its geographies from becoming shapeless dust. Monuments are like dream fragments, helping us to trace connections that might otherwise be lost, ignored, or forgotten.

VI

39, Elsworthy Road, London, N.W.3

I haven't been giving you much news these past weeks. Everything is still unreal, as in a dream. We didn't all leave at the same time, ourselves not until the Sunday before Whitsun. With us came Paula and Lün, the latter as far as Dover, where she was taken into quarantine by a friendly vet. We were spared the tedious Customs investigation in Kehl by a miracle. Over the Rhine bridge and we were free! The reception in Paris at Gare de l'Est was friendly, somewhat noisy with journalists and photographers. We spent from 10 a.m. to 10 p.m. in Marie's house. She surpassed herself in tender care and attention, returned to us part of our money and refused to allow me to continue the journey without some new terracotta figures. We crossed the channel by ferry boat and caught sight of the sea for the first time at Dover. And soon we were in Victoria Station where the immigration officers gave us priority.

Affectionate regards,

Sigm.

At Victoria Station, we spoke about platforms, timetables, rolling stock, and railway-related incidents in life and dreams. S.F. wrote: 'At the age of 82 and as a result of the German invasion, I left my home in Vienna and came to England, where I hope to end my life in freedom.'

Victoria Station represented the end of Freud's escape from tyranny and the beginning of his new life as a Londoner. Escaping Vienna was arduous. Trains. Boat-train. Train. Yet, Victoria – at the heart of Empire – held her arms open for this celebrated refugee. Nowadays, refugees are held at Calais, or further afield. Impractical Londoners would do well, then, to hold on to the painful experiences of the past – for these painful experiences continue, even if sometimes they seem very far away.

Londoners welcomed Freud. Perhaps as gifts, they launched their dreams at him. Perhaps in hope of an analysis, they offered up the rebus of their secret desires and fears, as if they were postcards from the unconscious. We do not know what Freud made of this. But the image of a garden bombarded by short-range missives might make us think again about the city. Like Freud's garden, London is littered with dreams wrapped around stone.

> With cities, it is as with dreams: everything imaginable can be dreamed, but even the most unexpected dream is a rebus that conceals a desire or, its reverse, a fear. Cities, like dreams, are made of desires and fears, even if the thread of their discourse is secret, their rules are absurd, their perspective deceitful, and everything conceals something else [...] Cities also believe they are the work of mind or of chance, but neither the one nor the other suffices to hold up their walls. You take delight not in a city's seven or seventy wonders, but in the answer it gives to a question of yours. (Italo Calvino, *Invisible Cities*, pp. 37–8).

AFTERWORD

At Maresfield Gardens a film shows S.F. enjoying a garden party. The only recording of his voice ends the film and his last sentence is: 'But the struggle is not yet over...'

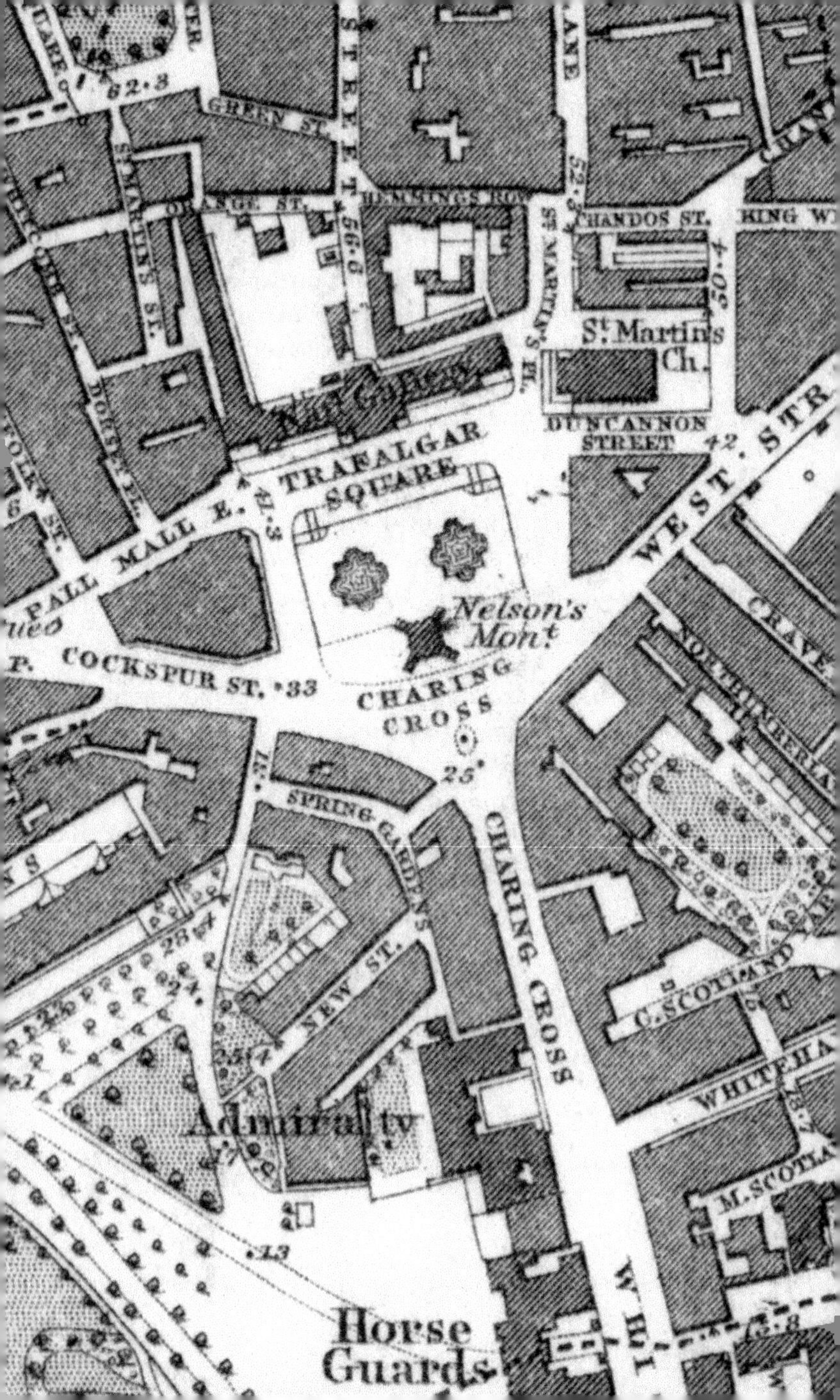

GREEN ST.
ST MARTIN'S ST.
ORANGE ST.
HEMMINGS ROW
CHANDOS ST.
ST MARTIN'S PL.
St. Martin's Ch.
Natl Gallery
DUNCANNON STREET
TRAFALGAR SQUARE
WEST STR
PALL MALL E.
Nelson's Mont.
COCKSPUR ST.
CHARING CROSS
SPRING GARDENS
NEW ST.
CHARING CROSS
NORTHUMBERLAND
G. SCOTLAND
WHITEHA
M. SCOTLA
Admiralty
Horse Guards

AHUVIA KAHANE

Walking Round Trafalgar Square

Temenos and Omphalos

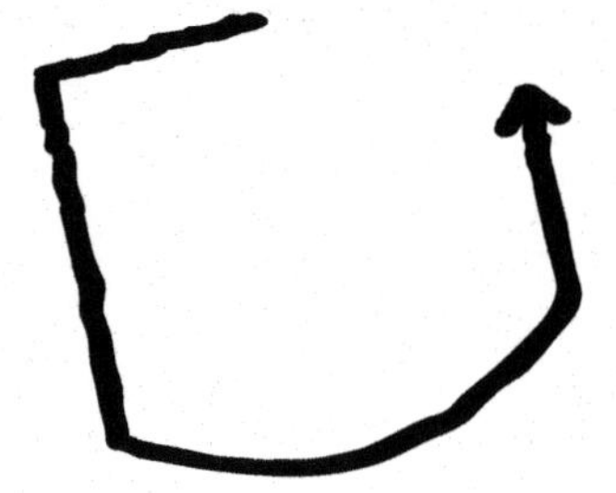

> Every universalizing approach, whether the phenomenological or the semiotic, will from the dialectical point of view be found to conceal its own contradictions and repress its own historicity by strategically framing its perspective so as to omit the negative, absence, contradiction, repression, the *non-dit*, or the *impensé*.[1]

1.

Walking is useful practice. We may walk for a reason, to get somewhere or to take exercise. But what is the *telos* of walking in itself? It seems to leave us with nothing to do, with a certain emptiness into which flow perceptions and thoughts, perhaps because they have nowhere else to go. To walk is to think.

Walking is, of course, a bodily activity, *kinêsis*, a movement, or, from a phenomenological point of view, movement perceived as *change*. Aristotle, for example, in the *Physics*, relies on this Greek term and the idea of spatial movement to grasp the idea of time.[2] The vehicle here is, of course, as important as the tenor. Ambulatory thought, because it is tethered to a body (or to a perception of a body) moving by its own unique force, gives space and time their human scale (unlike, say, the scale of the world as seen through a porthole by an astronaut, or the scale of the world observed through a microscope), their 'magnitude,' *megethos*, as Aristotle would call it.[3] The *kinêsis* of walking lets us see the world step by step yet as a *whole*, in scale, with its fragile contingency, its negatives, absences, contradictions and repressions, its particular moments and change, its things unsayable and its un-thought thought, the *non-dit* and *impensé*.

True walking, the walking that divests itself of illusory *telê* (the plural of *telos*), is ever conscious of movement even as it goes nowhere. It goes around in circles, like all true thought. It lifts the veils of illusion from our purposeful Apollonian actions and our busy metropolitan lives. Walking unconceals. Which is why, let me suggest, it is useful practice.[4]

2.

The Victorians who built London increased not only its size,[5] but also the scale of the city. Where once there were houses, they now created an imperial metropolis, a city of monuments. Powerful and overwhelming, these sites of illusion also moved the discourse, at least in part, from the unseen interiors of Privy Councils and into the open, civic space, where even the excluded could sometimes walk, and think, and move towards a different kind of future.

One of those Victorians was the architect Thomas Leverton Donaldson (1795–1885), a Londoner, if ever there was one. He was born in Bloomsbury Square. He died in Bedford Place. He was the son of a London architect, founder of the Royal Institute of British Architects, member of the Elgin Marbles Committee, and more.

On the 16th of July 1840, Donaldson gave expert testimony to the Parliamentary Select Committee on Trafalgar Square and reflected on the plan to erect a memorial column in honour of Lord Nelson on the site. The Square, Donaldson pointed out, was:

> One of the finest in the world. The best possible position for a lofty monument is when the spectator comes upon it unexpectedly, and when it can only be seen from a short distance: Trafalgar Square unites in an eminent degree both these requisites. To those approaching from the Strand and Pall Mall, it will come upon them by surprise and the column will present itself in all its grandeur. To those approaching from Westminster, it will appear majestically on a rising ground, with the contrast of the National Gallery behind it, to increase its apparent size.[6]

As Donaldson rightly saw, it is the urban geometry of Trafalgar Square, its environs and its interaction with the monumental column, then only a twinkle in the Empire's eye, that affected thought:

> The eye can embrace without inconvenience an area of 60 degrees; but it is no objection to the dignity of an object, that it compels an effort on the behalf of the beholder in order to embrace all its parts.[7]

Walking in the city today, one can indeed see the point. Nelson's monument arrests the linear movement from Pall Mall to the Strand, from Westminster to Charing Cross Road. It compels the viewer to walk around it in a circle. It invites us to engage in embodied, walking thought.[8]

Nelson's Column, Trafalgar Square.

3.

The grandeur of Nelson's Column, as Donaldson knew equally well, was intimately coupled with its upwards flight:

> ... the very circumstance of those approaching Trafalgar Square from the east or west being obliged to raise their heads, and use some exertion in order to see the full height of the column, will create an impression of dignity upon the mind; and the first emotion which a monument produces upon the spectator is all-important. When a lofty object is first seen from far and kept in view up to the moment that the beholder gets close up to it,

> the impression is not so overpowering, however small may be the other objects which may surround it, as when it bursts suddenly upon the view close upon him. The gradual approach to it from a distance begets impatience and weariness; the impressions of grandeur only progressively develope [sic] themselves ...

Furthermore, as a seasoned traveler to Greece and Italy, he was also aware of the classical precedents of such architecture and its effects.[9]

> The ancients well understood this; their temples were never seen isolated and from far; they were always surrounded by colonnades and enclosure walls. The Column of Trajan was on one side of a square court of small dimensions, probably not more than 100 metres square.[10]

4.

Donaldson was right to invoke antiquity and the Column of Trajan, which like Nelson's Column towers high above its square and is crowned by a statue of its eponymous hero. Dedicated in 113 AD by the Senate and People of Rome to the soldier-emperor Trajan (53–117), this column too is an imperial monument of overwhelming scale and grandeur.[11]

The Column of Trajan, Forum of Trajan, Rome.

Like Nelson, Trajan stands upright atop his perch, seeing *all*, observed and acknowledged by *all*, and yet himself acknowledging *no-one* in particular. The relationship between the man at the top of the erect column and the public below is invariably 'asymmetrical'. It needs no more saying today than it did in the 19th century or in antiquity, that the monument is a geometric metaphor of imperial power.[12] Nelson's erect, overscaled Corinthian column, guarded by its oversized lions (over 6 metres high; the work of Edwin Landseer RA, 1802–1873), dominates the centre of its large, open square. Together, so monumentally beyond human scale, they claim, seemingly absolutely, a sublimated space of public art, elegance, leisure and culture. Facing Nelson's

Column in Trafalgar Square is the National Gallery (founded 1824). Likewise, the Column of Trajan, dominating its own space, the Forum of Trajan, was flanked by architectural emblems of culture, Trajan's Latin Library on the one side and the Emperor's Greek Library on the other, both of which were built when the column was erected.[13] Both columns, of course, equally maintain the perfect pitch of their political message. Nelson's imperial simulacrum faces Westminster and Whitehall. At the north end of Trajan's forum lay the Basilica Ulpia.

5.

Donaldson, it seems to me, nevertheless left certain things unsaid when he spoke of 'impressions of grandeur'. Nor could he or the Victorians exert full control over their monument. His, and the Committee's, and Parliament's was an imperial enterprise. It is in the nature of the universal enterprise of imperial orders that they only speak of themselves, that they see, as it were, only the one statue at the centre of their Square. There can be only one Empire.[14] Yet, of course, if only on account of Nelson's Column's necessary reference to Roman imperial monuments and its emulation of Roman Imperial practice, there is more than one empire and there are other statues at the centres of their squares.[15] Already, then, within the Column's imperial heritage and its own imperial aspiration, lie the seeds of contradiction. Likewise, and perhaps more significantly for our specific discussion here, it is the very visual 'essence' of the column as a monument, its overpowering height and imperial scale, that seems to call to task its imperial claim.

The point (which needs no words) is impossible to miss, as even a quick walk-around will confirm: It is as difficult, indeed impossible, to see any of the features of Nelson's figure atop of his column (53 metres high) as it is to see the statue of Trajan atop his monument (44.07 metres).

From a distance, these statues, though visible, are only paltry outlines. The closer we draw to the columns, the more the monumental figures at their top are obscured, indeed, by the columns' pedestals and shafts themselves. Close up, the statues quite literally disappear from sight. Paradoxically, then, the all-important tenor of representation, the imperial master, slips out of sight precisely by the form of the monuments, by the representing vehicle, his monument, and by the process of 'reading'.[16] There are, of course, other prominent elements of Nelson's Column: the four large (5.5 metres sq.) bas-relief panels on the four sides of its pedestal, each depicting ('telling the story of') one of Nelson's battles, Cape St. Vincent, the Nile, Copenhagen and Trafalgar. These panels, cast in bronze from melted down French canon (scandalously adulterated with iron at the time of casting), are obviously there to tell the story of imperial triumph close up. Yet the detail of these visual elements too is not easy to see, first, due to their dark bronze colour, which prevents the proper contrast of chiaroscouro, and second, simply because without commentary their 'narrative' is rather hard to decipher even as they depict the most prominent events and figures.

Nelson's Column: The Battle of Trafalgar.

This, as we may by now suspect, is not simply an accident, but possibly yet another instance of what we might call 'the paradox of monumental reading'.

6.

To explore this idea further, consider briefly, first, some details of the Column of Trajan. Its main representational element other than the statue of the Emperor (and other than some less-important carvings at the base, which we will not here have room to consider) is a long *bas-relief* frieze that spirals all the way up the shaft, right up to the top. The frieze contains many varied scenes of Trajan's Dacian campaigns and, like the panels on Nelson's Column, comprises a visual narrative.[17] Trajan's Column is thus, like Nelson's Column, a prominent object that is clearly meant to tell an essential story in detail.

The Column of Trajan and detail of the spiral frieze.

Although the visual narrative is right there on the Column, in order to 'read' it the determined viewer must circle the monument some twenty five times, craning her neck, peering at small images that are ever receding as they spiral up towards the statue of Trajan and the heavens. Paul Veyne speaks about 'works of art without spectators' and the invisibility of the Column's contents.[18] Salvatore Settis rightly speaks of *'la difficoltà quasi insormontabile di lettura'*, the 'almost insurmountable' difficulty of reading this crucial visual narrative,[19] here as much visual/sensory as it is a hermeneutic/thematic difficulty! In other words, the story behind the Column's visual representation is almost 'illegible'.

One might note that Trajan's Column contains a set of spiral stairs, which visitors can ascend.

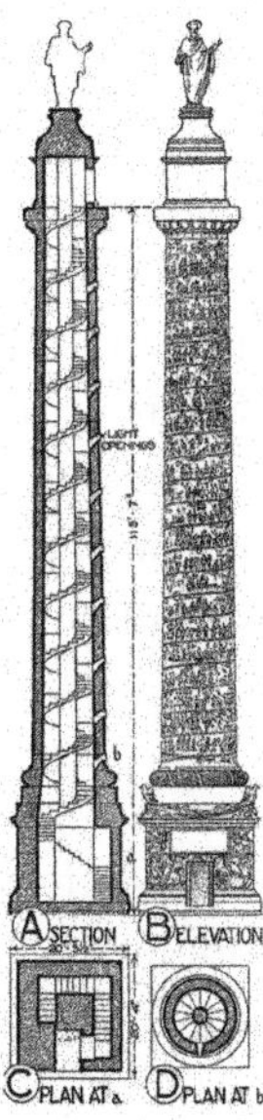

Internal Structure of Trajan's Column.

These stairs replicate the visitor's outside spiralling movement, but only stress the 'illegibility' of the visual narrative of the Emperor's exploits. From the top, one can of course see the main element of the monument, the statue of Trajan, without any difficulty. But such close viewing is again paradoxical. It strips the representation of its distance from the viewer and height, precisely its most important monumental attributes.[20]

7.

Did the imperial architect of Trajan's Column, Apollodorus of Damascus (fl. 2nd c. CE) and the Roman Senate, or the Victorian William Railton (1800–77) who designed Nelson's monument and the Committee on Trafalgar Square all get it wrong? Did they miscalculate the technical details of the construction and its visual effects? This is unlikely. We are not dealing with an accident of architecture but, as I've already suggested, with an essential pattern of 'monumental illegibility'. Furthermore, let me propose that this pattern is as necessary for the commemoration of Trajan as it is to the memory of Lord Nelson and, indeed, to the function of many other monuments which replicate the practice of 'asymmetrical perspectives'. This is a variant of a yet larger pattern of monumental veneration and illegibility.[21]

8.

In order to explain this idea, let us briefly take a look at two prominent examples of the pattern. These are 'paradigmatic' examples that deal with veneration in its most literal, religious form. They all concern essential church architecture from the 4th c. CE and the Constantinian era, that is to say from the time when Christianity became an established state religion in the lands where it emerged and thus a 'political force' that could define its own public space and erect substantial architectural monuments and visual representations of itself.[22]

The first monument is the Constantinian Church of the Holy Sepulchre in Jerusalem (the original Church was destroyed and rebuilt several times):

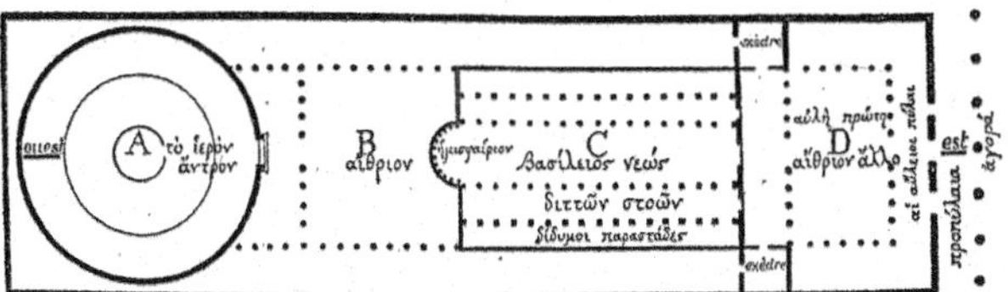

The Constantinian Holy Sepulchre, Jerusalem.[23]

and the Rotunda of the sanctuary of the Ascension on the site of the tomb:

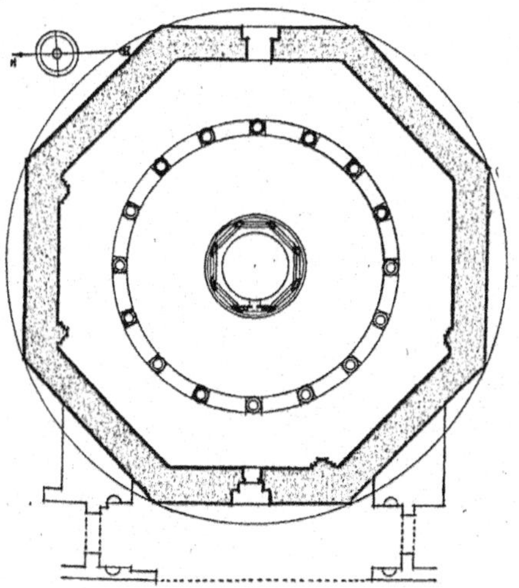

Plan of the Anastasis, Jerusalem.[24]

My second example is the Church of the Nativity in Bethlehem:

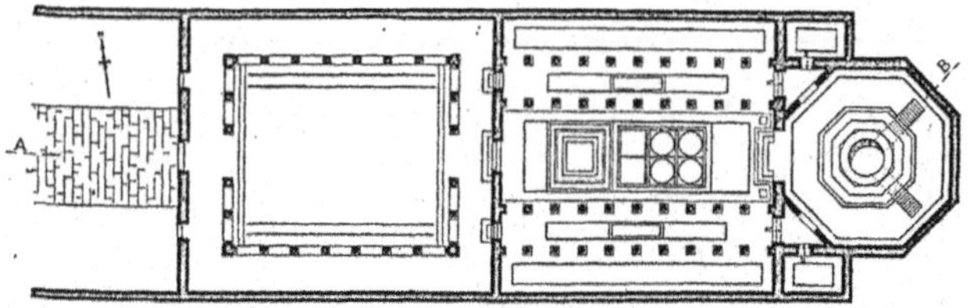

Plan of the Sanctuary of the Nativity, Bethlehem.[25]

In these physical structures, dealing with the birth, crucifixion and resurrection of Christ, we find, let me suggest, quintessential examples of the pattern of 'enclosure and shrine', a circular, polygonal or square space (the octagon is an intermediate geometric shape, linking the circle and square) surrounding a venerated middle-point, a *temenos* ('sacred precinct') round an *omphalos* ('navel', 'middle point', 'keystone', 'tomb'). The centre of this pattern is quite literally the focus of religious worship. In these structures, the centre-point is either below the viewers (Sepulchre/Anastasis) or on a level plane with them (Nativity), yet it is clearly celestial and much higher than even the very tip of Nelson's hat or the halo of St. Peter that nowadays rests above the Emperor Trajan's head. We are dealing with a spatial pattern, the geometric figure of veneration that represents the relationship between mortal and divine.

The centre-points of these ecclesiastical structures are empty ciphers by definition, notional points in the 'transcendental geometry' of religious worship. They do not contain the infant Christ or his manger nor, of course, the body of risen Christ or even a statue or a crucifix. To have placed a simulacrum on the spot would indeed have seemed strange. Absence is a paradoxical, yet essential element of these spaces, not merely because of the narratives they represent ('Christ is risen') or, on a more abstract level, because of the asymmetrical relationship between the Son of God and Man, but also because of their essential function as representations and signs. It is exactly the paradox of presence and absence that constitutes the nature of signs, 'present' signifiers that bear witness to an absent signified. The 'illegible' quality of the visible sign, the arbitrary nature of the signifier (as de Saussure would say) and the invisibility of its signified are the essence of its representational function. Signs provide us with a locus for meaning and, perhaps, more generally, with the model of all knowledge.

9.

We are are dealing with a very wide pattern indeed. As historian of early Church architecture Jean Lassus says:

> André Grabar has shown that although these commemorative monuments were of very different types, the intention was the same: to serve as a shrine for some holy place, to enable the masses to come as pilgrims and contemplate it without harming it and to assemble nearby for communal prayer. The spectators used to arrange themselves in concentric circles around a single point. The monuments were therefore either circular or polygonal and resembled the imperial mausoleums, which had a similar purpose.[26]

The permutations of this pattern of veneration are attested in many different sites, not only in the Eastern Church but also, as Lassus and others stressed, in the Mausoleum of Augustus and the Pantheon in Rome, and possibly, we might add, in the Kaaba square in Mecca, the Dome of the Rock on Temple Mount in Jerusalem, Hagia Sofia in Istanbul, perhaps at Stonehenge, and in yet other more-and less-important sites, including, mutatis mutandis, some 'ordinary' city squares with 'ordinary' commemorative statues or other objects at their centres.[27] Each of these shares in the general semantics of the pattern though it manifests a distinct configuration of the pattern's 'vocabulary'. Each, of course, can only be fully interpreted within its own contingent historical setting.

Nelson's monument is part of this architectural figure too. It plants the Column in the middle of a precinct, allowing the masses to come 'as pilgrims to contemplate it'. Like his Christian counterpart, Lord Nelson, is, of course, both Master and Martyr. Separate from the rest of humanity, he suffers alone, yet for a cause, for England and the Empire, atop of his column/cross.

As we have already noted, the column's scale or magnitude (*megethos*) is well beyond the human, well beyond what might have been the size of the Cross or the size of Jesus' tomb or the manger where he was born. This, it seems to me, is more than just an emblem of the scale of imperial aspiration. It is also, let me suggest, compensatory practice at a 'higher' metaphorical level. Try as the Empire might to celebrate the Hero of Trafalgar, it could not elevate him to the status of divinity.[28] Those whose task it was to commemorate him had to find other ways of raising him beyond ordinary mortals that did not have direct religious functions. Literal elevation of this magnitude was, I suggest, the perfect way to both mask their purpose and effect it.

Like the Column of Trajan (and, indeed, like memorial and triumphal arches too), Nelson's column is explicitly a structural architectural element. It is a column in the Corinthian style, such as normally support the roof of a temple or a neoclassical church. Yet Nelson's Column holds up no roof. What should we say, then, of a vast, oversized and solitary column in the middle of an open space? It transforms the whole of the 'Square' into an open-air chapel or temple for the veneration of its secular god, a god of the metropolis and of the Empire, a divinity that is invisible (quite literally, when we are up close), whom we are nevertheless certain is up there in the sky.

The Victorians were unlikely to have built a literal cathedral to Lord Nelson. This would have been something of an act of Christian sacrilege. It would have also partly misrepresented the Empire, which, though Christian by faith, was secular, political and commercial in essence. Even more importantly, the great cathedrals of England and Europe offered a model that was largely unsuitable for the purpose of imperial commemoration. The cathedrals of the Western Church were built as elongated cruciforms. Their altars were set at the eastern end of the building, facing the true centre of the Christian world, the Holy Land, far away in the 'East.' Such symbolic geometrical displacement was, let me suggest, unsuitable for the British Empire, whose centre was, of course, England and London itself. The builders of Nelson's imperial monument needed a pattern whose centre pointed nowhere else. This they found in precisely the pattern of a monumental column like the Column of Trajan, which stood in Rome, at the centre of its own empire, the Roman Empire. The basic geometry of the Column of Trajan is, as we have seen, reflected and indeed historically linked to the figure of the great architectural emblems of the Eastern Church, which were based on circles and octagons. The great sanctuaries and martyrions of the Eastern Church themselves were in the East (the most important literally in the Holy Land), in their own *omphalos*, and were thus meaningfully built in the pattern of the circle and its centre-point.

10.

Like Christ, like the 4th c. CE Syrian Martyr Simeon Stylites (Semaan Al Aamudi, 388–459, yet again a figure of the Eastern Church),[29] Lord Nelson has no space (no 'room' – a covered space) atop his column to sit down, no space to eat or defecate, to lie down to sleep or, indeed, to lie down to die.

The imperial hero who sees all atop of his column also has no space for walking. It is we, the spectators, who cannot see him, who walk round his monument. And this, let me suggest, is where the paradox of empire 'bursts suddenly upon the view close upon us', to turn Davidson's words to our own use.

In the closed spaces of cathedrals, we, the worshippers and spectators, mostly stand in silent reverence (conceptually, at least, one 'walks' in and out of enclosed spaces but one does not 'walk' indoors). Even in the ambulatories and rotundas of the churches and sanctuaries of the East, worshippers mostly gathered round, in essence so that they might stand still. In contrast, Nelson's open-air sanctuary, by its very nature and scale, invites us to walk around it and gives us ample space to do so. Such walking 'in circles' gives us time to think, to recognize our own human scale and the absurdly discrepant scale of our imperial surroundings.[30] Trafalgar Square and Nelson's Monument are thus, not surprisingly, places that enact both the convictions of imperial enterprise and their anxieties. Felix Driver and David Gilbert rightly stress that,

> In periods of mass political unrest, spaces which had been consciously designed to symbolise imperial power could also become sites of challenge and resistance. Mace (1976) provides a particularly compelling account of the ways in which Trafalgar Square, designed as an imperial space during the 19th century, simultaneously became established as a site of political demonstration and protest. These two dimensions to the square's history were of course related: the square's officially monumentalised status as an 'emblem of Empire' provided the rationale for its use by those who challenged the nature of the imperial order. Although Mace emphasises socialist and antifascist protest, the square also provided the location for explicitly anticolonial protests, such as those of the India League and Indian Freedom Campaign in the decade before Indian independence.[31]

Driver and Gilbert note that 'London has, of course, long been a site of international political activism' and that,

> It might therefore be concluded that London as a whole, like Trafalgar Square, is best thought of as a schizophrenic space, simultaneously 'imperial' and 'anti-imperial'.[32]

While I agree with their analysis, it seems to me that, at least when it comes to Trafalgar Square, their pathologizing term 'schizophrenic' may be slightly misleading. The prominence of Nelson's Column as an imperial space certainly attracted its opponents. But the paradoxes of imperial practice are an inseparable, and in this sense 'normal' aspect of its monumental architecture, as I hope to have shown and as, I hope, anyone taking a walk around Trafalgar Square can see.

ENDNOTES

1 Fredric Jameson, *The Political Unconscious: Narrative as a Socially Symbolic Act*, Ithaca, NY: Cornell University Press, pp. 109–110.

2 See Aristotle, *Physics* 219a.

3 See *Poetics* 1449b on the definition of tragedy; also *Physics* 206a.

4 See recently, e.g., Frédéric Gros, *A Philosophy of Walking*, London: Verso Books; Rebecca Solnit, *Wanderlust: A History of Walking*, London: Granta, 2014.

5 In the 19th century, the population of Greater London increased by more than a factor of six, from 1,011,157 to 6,226,494 (ONS and Census of Population. Summary in GB Historical GIS / University of Portsmouth, *A Vision of Britain through Time*. http://www. visionofbritain.org.uk/unit/10097836/ cube/TOT_POP. Accessed: 11th September 2015).

6 "Report from the Select Committee on Trafalgar Square, House of Commons, 27 July 1840", *House of Commons Reports from Committees*, Vol. XII, London: House of Commons, 1840, pp. 387–433. For a contemporary commentary on Trafalgar Square in the context of imperial London, see, e.g., Rodney Mace, *Trafalgar Square: Emblem of Empire*, London: Lawrence and Wishart, 1976; Felix Driver and David Gilbert, "Heart of Empire? Land-scape, Space and Performance in Imperial London", *Environment and Planning D: Society and Space* 16 (1998), pp. 11–28; cf. David Atkinson and Denis Cosgrove, "Urban Rhetoric and Embodied Identities: City, Nation, and Empire at the Vittorio Emanuele II Monument in Rome, 1870–1945", *Annals of the Association of American Geographers* 88, pp. 28–49.

7 This, and all following quotations from Donaldson's evidence below, are from the same Report of the Select Committee on Trafalgar Square.

8 Walking is clearly assumed. It is quite literally not possible to drive around the Column. Indeed, even in the abstract, the idea of riding in a brougham or a landau, let alone in a London Cab, bus or car round and round and round the Square seems dizzying and Chaplinesque.

9 See, e.g., Donaldson's contributions in William Clarke, *Pompeii: Its Past and Present State, Its Public and Private Buildings, Etc.*, London: M. A. Nattali, 1847.

10 Trajan's Column was well known to 19th-century architects (see, e.g., Mace, *Trafalgar Square: Emblem of Empire*, p. 16) and later, in 1864, plaster casts of the spiral frieze of the Column (for which see further below) were deposited in the Victoria and Albert

Museum. The Forum of Trajan was, in fact, significantly larger, about 200 by 120 metres.

[11] See Filippo Coarelli, Paul Zanker, Bruno Brizzi, Cinzia Conti and Roberto Meneghini, *The Column of Trajan*, Rome: Editore Colombo, 2000.

[12] The vertical is an essential element of the visual semantics of political architecture and public discourses of power. One might think of modern urban skyscrapers or the mediaeval towers of San Gimignano in Tuscany; see Ahuvia Kahane, "Image, Word, and the Antiquity of Ruins", *European Review of History* 18 (2011), pp. 829–850, for discussion in the context of antiquity. For the contemporary political debate, see, e.g., Stuart Elden "Secure the Volume: Vertical Geopolitics and the Depth of Power", *Political Geography* 34 (2013), pp. 35–51; Eyal Weitzman, "Introduction to the Politics of Verticality," (https://www.opendemocracy.net/ecology-politicsverticality/article_801.jsp, 2002); Eyal Weitzman, *Hollow Land: Israel's Architecture of Occupation*, London: Verso Books, 2007; Francis Sparshott, "The Aesthesis of Architecture and the Politics of Space", in Michael H. Mitias, ed., *Philosophy and Architecture*, Amsterdam and Atlanta: Rodopi, 1994, pp. 3–21

[13] See James Packer, *The Forum of Trajan: A Study of the Monuments*, Berkeley, CA: University of California Press, 1997.

[14] Where this fantasy is challenged, there is often imperial aggression, of course.

[15] For the inherent paradoxes of empire and the transition from empire to late modernity, which is essential to the thesis of this essay, see, e.g., Michael Hardt and Antonio Negri's classic work, *Empire*, Cambridge, MA: Harvard University Press, 2000.

[16] Cf. Jesper Svenbro's famous discussion, 'I write, therefore I efface myself,' in *Phrasikleia: An Anthropology of Reading in Ancient Greece*, Ithaca, NY: Cornell University Press, 1993, pp. 26–45.

[17] The campaigns are also attested in Trajan's *Dacica*, of which only a single line survives, in the works of the Roman grammarian Priscian (*Grammatici Latini* 2.205 K.1: *inde Berzobim, deinde Aizi processimus*. 'then [we advanced] to Berzobim, next to Aizi'. See Frank A. Lepper and Sheppard S. Frere, *Trajan's Column, A New Edition of the Cichorius Plates*, Gloucester: Sutton Publishing, 1988, p. 17. Generally, see Salvatore Settis, Adriano La Regina and Giovanni Agosti, *La Colonna Traiana*. Torino: Einaudi Editore, 1988; Coarelli et al. *The Column of Trajan*. Rome: Colombo, 2000.

[18] Paul Veyne, "Conduites sans croyance et oeuvres d'art sans spectateurs", *Diogène* 143 (1988), pp. 3–22; cf. Veyne, "Propagande expression roi. Image, idole, oracle", *L'Homme* 114 (1990), pp. 7–26; Veyne, "Post-scriptum, la Colonne Trajane comme monument cérémonial", in *La société romaine*, Paris: Éditions Seuil, 1991, pp. 338–342.

[19] See Settis *et al.*, *La Colonna Traiana,* pp. 86–87. Even when viewed up close, the meaning of the frieze is unclear and disputes over its interpretation are as intense today as they have ever been.

[20] Jás Elsner has drawn my attention to some further key intertexts of Trajan's Column such as The Monument, Christopher Wren's monumental column in London, commemorating the fire of 1666 (see John E. Moore, "The Monument, or, Christopher Wren's Roman Accent", *Art Bulletin* 80 [1998], pp. 498–533) and the Column of Marcus Aurelius in Rome (193 AD? See John Scheid and Valérie Huet, eds., *Autour de la colonne Aurélienne: Geste et image sur la colonne de Marc Aurèle à Rome*, Brepolis: Tournhout, 2000). Elsner says: 'If Marcus is no. 2 to Trajan, then arguably Nelson is no 2 to Wren [i.e. to the 1677 Monument]. Both London columns are "salvific" [one from natural disaster, one from political/military disaster].' These two sets of memorial columns, unmissable, especially in their time, because of their extraordinary height, create intense tensions and affinities among themselves. Elsewhere Elsner writes of the Column of Marcus Aurelius: 'Hardly any monument in Roman art is – on the face of it – so carefully constructed as a creative imitation of a distinguished predecessor. Yet, despite the patently obvious conservatism... of this great Antonine genuflection to Trajan's column, the art-historical literature on the... monument is devoted... to ... its radical stylistic innovations...' (Jás Elsner, "Frontality on the Column of Marcus Aurelius", in Scheid and Huet, *Autour de la colonne Aurélienne*, p. 251).

[21] On asymmetry and problems of visibility in in Roman monumental art, see Jennifer Trimble, "Visibility and viewing on the Severan Marble Plan", in Simon C. Swain, Stephen J. Harrison and Jás Elsner, eds., *Severan Culture*, Cambridge: Cambridge University Press, 2007, pp. 368–384.

[22] See discussion in Ahuvia Kahane, "Cavafy's Last Act: Death, Martyrdom, and the Problem of Bearing Witness to the Past", *Classical and Modern Literature* 23 (2003), pp. 143–160; Vered Shalev-Hurvitz, *Holy Sites Encircled: The Early Byzantine Concentric Churches of Jerusalem*, Oxford: Oxford University

Press, 2015, pp. 9–10, with further references on the iconography of architecture.

[23] Jean Lassus, *Sanctuaires chrétiens de Syrie: essai sur la genèse, la forme et l'usage liturgique des édifices du culte chrétien, en Syrie, du IIIe siècle à la conquête musulmane.* Paris: P. Geuthner, 1947, p. 104; Lassus, *The Early Christian and Byzantine World*, New York: McGraw-Hill, 1967, p. 33; see André Grabar, *Martyrium: Recherches sur le culte des reliques et l'art chrétien antique*, Paris: Les Éditions d'art et d'histoire, 1943–6.

[24] Lassus, *Sanctuaires chrétiens de Syrie*, p. 107; *The Early Christian and Byzantine World*, p. 34.

[25] Lassus, *Sanctuaires chrétiens de Syrie*, p. 105; *The Early Christian and Byzantine World*, p. 34.

[26] Lassus, *The Early Christian and Byzantine World*, p. 36. Cf. Grabar 1943–6; Shalev-Hurvitz, *Holy Sites Encircled*, pp. 9-10.

[27] See, e.g., Lassus *Sanctuaires chrétiens de Syrie*, p. 105 (but mentioning only the Christian monuments).

[28] Note that in early heroic epic, for example in Homer, even heroes who have an immortal parent (Achilles, son of Thetis; Sarpedon, son of Zeus) and who are often described as 'godlike', are *not* immortal themselves.

[29] Simeon Stylites provided an important model for the Victorians and, for example, for the Poet Laureate Alfred, Lord Tennyson. See Herbert F. Tucker, "From Monomania to Monologue: 'St. Simeon Stylites' and the Rise of the Victorian Dramatic Monologue", *Victorian Poetry* 22 (1984), pp. 121–137.

[30] I may *walk around the house* (or even take the National Trust's guided tour), but walking *stricto sensu* is, let me suggest, something one does *outdoors*, under the heavens and the stars. Compare, e.g., the Kaaba, a shrine surrounded by an *open* space where the public at large *do* ritually walk round and round. But this important example requires extended, separate study of its contingent theology, politics, iconology and architectural dynamics.

[31] Felix Driver and David Gilbert, "Heart of Empire? Landscape, Space and Performance in Imperial London", *Environment and Planning D: Society and Space* 16 (1998), p. 27.

[32] Felix Driver and David Gilbert, "Heart of Empire? Landscape, Space and Performance in Imperial London", *Environment and Planning D: Society and Space* 16 (1998), p. 27.

Music

STRAND
THAMES
LONDON
Somerset House
Temple Pier
Police Station
City & County of the City of London By.
Parly. & Munl. Boro. By.
Waterloo Bridge
Blackfriars Bridge
Southwark Bridge
Southwark Bridge Stairs
St. Paul's Station
St. Paul's Pier
L. C. & D. RY.
Landing Stages
Landing Place
Landing Stage
Jetties
Lead Works
Lion Brewery
Saw Mills
Waterloo Station
Waterloo Road
York Road
New Cut
Commercial Road
Stamford Street
Blackfriars Road
Southwark Street
Lavington Street
Union Street
Charlotte St.
Gt. Charlotte St.
Nelson Square
Marshalsea Road
Borough High Street
Queen St. Pl.
Upper Thames Street
The Approach
Hospl.
Ch.
Sch.
Chap.

AMY BLIER-CARRUTHERS

The Travelling Mindset: A Method for Seeing Everything Anew

Images by Alan Douglas Carruthers

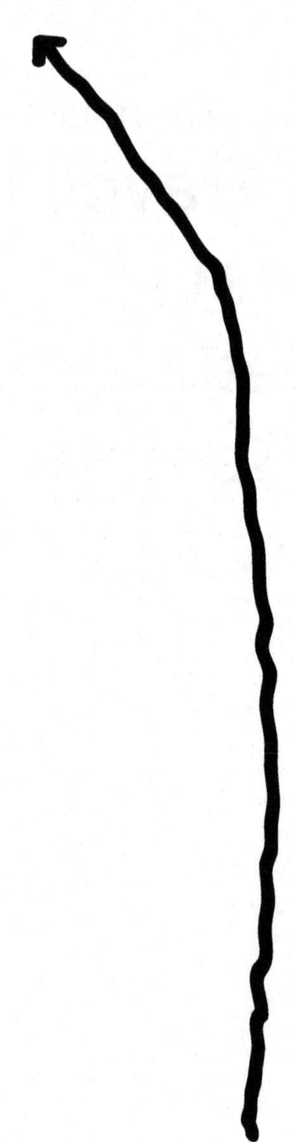

All too often as artists and musicians we take the spaces which we inhabit for granted. We believe that we know all we need to know about a place, event, or situation because of long acquaintance, and therefore unthinkingly accept the expectations, ceremonies, or behaviours associated with them. However, this stance could be questioned. What if instead we adopted the 'travelling mindset'[1] suggested by the 18th-century French 'armchair philosopher' Xavier de Maistre? Might this enable us to begin to see familiar things anew and perceive things differently? Walking is a good way to help train oneself to use this travelling mindset. How, by taking a walk, might we learn this technique for observing our surroundings, and thereby perhaps learn to reconsider the often controlled and managed spaces in which we habitually operate?

Our walk took place along the south side of the river Thames, the cultural quarter of London known as the South Bank. It began at the Tate Modern museum with a stroll through the galleries, and continued on to the Royal Festival Hall for a short early-evening concert of classical music.[2] It was late afternoon and we met in the vast Turbine Hall of the Tate Modern. This cathedral-like industrial space, with its smooth concrete sloping floor and dark steel girders, rising to skylights 35 metres above, houses the Tate Modern's rolling exhibition of larger sculptural pieces and art installations. I was there to lead a walk based on the theme of 'Temporality and Space in Art and Music', and was joined by practitioners of music and the arts – academics and post-graduate students from the Royal College of Art and the Royal Academy of Music. The themes I was drawing out centred on the different types of spaces in which art and music are prepared for and exhibited–the spaces and the teleologies of these art forms affect us differently, both as practitioners and observers.[3]

At an art gallery, as a member of the viewing public, you are free to move through the space, you can walk at your own pace. You can choose the order in which you see things. You can stand and linger, looking closely at the details of the brush-strokes or sculpted lines, or you can walk straight past a piece. You vote with your feet–*you* create the tempo. There are, of course, instances where this is not the case, for instance when people stand in your way, or in the case of performance art–I heard someone say at an exhibition recently 'that's the problem with video-art: it takes time to watch it'. At a concert, once the music starts, you are committed–you have no freedom to walk past something like you do in a gallery. If you find you don't like it, or you've heard it before and don't feel like experiencing it just now, you're stuck. The thing is, music takes *time*: it unfolds, it develops, it is structured to be listened to from start to finish, and in a live concert setting you are compelled to do just that–stay and pay attention. Does this put people off taking a risk with classical music they're not sure they will like, or classical music they don't know at all? Perhaps. However, music does have a magical quality of capturing your attention, and even when your mind wanders, it is free to do so, accompanied by the sounds you are hearing. It is a different kind of freedom–one you can take advantage of whilst sitting in your seat, hearing new or familiar sounds.

These were some of the subjects that we were considering whilst walking. But why, one might ask, would a group of artists and musicians be taking a walk at all?

What has walking got to do with it? Wouldn't we be better off to stay in our practice rooms and studios, surrounded by our instruments, tools, and materials, and just keep working? Maybe not. Perhaps there are times when this just won't suffice. Perhaps sometimes we need to get up, go out, see something else, get a different perspective, get our minds thinking along unexpected tracks. There are many different kinds of walk that one might embark upon. You can walk to get from A to B; you can walk to think through a problem; you can walk to recharge, to combat lack of inspiration or depression–what Vincent van Gogh called 'the meagreness';[4] you can walk to clear your mind, often coming to some solution without having been consciously thinking about it–Barbara Ueland in her book *If You Want to Write* calls this 'moodling'[5]–it helps the sediment to settle in your mind, leaving you with some clarity; you can walk for enjoyment, thinking of nothing at all except the act of walking and being; or you can walk to observe with curiosity the details around you. Many musicians, artists, and writers have walked to help them get ideas and work through problems. I recently came across a piece about walking by Will Self in which he quoted Nietzsche who said 'I never trust an idea that didn't come to me on a walk'.[6] Van Gogh was an avid walker and observer,[7] Charles Dickens walked the streets of London every day gathering material for his stories,[8] and Ernest Hemingway walked around Paris to help him think.[9] Virginia Woolf used to walk, once citing the desperate need of a new pencil as the excuse to leave her desk and refresh herself by treading the streets of London:

> No one perhaps ever felt passionately towards a lead pencil. But there are circumstances in which it can become supremely desirable to possess one; moments when we are set upon having an object, an excuse for walking half across London between tea and dinner [...] when the desire comes upon us to go street rambling the pencil does for a pretext, and getting up we say: 'Really I must buy a pencil,' as if under cover of this excuse we could indulge safely in the greatest pleasure of town life in the winter–rambling the streets of London.[10]

Despite these many reasons for walking, and despite the ostensible theme of my walk, my *main* aim for this walk was actually to propose a *mindset* for walking, a possible *way of seeing*, a method for *observing*. It's the how we're looking at things that I want us to focus on, and going for a walk is an ideal way of practising this method for perceiving the world around us. As artistic practitioners, be it in the arts or in music, there is of course the act of making or doing, in which we are nearly constantly engaged, so much so that we might often no longer be able to see the wood for the trees–we're always so busy *doing*. But how might we capture that process, in order to be able to look at it more objectively and learn something from it? To be able to do this is especially important to academics or postgraduate students engaged in research into their own artistic practice (often known as practice-as-research or artistic research), but it can also be very useful as a teaching tool, or as a way of developing one's awareness of one's own practice. Awareness of our environment enables us to look at music or art as social practice, and to look at what we do and the spaces we inhabit more objectively, to see how they actually influence us and our creativity.

To achieve this level of objectivity with regards to something so familiar, we might think about studying our own practice as if we were anthropologists or ethnomusicologists studying the daily life, cultural practices, or music-making traditions of a community in an unfamiliar faraway place.[11] Traditionally these researchers journey to foreign lands and their fresh view and objective stance come as a matter of course; it is an integral part of their method to approach their fieldwork subjects with openness, a lack of judgement or preconceived ideas, and to try to view and understand the situation from the point of view of the people they are studying. You might wonder why we might need to emulate this kind of work when thinking about music or art. But the fact is that the techniques we need to employ are very similar. Their journey takes them to an unfamiliar place, but we need to try to see our immediate surroundings as if they were far away, unfamiliar, and strange.

A painting or photograph, or a recording of music, are fixed and can be looked at or listened to and examined repeatedly. Live performance events, or our own artistic practice, are fleeting, so we need different techniques to analyse them. We need other ways of capturing these processes in order to be able to examine them self-reflexively. There are several tools we can use to capture creative processes in action, and anthropologists and ethnomusicologists have used these for a long time:

various forms of experiential writing, including practice or work diaries, reflective commentaries, notes from lessons or other interactions; and fieldwork observation, field-notes, or interviews with people with whom we work. We can also capture documentation of our experiences through audio or video recording.

There has been a marked increase in this kind of approach to studying classical music in the last decade or so.[12] Some time ago Jonathan Stock[13] called for further work to be done in this area, explaining why those working in the tradition of Western Art Music would benefit from borrowing ethnographic techniques: 'It is self-evident that music is more than simply sets of sounds [...] Music is process as well as product, an arena for both social action and personal reflection.'[14] He quotes Anthony Seeger who writes that music is 'emotion and value as well as structure and form'.[15] Stock continues: 'The musicologist that analyzes what musicians and others actually do on particular musical occasions, and how these individuals explain what they do, is likely to gain enlightening perspectives on the sounds that emerge.'[16]

Ethnographies of music colleges have been written by Bruno Nettl[17] and Henry Kingsbury,[18] and the further growth of research in this area is evidenced by the work of Stephen Cottrell,[19] Stephanie Pitts,[20] and the publication of the special issue of *Ethnomusicology Forum* on 'The Ethnomusicology of Western Art Music', edited by Laudan Nooshin.[21] I would urge anyone to look at these sources in order to get an idea of what the possibilities are in terms of thinking and methodologies–it quickly becomes quite clear that these ideas can easily be employed across disciplinary boundaries.

Another useful volume, *Shadows in the Field*, contains several articles which offer insights into how to undertake this type of research.[22] These authors offer suggestions as to how to write up observations, how to be self-reflexive in one's research, and techniques for dealing with problems of advocacy, anonymity, representation, and interpretation when writing up one's findings.[23] The work of Anthony Seeger has helped me to think about the researcher's place in relation to his research subjects,[24] and Gregory Barz[25] offers a useful model of a trinity of ethnography, describing the flow of ethnographic research as: 'Field research (Experience)–Fieldnote (Reflection)–Ethnography (Interpretation)'.[26] Barz also suggests that:

> Field research is performed [...] Fieldnotes are for many ethnomusicologists an essential aspect of knowing; they are not only critical in determining what we know, but also illustrative of the process of how we come to know what we know. [...] fieldnotes inscribe action while simultaneously affecting and reflecting that action [...] The process of writing notes in the field presents a significant opportunity to pivot between experience and understanding, explanation and knowing.[27]

So the question now is: how can we as artists and musicians (or in fact any kind of thinker or practitioner) train ourselves to do this kind of work? If ethnography[28] is a 'scientific description of the races of the earth', and 'ethnomusicology is to make a study of music [...] in relation to the culture in which [it is] found',[29] my own definition of an ethnography of classical music or of artistic practice more broadly conceived is to look at something incredibly familiar but opening your eyes and mind and *trying to see it as if for the first time.* Bruno Nettl calls this doing 'ethnomusicology at home', by looking 'at the familiar as if it were not, at one's own culture as if one were a foreigner to it'.[30] He sets up the example of an 'extraterrestrial ethnomusicologist from Mars'[31] appearing in a cultural institution, with no prior contextual knowledge of the milieu being observed.

If you're going to examine your own practice in this way it helps to be at once subjective and objective, to be on the inside looking out and on the outside looking in, reflecting on your own practice, being self-reflexive, *by looking at everything anew.* We could take as inspiration someone who tried this in the late 18th century. Xavier de Maistre, an aristocrat and army officer, was once confined to his apartments for several weeks as punishment for engaging in illegal duelling. His movements thus restricted, he began to think about travelling, and his musings became a book called *Journey Around My Room.*[32] Remaining in his bedroom, attired in his dressing gown, he took a journey from where he sat. He advised this as a method of travelling that might be 'infinitely more practical' for those neither 'brave nor [...] wealthy'. He 'particularly recommended room travel to the poor and to those afraid of storms, robberies, and high cliffs'.[33] De Maistre exclaims:

> What a grand resource this way of travelling will be for the sick! They won't need to fear the inclemency of the air and the seasons. As for the cowards, they will be safe from

> robbers; they will encounter neither precipices nor quagmires. Thousands of people who, before I came along, had never dared to travel, and others who hadn't been able to, and yet others who'd never even dreamt of travelling, will be emboldened to do so by my example.[34]

He asks us to look at familiar everyday things in the same frame of mind as if we were embarking on a journey to a foreign destination, a frame of mind which is usually much more attuned to the myriad small details of our surroundings.

> Don't let anyone start telling me off for being prolix in my details: all travellers behave the same way. When you set off to climb the Mont Blanc, or when you go to visit the wide open tomb of Empedocles, you never fail to describe the smallest details precisely; the number of people, the number of mules, the quality of the provisions, the excellent appetite of the travellers–everything, in short up to and including the times your mounts stumble, is painstakingly recorded in your diary, for the instruction of the sedentary world.[35]

De Maistre begins by telling us that his room is rectangular, extends from east to west, and is 36 paces in circumference. He begins his journey by the table, and sets out obliquely towards the door, soon encountering his armchair, in which he settles comfortably for a time. He advocates being open to following different paths during your journey:

> I will be crossing [my room] frequently lengthwise, or else diagonally, without any rule or method [...] I don't like people who have their itineraries and ideas so clearly sorted out [...] My soul is so open to every kind of idea, taste and sentiment; it so avidly receives everything that presents itself! [...] There's no more attractive pleasure, in my view, than following one's ideas wherever they lead, as the hunter pursues his game, without even trying to keep to any set route.[36]

From his armchair (in which he likes to sit by the fire with books and pens, free to read, write, or dream) he is delighted by the view of his bed, which is 'situated in the most pleasant spot imaginable',[37] and from which he recalls watching the morning sunlight moving along the wall, with the shadows from the trees fluttering on his pink-and-white sheets. He meditates on the scenes that are enacted in beds: 'A bed witnesses our birth and death; it is the unvarying theatre in which the human race acts out, successively, captivating dramas, laughable farces and dreadful tragedies. It is a cradle bedecked with flowers; it is a throne of love; it is a sepulchre.'[38] The objects he encounters along his journey – be it a series of paintings, his dog Rosine, a plate of toast and a cup of coffee, his mirror, or a dried rose – inspire direct descriptions, related memories, moments of reverie, and tangential departures into remote ruminations.

In his book *The Art of Travel*, the modern philosopher of everyday life Alain de Botton explains that de Maistre interrogated the concept of what de Botton calls the 'travelling mindset':[39] 'de Maistre's work springs from a profound and suggestive insight that the pleasure we derive from journeys is perhaps dependent more on the mindset with which we travel than on the destination we travel to. If only we could apply the travelling mindset to our own locales, we might find these places becoming no less interesting than the high mountain passes and butterfly-filled jungles of Humboldt's South America.'[40]

To get a fuller picture of the state of mind that de Botton is describing, we might let him elaborate, though remembering that he is writing in the 21st century, so the examples he uses are contemporary. He asks:

> What, then, is the travelling mindset? *Receptivity* might be said to be its chief characteristic. We approach new places with *humility*. We carry with us *no rigid ideas* about what is interesting. We irritate locals because we stand on traffic islands and in narrow streets and admire what they take to be *strange small details*. [...] We *dwell at length* on the layout of a menu or the clothes of the presenters on the evening news. We are *alive to the layers of history beneath the present and take notes and photographs*. [...] Home, on the other hand, finds us more settled in our expectations. We feel assured that we have discovered everything interesting about a neighbourhood, primarily by virtue of having lived there a long time. It seems inconceivable that there could be anything new to find in a place which we have been living in for a decade or more. We have

> become habituated and therefore blind. De Maistre tried to shake us from our passivity.[41]

We as musicians and artists can apply this mindset to all the habits and behaviours that we experience every day but don't question–our own activities and thought patterns, assumptions, learnt behaviours related to our art, the etiquette of the spaces where work is performed or exhibited, or the accepted ways of talking and writing about our milieu. We might ask ourselves if these habits and expectations help to structure our working lives in positive ways, or whether they perhaps restrict our creativity. In this way, walking or engaging in fieldwork observation can trigger processes of thinking, making, and researching. I do this regularly with my students, whether undergraduates or doctoral researchers. We go on a field trip to an event with which we are intimately familiar–in my case a concert of classical music at a high-profile concert hall. Students of music in conservatories or university music departments have usually internalised the habits and expectations of such an event from having spent well over a decade, in most cases, regularly performing in these kinds of concerts. By setting out to observe in detail and to confront our ingrained expectations and assumptions we can really help ourselves to see things anew and question the status quo.

Returning to the idea of walking as a way of practising having a travelling mindset, if we choose to go for a walk and question the institutions in which our arts are exhibited and performed, what details might we notice? Some of the things we might look out for are the exteriors of the buildings and the entrances–each façade gives a message: do they feel imposing, inviting, or both? Once inside, what are the liminal spaces like, the spaces in between the outside world and the display space–the foyers, the cafés, and shops? We might look more closely at the exhibition or performance spaces–how is the work presented; is there a separation between art/artist and audience, or are they brought together on the same plane? Who is there–what is the demographic, how do people move and settle? What are the expected behaviours and dress codes, and do people adhere to them? We might imagine the making or creating spaces that precede these presentation spaces–the places where the artists and musicians make or rehearse before exhibiting the fruits of their art. Once in a gallery or concert hall, how do we experience that exhibition or performance–what does the particular medium demand of us as observers and consumers? Are the performers enacting the performance, or is the art displayed, according to our expectations, and if not, how are they subverting those expectations? What is the content of the art exhibition or concert–is it traditional or innovative, does it surprise or bore us, does it successfully meet its stated aims, does it interact with or react to the venue and audience? How does the venue market itself–does the marketing match the sense you have of the place? Is it a purely cultural space, or is there a combination of leisure and culture; do people use it in the way it was intended, or do the public discover other ways of using the space? As you depart, what overall impression are you left with?

This may seem like a long list of questions, but it might enable you to recreate our walk from art gallery to concert hall for yourself or in fact any other walk or process of observation relevant to your particular setting. You can also take this a step further by considering your own practice. By using a travelling mindset, detailed observation techniques, note-taking, and self-reflection, you have a better chance of capturing your thought processes, your artistic decision-making, and the minute instantiations of your craft in such a way as to be able to bring this tacit knowledge to the foreground. These ethnographic techniques can help you to present the ephemeral but centrally important evidence of your working process in a way that more clearly and convincingly presents its validity and value.

By developing a critical stance towards our own practice, and by being willing to ask ourselves questions about what we do, we might find a deeper and clearer understanding of what we want to articulate as practitioners. By taking a walk through the spaces of art and music, and learning to use a travelling mindset to see things anew, I hope we may all begin to discover a new objectivity, self-awareness, and a new view of space, time, and self.

MUSICIANS
CREATORS

ENDNOTES

1 The term 'travelling mindset' is used by philosopher Alain de Botton to describe de Maistre's experimental approach to embarking upon an imaginary journey. Alain de Botton, *The Art of Travel*, London: Penguin, 2003, p. 246.

2 Photo credit: The images in this article are details from the Tate Modern and Royal Festival Hall. Photographer: Alan Douglas Carruthers, © 2010/2011/2016. Reproduced with permission.

3 My theme of temporality and space is somewhat echoed in the themes of porosity and presence in Richard Sennett's article 'Good Homes for Art', in Kiera Blakey, *Music and Architecture: Ways of Listening*, London: Theatrum Mundi, 2014, pp. 25–37. http://thea-trum-mundi.org/wp-content/uploads/2014/02/T-M-Publication.pdf – accessed February 13, 2016.

4 Barbara Ueland, *If You Want to Write*, (1938), Saint Paul, MN: Graywolf Press, 1987, p. 42.

5 Ueland, 1987, p. 38.

6 Friedrich Neitzsche as quoted by Will Self, 'King of the Road', ES Magazine: *Evening Standard*, February 12, 2016, pp. 26–28.

7 Barbara Ueland, *If You Want to Write*, (1938), Saint Paul, MN: Graywolf Press, 1987, p. 21, 42. There is a famous self-portrait of him walking through the countryside near Arles carrying his easel and painting equipment entitled 'The Painter on His Way to Work. http://www.vangoghgallery.com/catalog/ Painting/374/Painter-on-His-Way-to-Work,-The.html–accessed April 28, 2016.

8 Peter Ackroyd, *Dickens*, London: Vintage, 1999, p. 163. He opens his short story 'Night Walks' with: 'Some years ago, a temporary inability to sleep [...] caused me to walk about the streets all night, for a series of several nights [...] In the course of those nights, I finished my education in a fair amateur experience of houselessness.' Charles Dickens, 'Night Walks', in *Night Walks*, London: Penguin, 2010, p. 1.

9 'I would walk along the quais when I had finished work or when I was trying to think something out. It was easier to think if I was walking and doing something, or seeing people doing something that they understood.' Ernest Hemingway, *A Moveable Feast*, (1964), London: Arrow Books, 1996, p. 38.

10 Virginia Woolf, 'Street Haunting', (1930), in *The Death of the Moth and Other Essays*, (1940), London: Penguin, 1965, p. 23.

11 People who have done this include: Anthony Seeger who went to study the music and social organisation of the Suyá Indian tribe of Mato Grosso, Brazil; Michelle Kisliuk who looked at the singing

and dancing of the Baka people in the Central African Republic; or anthropologist Nigel Barley who went to North Cameroon to observe the coming-of-age circumcision and rainmaking rites of the Dowayo tribe. (Anthony Seeger, 'Theories Forged in the Crucible of Action: The Joys, Dangers, and Potentials of Advocacy and Fieldwork', in Gregory F. Barz and Timothy J. Cooley (eds.), *Shadows in the Field: New Perspectives for Fieldwork in Ethnomusicology*, Oxford: Oxford University Press, 2008, pp. 271–288. Michelle Kisliuk, '(Un)doing Fieldwork: Sharing Songs, Sharing Lives', in Gregory F. Barz and Timothy J. Cooley (eds.), *Shadows in the Field: New Perspectives for Fieldwork in Ethnomusicology*, Oxford: Oxford University Press, 2008, pp. 183–205. Nigel Barley, *The Innocent Anthropologist: Notes from a Mud Hut*, London: Penguin, 1983/1986).

12 Though music psychologists had also already been working in the area of music-making as social practice.

13 Jonathan Stock, 'Documenting the Musical Event: Observation, Participation, Representation', in Eric Clarke and Nicholas Cook, (eds.), *Empirical Musicology*, Oxford: Oxford University Press, 2004, pp. 15–34.

14 Stock, 2004, p. 19.

15 *Ibid.*, p. 19.

16 *Ibid.*, p. 19.

17 Bruno Nettl, *Heartland Excursions: Ethnomusicological Reflections on Schools of Music*, Urbana and Chicago: University of Illinois Press, 1995.

18 Henry Kingsbury, *Music, Talent & Performance: A Conservatory Cultural System*, Philadelphia: Temple University Press, 1988.

19 Stephen Cottrell, *Professional Music-Making in London: Ethnography and Experience*, Aldershot and Burlington, Vt: Ashgate, 2004.

20 Stephanie E. Pitts, 'What Makes an Audience? Investigating the Roles and Experiences of Listeners at a Chamber Music Festival', *Music & Letters*, Vol. 86, No. 2, 2005, pp. 257–69.

21 Including salient articles by Amanda Bayley, Melissa Dobson and Stephanie Pitts, Tina K. Ramnarine, and Rachel Beckles Willson. *Ethnomusicology Forum*, Vol. 20, No. 3, 2011; Laudan Nooshin (ed.), *The Ethnomusicology of Western Art Music*, London and New York: Routledge, 2013. Another useful text which argues for an ethnographic approach is Nicholas Cook, *Music: A Very Short Introduction*, Oxford: Oxford University Press, 1998, pp. 99–101.

[22] Gregory F. Barz and Timothy J. Cooley (eds.), *Shadows in the Field: New Perspectives for Fieldwork in Ethnomusicology*, Oxford: Oxford University Press, 2008.

[23] Such as Kay Kaufman Shelemay and Michelle Kisliuk: Kay Kaufman Shelemay, 'The Ethnomusicologist, Ethnographic Method, and the Transmission of Tradition', in Barz and Cooley, 2008, pp. 141–156. Michelle Kisliuk, '(Un)doing Fieldwork: Sharing Songs, Sharing Lives', in Barz and Cooley, 2008, pp. 183–205.

[24] Both in his article in this volume and in his paper given at the RMA/ CHARM Conference, Royal Holloway, University of London, September 13, 2007. Anthony Seeger, 'Theories Forged in the Crucible of Action: The Joys, Dangers, and Potentials of Advocacy and Fieldwork', in Barz and Cooley, 2008, pp. 271–288.

[25] Gregory F. Barz, 'Confronting the Field(note) In and Out of the Field: Music, Voices, Texts, and Experiences in Dialogue', in Barz and Cooley, 2008, pp. 206–223.

[26] *Ibid.*, p. 215.

[27] *Ibid.*, p. 206.

[28] For a useful overview of the history of ethnomusicology, see: C. Pegg, H. Myers, P. V. Bohlman, and M. Stokes, 'Ethnomusicology', *Grove Music Online*, Deane Root (ed.), http://www.oxfordmusi-conline.com – accessed April 20, 2016.

[29] Catherine Schwartz (ed.), *The Chambers Dictionary*, Edinburgh: Chambers, 1993, p. 578. The definition of anthropology is: 'the scientific study of human beings and their way of life, the science of man in its widest sense', *The Chambers Dictionary*, p. 65.

[30] Nettl, 1995, p. 11.

[31] *Ibid.*, p. 1.

[32] Xavier de Maistre, *A Journey Around My Room* (1790), Richmond, Surrey: Alma Classics, 2013. The original French title is *Voyage autour de ma chambre*. He followed this up in 1825 with *A Nocturnal Voyage Around My Room (Expedition nocturne autour de ma chambre)*.

[33] de Botton, 2003, p. 245.

[34] de Maistre, 2013, p. 4.

[35] *Ibid.*, p. 24. The notes for this passage explain that 'The ancient Greek philosopher Empedocles, according to legend, threw himself into Mount Etna, (notes, p. 138).

[36] *Ibid.*, p. 7.

[37] *Ibid.*, p. 8.

[38] *Ibid.*, p. 9.

[39] de Botton, 2003, p. 246.
[40] *Ibid.*, p. 246.
[41] *Ibid.*, pp. 246–47. The italics are mine.

CHISWICK
Old Deer Park
HOUNSLOW
TWICKENHAM
RICHMOND
RICHMOND PARK
Putney
Roehampton
Putney Heath
Wimbledon Common
WIMBLEDON
Petersham
Ham
Ham Common
TEDDINGTON
Hampton
Hampton Wick
KINGSTON UPON THAMES
Hampton Court Park
West Molesey
East Molesey
SURBITON
Thames Ditton
Long Ditton
Tolworth
Malden
Worcester Park
Hook
Chessington
Esher
Sandown Park
Ewell
Cheam Common
Cottenham Park
L. & S. W. R.

PETER SHEPPARD SKÆRVED

Practise. Walk

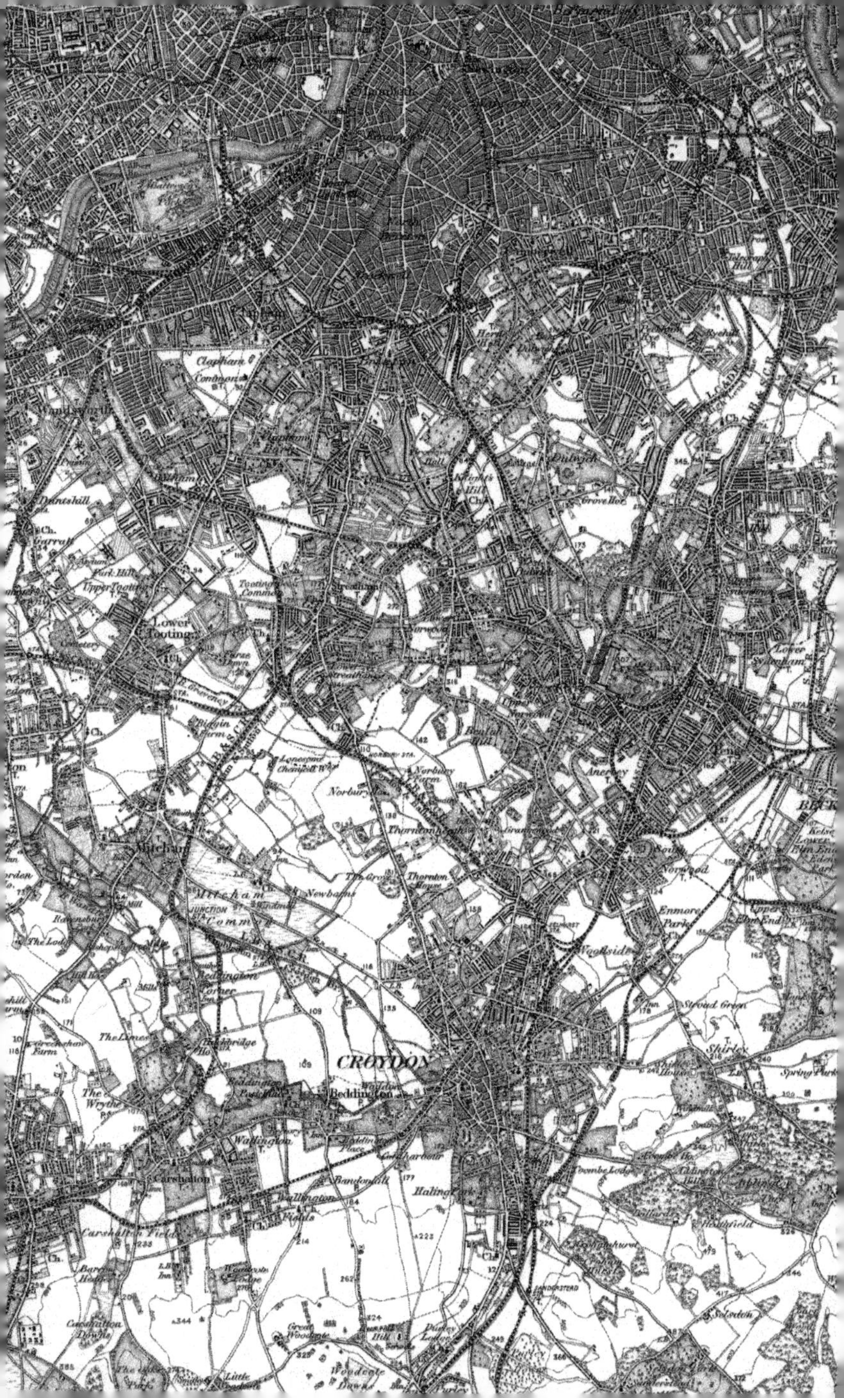

Clapham Common
Wandsworth
Tooting Common
Upper Tooting
Lower Tooting
Brixton
Streatham
Dulwich
Norbury
Norbury Farm
Thornton Heath
Anerley
Norwood
Lower Sydenham
Mitcham
Mitcham Common
Newbarns
Woodside
Enmore Park
Stroud Green
Shirley
Spring Park
CROYDON
Beddington
The Limes
The Wrythe
Wallington
Carshalton
Bandon Hill
Haling Park
Coombe Lodge
Heathfield
Selsdon
Carshalton Downs

I'm standing on the bridge over the river Wandle, a cold paper cup of espresso in my hand, enjoying the wrecked boats in the mud. Squinting at the ooze beneath me, I wish for a Saxon sword blade to emerge, or better still, a pristine ceremonial object, like the 'Mortlake Axe' (made of precious Jadeite mined in the Alps) thrown into the Thames for the God. I am a violinist, an artist, a writer (of sorts) and a walker.* How these activities tie together is not entirely clear to me. Or rather, to put it better: I am not sure how to articulate how these ways of being interact, but it seems simple enough, from where I sit (or stand), that they do. However, the various aspects, the things, which make this up are clear. And they seem to behave in the way that filmmaker Sergei Eisenstein defined 'overtones':

> For the musical overtone (a throb) it is not strictly fitting to say: "I hear." / Nor for the visual overtone: "I see." / For both, a new uniform vocabulary must enter our vocabulary: "I feel."[1]

I live on a cobbled street in Wapping, by the tidal Thames. I feel my ancestors, refugees from Spain and France, by this river, under my feet, their voices in the air around me, every day. My wife, a Dane, hears her forbears, in the "Ta" of shopkeepers, and the place names of Viking saints (Magnus, Olaf), and the shopping street ('Købe-side' – Cheapside) that they left behind. Wapping is named for a Saxon prince, or princess,

* For audio and video musical examples, please see: http://www.peter-sheppard-skaerved.com/2016/02/a-2/

Wæppa (no-one agrees), and amongst the stone tools, broken Roman glass and clay pipes which I have fished out from the river 50 metres from my door, is a bone knife handle, carved by a Saxon fisherman (setting his traps in the river) in the shape of his quarry.

The eight-metre tide, the salt stench of the river, the memories of shipping, the over-layering and palimpsest of cultures which is London, led me to feel that this was a place to leave, to travel great distances from. And so I did. Gradually, I realised that travelling had created an unexpected fascination in me, in the paths which led from my front door, around, in and out of my city. Sensing the voices of French refugees from the 'Terror', not only on the streets of Marylebone, but in the beech and hornbeam woods of Epping Forest near my parents' home, offered me a sense of a to-and-fro to the city. I began to sense the tracks of travellers for trade, for war, in ceasefire, for pilgrimage, for visiting, for escape. The relationship to the practice of my art became vital to me.

A memory: walking in woods somewhere between Sarajevo and Banja Luka, with **Beethoven's** *Horn Sonata Op 17* [musical example] and Dante, both ringing in my ears:

> Nel mezzo del cammin di nostra vita / mi ritrovai per una selva oscura / ché la diritta era smarrita (In the middle of this journey (our life) / I found myself travelling through a dark forest / where the correct way was obscured).

Also in my head, a concerned admonition from my escorts: "Don't go off the path. Landmines." Initially, my reaction would have been that the music was little more than a sound-track to the experience. But I came to realise that the paths under my feet were not only eliciting responses, in music, in images, but conditioning them, affecting not only the way I hear and see, but the music that I make. And of course, the 'path under my feet', in many manifestations, offers constantly changing catalogues, casts, of characters, objects, stories, memories and suggestions, counterpointing with the ideas which fascinate me.

Walking is quotidian and often disrespects scale or distance. The walk around my street corner in Wapping, to the butcher, or to the station – just a few steps – evokes so much: Samuel Pepys comes to have his Viol repaired or to talk to striking sailors and their militant wives.[2] Earlier, Dutch engineers working for Henry VIII, drained the High Street, which, during the Blitz, briefly became a river of molten rubber. Any sense of accumulations of stories, or resonance, of overtones on a path, are directly proportional to the frequency with which we tread it, so the greatest layering of our myths and tale-telling will be where we walk the most; the shortest paths. If I walk west from this room, I will have Captain Bligh, Alastair Sim, Wedgwood Benn, Helen Mirren, Thomas Moore, Captain Kidd, Judge Jeffreys, Dickens, Whistler, Graham Norton, Jack the Ripper, Mrs Booth and Turner, and Lord Shaftesbury in my ear before I have gone 100 metres. By contrast, the longer walks can seem less peopled, as we pull on our five-mile boots and mark out thirty miles plus in a day. But this is like music. As I feel it, that's the difference between the concentration of **Britten's** ***Lullaby Op 6*** [musical example] which is so 'peopled' with memories, a (not so harmonious) colloquy between the composer's and my own, and the long view, of say the **Tchaikovsky violin concerto** [musical example], whose second subject spins around the same melody again, and again, as the great violinist Manoug Parikian pointed out to me, finding its lyricism, its memory, in the reach for an unattainable, flat horizon, in a longing for home, which its composer could not feel, or even articulate, except when he was far from it, be it in Clarens or Florence. I'm not sure that I could even begin to crowd that endless theme.

Friday, Waterloo station. I buy bread and coffee and take the 09.36 to Hampton Court. Forty minutes on the train; time enough to read the paper, and let care drop away, be unreachable. No mobile (I have never owned one), just cash, train ticket, water, *Gawain and the Green Knight* and notebook. At the final stop, there's a moment of doubt; should I change my route, and walk south-west down the river Mole ('Sullen Mole'), to Dorking, to the North Downs, onto another familiar route, maybe Box Hill...? I poke around the gardens east of the station, momentarily unsure, looking for the energy not to change my mind. The walk home is a known quantity, as is the pain that goes with it. I turn away from the daffodil-filled Elmbridge Gardens, and cross the river to Cardinal Wolsey's former palace and the 30 miles home. Perfect walking weather, although I realise that I am going to have to take off one of my pairs of socks. This will demand a five-minute stop, something which I resent. I put it off until it's necessary, a sunny bench near Kew, a misspelling of 'Key' (Quay). In 1658 Edward Phillips described it:

> Key of a River or Haven, a place where ships ride, and are as it were lock't in. Some deduce it a quiescendo, i.e. from resting, or from the old Latin Casare, i.e. to restrain.[3]

Phillips says nothing about sock-changing. I also realise, to my chagrin, that I have not marked, checked the time. I know that I will be able to see the clock on St Raphael's romanesque tower on the opposite bank of the river, as I come into Kingston, but until then, I am uncalibrated, floating. My life is carefully broken down into temporal units, bars, crochets, quavers, and most importantly, the division of my three hours of daily practice after midnight, and I am aiming at hitting Westminster in round about six hours. There's a deal of frustration that I can't get this outset, this setting out, precise.

The riverbank is pristine, and the first of hundreds of robins which will beautifully protest my passing all morning, is somewhere at my feet. I am always moved by the attention of 'lovely Robin', accompanying, it seems, every step through hedgerow and woodland. I always find myself talking to the bird, and then remember John Webster's more morbid perspective: 'Call for the robin-red-breast and the wren / since o'er shady groves they hover, / and with leaves and flowers do cover / The friendless bodies of dead men'.[4]

Hampton Court on my left, and the 'splendid wall, too, that bounds the Home Park'.[5] At a river door, two English Heritage employees, gossiping: "I did not want to go to that party ...". The first of the musics which wreathe around my walk rises, the Mendelssohn *D minor Piano Trio*, which I had been teaching in a front room in Highgate the day before, prefacing an unexpected walk along a lost railway line from Muswell Hill to Alexandra Palace, part of it on a busy viaduct, high above the terraces below. Victorian London, without Gustave Doré's grime. By the time I reach Pimlico, I find that I am listening to the theme of the second movement (**'Andante con molto tranquillo'**) and a countersubject the violin plays in the first (**'Molto Allegro Agitato'**) [musical example] at the same time. The obvious dawns on me: they are the same. A small gift of the time, rhythm and distance on foot, a lesson in Mendelssohn's thematic unities. From Pimlico to Auguste Rodin's *Les Bourgeois de Calais* at the Palace of Westminster, I obsess over whether this apparent stunt was actually the germ which initiated the piece. Even though I think at various times during the walk that Mendelssohn is <u>not</u> in my mind (the trio that is), I am, in retrospect, completely unable to shift him; garrulous as ever, he keeps popping up. As I pass a number of hollowed out tree trunks on the path, 'Mendelssohn's Tree' (a felled beech tree bizarrely stranded on a walkway above Barbican Station) flits in and out of my mind. I wonder, worry even, how long it can last. It also strikes me as bizarre that a 500-year-old tree is marooned in concrete and brick, not for being a natural wonder, a tree, but because when it fell in the 1880s, rumour spread that it was one of the Burnham Beeches where Felix had sat, dreaming his *Ein Sommernachtstraum*.

I walk on; a good pace. Tower Bridge, 29 miles, the sign says. The other morning walkers are happy and smiling, this dissipates before midday, and certainly has gone by the time I am in the city. Walking around the great ox-bow on which Wolsey built his palace, later his frantic bribe to Henry, I resent the manicured gardens and topiary on my left, the *grotesquerie* of nobility and royalty, carving out such a segment of the lovely Thames for themselves. In younger, more restful days, I would come to be still, to be alone, to sit and draw Wren's extension with my feet in the reflection pool. I was also thrown out of the palace for drawing in 1995, on the grounds that the Royal Family had copyrighted every inch of it. I once painted a grey autumnal view of this piece of the river, before I knew how to walk it, and gave it to a girl I was trying to impress. I stole a bit of Eliot for the title: 'Now and in England',[6] and inscribed it thus, to impress her. It didn't work. When and where was it thrown away?

Setting out fascinates me, both in terms of its adventurous, and everyday, qualities. We get up, have breakfast, put on shoes and coats, gather our things, and set out. In my life, it's difficult to articulate the difference between such settings out and musical ones. But I have two simple types–setting out to practise, and setting out of a piece, which, of course, offer typologies, between composition, performance and study. But the setting out of my desk, to work, each night, is the simplest place to begin. There's no foot on the path, of course, and that which is set out, are the tools of my work. Music on the desk, pens, pencils of various types, ink, pencil sharpeners, pot of tea. Verbena; my little homage to the Romans, who crowned their victorious heroes with the leaves. Laurel was just for athletes.

My nocturnal work routine is static, and despite the violin, essentially silent. My practice table is set up in a high-ceilinged room of an old factory in Wapping. The large windows face south-west, towards the river, which is just beyond the park beneath. Most of my work, violin in hand, is done at this desk, between midnight and 4 in the morning. Each night, my family goes to bed, and I sit down to work, my back to the window. Practice is emphatically non-visual, and I certainly don't feel isolated from the world, but while working, I hear it. By 2 am, the chimes of Big Ben are clear, and the loudest noise will be the family of foxes that play under my window.

Passing Tagg's Island, I start to worry about the etymology of Kingston. The romance of the stone on which nine Saxon Kings were crowned is irresistible, of King Egbert's gathering of his thanes at 'Kynigestun' in 838, but so is the doubt. If this is 'stone' and not 'town', then what about every other '-ton'. And of course, there are so many other 'King's Stones', such as the one at Belton (Rutland) where Charles I is supposed to have rested after the Battle of Naseby.[7] The way marker that I had been waiting for, Charles Parker's St Raphael's Church, on the Surrey bank, gives me what I need. A clock: '1050'. I can start counting my steps, start the ***passacaglia*** which will bring me home, like Biber's pilgrim[8] [musical example]. For the last 20 minutes, there has been a counterpoint of young rowers, three in single sculls, a coxless four and as the river begins to turn, towards the first hint of the tide, more beginners on the river; one of them a nervous young woman being coached by an overweight man on a bicycle. He's riding slightly slower than my walking speed, a wheezing hazard lurching behind me on the towpath, so I am very glad when his charge admits defeat and turns back upstream. Teddington, and Traherne, a footfall in the memory:

> I felt a vigour in my strength / that was all
> spirit.

I have no idea which poem that is from; I saw it when I was a child, on a gravestone on the Lizard Peninsula.[9]

And then, other dreaming drifts in; I start to muse on my lifelong obsession with various musical sequences, variations, cycles ... Bach, Telemann, Paganini ... César Cui's *Kaleidoscope* ... **George Rochberg's *Caprice Variations*** [musical example], which he told me was an homage to Wordsworth's method of walking and writing. Then more dreaming, lulled into a kind of doze by the walking; music that marks out time, and composers using the composition of music to mark out their lives. Some of 'my' composers incorporate walking into their practice; Michael Alec Rose in Nashville is writing a series of pieces based on our wanderings on Dartmoor, and David Matthews has written me a ***Ranz des Vaches*** ('Cow Call') [musical example] on top of a mountain in Liguria. But one of the fascinations for me is what happens to us, as people, as artists, when we 'take time'. With walking and music, 'taking time' is the only option. Nothing can, or should happen fast. Walking the Thames, there's an element of masochism to this, heightened by the foreshortenings of river bends and strange light effects on water. As I have come to know this path well, the *longeurs* of certain stretches have increased. I pre-empt the ennui that sets in, for instance, when I cross the miniature delta of the Wandle River (where I finish my coffee this time), behind the waste recycling plant, and start the haul towards Battersea Park, where Battersea Power Station forces the third crossing of the Thames, over Chelsea Bridge (my least favourite). I once made the mistake of walking in spring without protective gear, and was caught in a storm on this bridge. I spent the next hours soaked and shivering, blisters bursting, toes bleeding. There's little doubt that experience has coloured my lack of affection for this part of the river.

But this time, all is sunshine, and, as I came into the shadow of the Battersea Park Pagoda (noting the old Coastal Patrol Boat moored in the river there for years), I remembered that here I saw my first ballet. My primary school teacher, Mrs Morgan, got some of us tickets for the Royal Ballet's *Giselle*, in a tent in the Park. She did me (and I suspect many of the other children) a huge favour, and taught us the meaning of the classical ballet gestures. I walked into that theatre ready to read dance as a language, excited at the grammar and storytelling. It all seemed, I remember, so clear and obvious. Today, I am not sure whether the Royal Ballet had their tent, but the fountains blowing rainbows on the lake seem most appropriate, and I am thankful to Mrs Morgan.

But the discomfort doesn't go away. Anyone who really walks knows that there is no way to do it which does not involve loving the pain. There's always a moment when I wonder about the state of my feet inside my boots. I will find out later the bodily extremities become less refined, walking. I look at my hands, and realise, 20 miles in, that there is no way that I could pick up a violin at that moment. My fingers have lost their dexterity–my hands are mere clubs. Part of this is simply practical; the body marshalling resources, just like the 'butterflies' which some performers experience going on stage–signalling that the digestive system is powering down; it's not going to be needed for a while. But, with the feet, there are blisters, and bruising, and there is pride in this. I know that I was not alone, as a young violinist, in admiring the damage which playing did to my body. My 'violin mark', a running sore on my neck, was a source of disgust and admiration for school friends. But it was the track marks on my left hand, the 'ringing grooves of change' [10] on my fingertips, which I cherished and cultivated. There was always a worry, particularly after what seemed a particularly effective practice session, that my perfectly lined callouses, might soften up, or wash off in the bath, that the 'magic' would be lost. I did not stop washing my hands; this, I later learnt, was, and perhaps is, remarkably common. But when I get home from this walk, I run a bath, and sit on the edge of the tub to take my socks off. No blisters, not on the right foot. But the left sock is soaked in blood: triumph. But at Kingston, these thoughts are very far from my mind.[11]

My walks along the river, from haunted Faversham west from the Estuary, east from Hampton, to Windsor, Thame and Henley, reach out, and intertwine, with other paths.

The Thames is Liquid History, Spring 2015.

Two months earlier, I was in New York City. Winter had come late to the East coast, but it had arrived with fury. The bitter cold matched my mood; I was back in the city for my friend, the poet Guy Gallo, who had died a month earlier, after a year-long fight with cancer. So I was here to sit with his family, to play for his memorial at Barnard College, and to walk. With me, to practise, and to perform hard on my return to London, was a walking violin piece which I had put off playing for two decades. Luigi Nono's final work ***La Lontananza Nostalgica Utopica*** [video example]. It *matched* my mood perfectly; unsustainable, impoverished lyricism in a desolate, intimidating landscape. And, like **Philip Glass's *Strung Out*** [video example], or **Jim Aitchison's *Shibboleth*** [video example], the violinist walks, in this case, amidst a forest of music stands. I had been hunting for the landscape in which to place this piece, a 'selva oscura' in which it might happen, for a number of weeks. My score had become encrusted with images and writing, from Marx to Colonna, as I scrabbled fruitlessly for handhold, for purchase. Midwinter in Manhattan offered clarity, if not solace.

So many paths which we tread are conversation, discourse, with friends, lovers, spouses, with our children. They are all temporal, temporary. They all end. And we learn, bitterly, or sweetly, that there is no ideal ratio of intensity to importance, which might yield significance. I had tracked nearly two decades of conversation with my friend, Guy: 19 years colloquy, about poetry, music, architecture, history, writing, and the unanswerable question, of how to be, as an artist. It seemed that Guy was just about to find an answer, and then he was taken. Early each morning, I set out to walk the long way, around Central Park, from West to Eastside, but around the circumference, with Christina Rossetti on my mind:

> In the deep midwinter / Frosty wind made moan / Earth stood hard as iron / Water like a stone.

I left the 'El Dorado' building, past its murals of gilded flappers crossing into the 'city of gold' (a venture capitalist's *Pilgrim's Progress*) to walk into the empty park. Fifteen centigrade below, and it was more like the Claude Lorrain and Salvator Rosa which had inspired Frederick Olmsted and Calvert Vaux. I discovered that I did not know how to walk on deep, frozen snow, and that every bird expected feeding. Nono was in my mind (frankly, I would have preferred Schubert), warping around memories of Guy. He loved early baroque violin music, so I began an incoherent, freezing, musical conversation with him about landscape gardening and music, replaying one which we had had about 17 years earlier, but this time, interspersed with snippets of the Walther *Hortulus Cheliculus*, and the Biber *Passacaglia* [musical example], which did not suit, as there was no *Schutzengel* (guardian angel) for me. Answers to the problems that Nono was posing me loomed up, in the fractal beauty of the edges of ice and snow against the black stream flowing under Glen Span Bridge, into rock-hard Harlem Meer. And gradually, colour began to find its way, the slightest touch of roseate sunlight reflecting on the reservoir, a hint of robin's-egg blue on the westerly horizon beneath snow-fraught clouds, with the water-towers of the Upper West Side *in relievo*.

Practising the violin, every day, hour after hour, for the whole of my life, offers many such moments of clarity, of cloud-clearing. And it doesn't matter how many times we set out, often in an apparently disappointing dawn, crestfallen, initially, like Leonard Bast even if we are not offered a radiant sun-up, there will be other gifts, a ford worthy of Ruisdael in the woods south of Ware or a moment of understanding, chained to the practice desk, violin in hand, where the mind, or the hands, find a way, and we are given insight, offered something which is in front of us the whole time. A few days into my cold sojourn in the Big Apple, I was offered a curious way home, by way of Norway. I need to step back, to step forward.

Living in what was once the Wapping orchards and kitchen gardens drained by the Dutchman, Cornelius Vanderdelft in the 1530s, my constant walk has been west, into the nearby Square Mile, trampling absurdly rich layerings of history, finding ever more serpentine routes through the labyrinthine shambles and back alleys where my immigrant ancestors have made their lives over the past four centuries. Little Britain, Pinners' Passage, St Mary at Hill, Watling Street, Drapers Alley, Fish Street Hill. Hundreds of years of merchants, street sellers, fish-porters, mountebanks, thieves, churchmen, footpads, wide boys and pickpockets cluster around, whispering in my ears. Some of them rose, some of them fell, all of them touched by the mud which, as Dickens noted, ever adds 'new deposits to the crust upon crust...'[12] on all who live near the Thames. One of these was about to rise, and find his way into my imagination, and into my hands. On my third day in New York, I was in the galley kitchen on Central Park West. The normal routine: up very early to deal with administration back home, and a cup of coffee to kick-start the day, before setting out like Fridtjof Nansen across Central Park. An e-mail address which I did not recognise:

> Would you be interested in seeing the 1647
> Amati violin which Ole Bull owned?

I looked at the screen, shocked, to say the least. Another path in my life had swerved and forked into the track I was on. I had written about this violin, taken pictures of the embroidered coverlet which Bull made for it, and which sits in his exquisite music room in Lysøen, outside Bergen. I knew that he called the violin 'my pearl', and that he had bought it for an enormous amount of money in 1864. I also knew that the violin had basically disappeared into a Boston bank vault, in 1910. It had been unheard, since 1880. Bull is one of my heroes, not just as a musician, but as an artist who was prepared to offer a new model as to what, or who, an artist should be.

He was a pioneer, an explorer, an athlete, a builder, an activist, a freedom fighter, a storyteller, a craftsman, a thinker, a challenge to any living musician, whose response to adversity was indefatigability. He was, perhaps, the first musician to live a transatlantic life, with houses in Norway and the USA, and is regarded with as much reverence in Minnesota as he is in Norway, where he is a national hero.

Two weeks later, I meet this violin in London, and it proves miraculous, as I had hoped. But by then, the story had looped back, right onto my stamping grounds, to where I am writing this, now. The history of this beautiful violin in the 19th century reached an initial climax in 1827, when it was bought, for an outrageous sum, by a City business man, determined to make sure that King George IV did not further weaken the parlous Royal Household finances, by purchasing it. In fairness, it was the king's brother, Adolphus, Duke of Cambridge, who was the true connoisseur of instruments, purchasing 'Cremonas' found for him by the greatest of all amongst violinists, Giovanni Battista Viotti. After a fire broke out at St James Palace on 20th January 1809, he wrote immediately, reassuring Viotti that he had saved the violins first of all, carrying them out of the palace, under his arms, from the flames.[13] But it was the seller of this violin that brought it, quite literally, close to home. I should not have been surprised, of course. Ever since the 1500s, fine violins had been traded across Europe, famously beginning with the set of ornamented violins, which the inventor of the modern violin, Andrea Amati, made for Charles IX of France. And before the days of the traveller's cheque, itinerant musicians carried their currency in the form of violins and fittings (leaving Dover in 1499, Erasmus was horrified that he could not take more than 6 'angels' (gold coins) with him).[14] In 1702, the violinist Nicola Cosimi travelled to the UK to work as musician for the Duke of Bedford. He brought with him Cremonese violins by the Amati family. These all stayed here; when he left three years later, he exported violins by the London-based Robert Cuthbert, who had made instruments for Henry Purcell's ensemble. So it's likely that is how the 1647 Amati found its way into the hands of its first famous London owner, Sir William Curtis.

Curtis was best known in his lifetime by the affectionate moniker 'Billy Biscuit'. He was born in Wapping, no more than fifty metres from where I am writing this, and when his father died he inherited a bakery, backing on to the river on what is now called Wapping High Street. He was a gifted man of business, and parleyed his bakery into a primary supplier for 'ships biscuits' for the Royal Navy as the smaller conflicts with pre-revolutionary France found their way to the Napoleonic War. This little corner of Wapping, whose cobbled streets and customs walls still preserve much of the atmosphere of the 18th century, was the shipping goldmine of the age, with local businessmen cornering the market for sugar, of course, profiteering from slavery, and beer. Curtis became as rich as Croesus, Lord Mayor of London twice, revered in the annals of the Square Mile, and a member of parliament, where, unlike many of his peers, he actually voted once in a while. But most of all, he is remembered as a massively overweight bon viveur, and for his tenuous grasp of the 'King's English'. His most famous *bon mot* was the expression the 'Three Rs', trotted out as part of one of his many enthusiastic and unsuccessful toasts. It seems that he genuinely thought that the Writing and Arithmetic did begin with 'R'. He was a keen amateur musician, playing chamber music on more than one occasion with Viotti, who admitted that he had a good hand at the cello, if no more. As a socialite (chamber music played a central role in salon life in the early 19th century), it was necessary that Curtis had instruments. Even professional players did not travel around more than was necessary with their own instruments, and for good reason. Musicians 'roped in' to add *bon ton* to parties, at Carlton House, or Elisabeth Vigée-le Brun's little apartment at 5 Upper Berkeley Street (where the Prince Regent listened from under the fortepiano), could not afford a carriage, or a litter, and maybe not even a 'link man' to light them home to the growing suburbs of Marylebone and Fitzrovia where they had cheap lodgings. It was not worth the risk of carrying instruments in the undoubtedly dangerous London streets at night. So it was normal for a host to have a set of violins (echoing the 'chests' of viols of earlier times), consisting of at least two violins, one viola and two cellos. When the 1647 Amati was sold two years before 'Billy Biscuit's' death in 1827, it was the start of the greatest collection of instruments ever sold in London, a sale still written about in hushed terms, nearly a century later. Little did I know that that first e-mail, read at a kitchen table in Manhattan, before walking across the frozen park, this winter, would bring me, first of all, right back to my home, to the 'setts' of the streets that I walk the most, and to a man known by my London ancestors, traders at Billingsgate Market, on the river near his bakery (those who weren't footpads, and housebreakers, of which we had a few). But it also took me to the outdoor pursuits of violinists.

Ole Bull, like his protégé Edvard Grieg, was an outdoorsman, and would, like I love to, when I am there, walk from the front door of the apothecary's shop where he was born, near Bergen fish market, up the steep wooded hill that shadows the north of the old town, up, through the beech and oaks, to the lines of spruce and larch, and higher, out up onto the *Vidder*, the mountain plateau, and to the *saeter*, the mountain pastures which inspired his most famous tune, the sound of the Norwegian resistance in World War II. When I first had this violin in my hands, in a room a few houses down from Berlioz's London digs, the very first thing that I played on this gem of a violin was this aching melody, which sings of distance and enchantment, and the blue empyrean. It is, I suspect, this sense of other people's footsteps that draws me to old instruments. The violin is a malleable, almost squishily organic tool. Every player of honesty knows that it is impossible to play any instrument without leaving traces, marks, damage. Some of this will be irreversible, and much of it can be read, testament to previous players, akin to footprints on a path. It's easy enough to see the generic abrasions and scratches: the rubbing away of varnish on the scroll by the left thumb, the chips and indentations on the 'C-bout' of the violin, from the 'heel' of a modern bow. Then there are historical marks, strata relating to changing practice and social mores. Most violins older than 200 years will have the back of the scroll worn down, a memory of when the 'non-travelling' instruments mentioned earlier were slid into shelves in cupboards and cabinets for storage (only shops and non-players would ever hang a violin up, exposed). Then there's memory of the beard-boom of the mid-1800s, when Joseph Mechi, who had made his fortune on razor-strops, had to change business, and make jam instead, and Johannes Brahms and Joseph Joachim made a duet out of their burgeoning facial hair. This resulted in the varnish being brushed away on the right hand side of the tail-piece, under the chin. And then, in our time, the violin equivalent of mountain-bike damage to ancient foot-paths, the gouging in the back of a violin, legacy of a collapsing shoulder rest, and a high-pressure clamping of the instrument between head and body. But these are not really the marks which players are looking for on an instrument, any more than we really expect to find the footprints of John Clare north of Epping Forest, or the conversation of Alexander Pope in the tow path near Twickenham. But we all sense that something is there; I put the 'Bull' violin under my chin with the barely whispered expectation that, maybe, he has left something, an echo, a timbre, which I can learn, and voice. Sometimes, the sense of presence is palpable, often revealed by symbols. Walking the North Downs, East towards Shoreham, I felt a presence behind me, and turned, to see a Church spire rising from the white of a ploughed field of chalky soil. Suddenly, the Samuel Palmer of the 1824 notebook was stalking me. Many years ago, giving my first cyclic performances of the Bach Sonatas and Partitas in a church in Norwich, the candles burnt down during the performance, revealing the carving in the gravestone at my feet, in sharper and deeper relief:

DEATHE.

I have experienced such symbols, to greater or lesser degrees, with the instruments of Paganini, of Viotti, of my teacher, Ralph Holmes. Initially, I don't notice it with the Bull Amati. But my son is with me, entranced at seeing such a first meeting, for the first time. He films the first notes on the violin. We walk home to Wapping, snaking through the west–east alleys of Soho, Lincoln's Inn Fields, Inner Temple, Billingsgate, the Tower, and past the Hermitage, now a charming modern school, but named for a John Ingham, who lived there in splendid isolation in the 14th century. My wife is waiting: "What was it like?" I can't say anything, but put the film on. "My god, it's so pure", she whispers. She's right. I had not noticed. That's what had drawn Bull, the countryman, the nature lover. This was a violin sound with the clarity of a mountain stream, of the ice melt in Lysekloster, near where he would build his home. This was the voice he was seeking.

Back on the path, I realise that I am walking through the preparations for the Oxford / Cambridge boat races. As I take a picture of the white iron balconies of Gustav Holst's house, I notice a camera set up on the river ('No. 24'). And then, the torture of the long curl of the river, on the Surrey Bank, to the cup of coffee which I have promised myself at Putney. The Oxford women's team literally fly past me on the river, barely touching it, communicating like a string quartet. Oars, backs, heads, arms, even spray, in exquisite choreography. The last mile before my coffee (I'm not tired, just thinking about caffeine) is pure torture, and then the two sisters of Putney divert me, or rather, the two sisters of Putney and Guildford, and two paths, merge into one. The westerly arm of the North Down's trail is a geological wonder, as the path slips from the chalk line of hills, which support the roaring Hogs Back to the north, quite literally, on to the beach, cutting its way, as it rises west from crossing the river Wey, through miniature canyons and grikes of yellowest sandstone, deep enough, even in the driest weather, to form and protect astonishing ecosystems, microclimates, tropical clustering of lush fern and moss, and lurid green and blue moulds and slimes which glint and glister in the light, finding its way through the ash and pine. No-one, approaching Guildford or Putney on the river, from the South, can fail to see the paired churches, the chapels of St Catherine and St Martha-at-Chilworth on their bluffs over the Wey, and All Saints and St Mary's on the Fulham and Putney Shores. They were all built by twin giantesses, with the same *modi operandii*, preserved in the very apocryphal etymology of Putney–'Put it Nigh', and Fulham–'Heave it Full Home'.[15] In his 'Bygone Surrey' George Clinch noted that the two churches over the Wey were built by giant sisters, who only had one hammer, which they threw the three kilometres or so, over the river 'backwards and forwards as they required it'.[16] In 1781, Francis Grose noted about the Putney Fulham churches: '...two sisters, who had but one hammer between them, which they interchanged by throwing it across the river, on a word agreed between them'.[17] Hence the names. My coffee is waiting for me, behind All Saints Putney, which seems to be taking longer and longer to arrive, and I have to pick my way through the women's rowing squads, now washing their boats on the slipways. None of them, it strikes me, would have any trouble flinging a hammer across the river. I quicken my pace, remembering my wife's favourite joke. She's very much a Viking, so it comes with war hammers. 'How many feminists does it take to change a light bulb? That's not funny.' Putney was where one of my lifelong musical passions began, violin-piano duo playing. In my mid-teens, I gave some concerts with Australian pianist Piers Lane, newly arrived, and living in a little house a few blocks in from the rowers. His practice room was filled, as I remember, with postcards of beaches back home. We played Prokofiev, the wondrous ***Cinq Melodies*** [musical example] which the composer transcribed for American (Spalding), Polish (Kochanski), Hungarian (Szigeti) and Norwegian (Hansen) violinists. But the original set was composed as vocalises for the soprano Nina Koshets, who was in love with the unresponsive composer. Koshets followed Prokofiev to America, who advised her, when she prepared her publicity material, to transliterate her name as '-shets', not '-shits', which as he noted 'means something else'.[18] But now, with the giants throwing hammers over two rivers, my memory of a brilliant young pianist playing Prokofiev, and being very tolerant of a teenage upstart, and the river alive with small boats, measuring out the starting line, I finally get my coffee, and set my feet on the path home.

It doesn't really seem to matter, to me, where I walk, whether I get there, or in what direction I go. I probably have to blame Geoffrey Chaucer and/or Oliver Statler for this. 'When that zephirus with his shoures sote…', has very often marked the beginning of my walking season, an urge to cross the Thames to Southwark, and walk East, past Edward II's ruined manse at Rotherhithe, along the lost Thames Road, and then down to the chalk hills for Canterbury, turning left at Wye, with a wave to

Aphra Behn, and then back south-east to Dover, and maybe, with Turner on the Channel packet, to points beyond. I 'longe to go on pilgrimages', like Geoffrey's troupe, even though they only made it from being blessed at the old St James Church on Garlick Hill, over London Bridge, to the 'Boar', for rest and refreshment, after, generously, half a mile on horseback, barely breaking into a 'canter' en route. I discovered Statler not long after Chaucer; in his *Japanese Pilgrimage* he observed that pilgrimages are not endurance tests, and for the Japanese, he observed no particular virtue, or merit, in walking the whole path, rather than just part of it, a month any more than an afternoon. Indeed, as so many of the pilgrimage routes in Japan are circular, end or beginning, start or finish–it's all moot. Cheerfully being on the road, putting one foot in front of the other, is the thing.

For me, it's analogous to violin practice, to my relationship to the music on my work desk. To much of it, I return again, and again, at irregular intervals, the only constant the happy, or not so happy recognition of well-trodden paths, offering renewal and surprise, despite, or perhaps because of their familiarity. So the getting there, whether it's arriving home, or at the final destination, usually a railway station, does not interest me so much. At the beginning of his *Four Quartets* a proem to *Burnt Norton*, T. S. Eliot inserted a quote from Heraclitus: ὁδὸς ἄνω κάτω μία καὶ ὡυτή ('the road out and back is the same').[19] As a classics-obsessed teenager, it seemed to me the meaning of this had been subsumed by the 'In my end is my beginning', which emerges later. Of course that was a youthful misunderstanding. But still I cling to the Heraclitus; 'the way up and the way down are one and the same', and I come home, and know it for the first time.

ENDNOTES

1 Sergei Eisenstein, *Film Form*, tr. Jay Leyda, New York: Harcourt Brace Jovanavich, 1949, p. 71.

2 14th June 1667. *Pepys' Diary*, Volume III, eds. Robert Latham and William Matthews, London: The Folio Society, 1996, pp. 81–2.

3 Edward Phillips, *The New World of English Words: Or a General Dictionary, containing the Interpretations of such hard words as are derived from other languages*, Printed by E. Tyler for Nath. Brook at the Sign of the Angel in Cornhill, 1658, (no pagination).

4 John Webster, *The White Devil*, (originally published 1608), London: Reeves & Turner, 1857, p. 127.

5 Robert Gibbings, *Sweet Thames Run Softly*, London: J M. Dent & Sons, 1940, p. 167.

6 T. S. Eliot, *Four Quartets*, London: Faber & Faber, 1944, p. 42.

7 Jennifer Westwood & Jacqueline Simpson, *The Lore of the Land*, London: Penguin, 2006, p. 601.

8 Every step the same, each beat and *taktus* the same, whilst melody and decoration, ornaments abound everywhere. At Kingston, the second bridge, I resume a measured pace after a momentary attack of spleen, that the mooring next to the bridge is 'Royal Parks' and *(non-sequitur)* therefore, private.

9 St Anthony-in-Meneage, Cornwall.

10 Alfred Tennyson, *Locksley Hall (Poems of 1842)*, Eds. Christopher Ricks, Plymouth: MacDonald and Evans, 1981, p. 208.

11 I mention this to a dancer friend the next day, who admits that she still has some of her shoes from younger days, which she had kept; bloodied trophies.

12 Charles Dickens, *Bleak House* (1853), London: Penguin, 1971, p. 491.

13 Denise Yim, *Viotti and the Chinnerys: A Relationship Charted Through Letters*, Aldershot: Ashgate, 2004, p. 145.

14 John Booker, *Travellers' Money*, Dover: Alan Sutton, 1994, p. 21.

15 Peter Ackroyd, *Thames*, London: Chatto & Windus, 2007, p. 436.

16 Jennifer Westwood & Jacqueline Simpson, *The Lore of the Land*, London: Penguin, 2006, pp. 718–9.

17 *Ibid.*, p. 482.

18 Harlow Robinson, *Sergei Prokofiev, A Biography*, Boston: North Eastern University Press, 1987, p. 175.

19 Heraclitus, *On the Universe*, Trans. W. H. S. Jones, Loeb Classical Library 150, Cambridge, MA: Harvard University Press, 1931, pp. 492–3.

Dialogue

Paddington Station
Great Western Terminus
All Saints Ch.
Praed Street Sta.
Royal Oak P.H.
Bayswater
Cleveland Square
Upper Hyde Park Gardens
Christ Ch.
St. James's Ch.
Westbourne Gate
Bayswater Road
Lancaster Gate
Water Works
Speke's Monument
Boundary of the Liberty of the City of Westminster
Nursery
KENSINGTON GARDENS
The Temple
Serpentine Br.
Round Pond
The Broad Walk
Water Meter
Kensington Palace
Kensington Pal. Green
ST. MARGARE
WESTMINST
(Detached)
Acres
390·944
Band House
Nursery
Kensington
St. Govor's Well
Black Pond Wood
The Flower Walk
The Prince Consort Memorial
The Royal Alcove
Coalbrookdale Gate
The Queen's Gate
Lodge
Parliamentary Boundary
Kensington Road
Eden Lodge
Royal Albert Hall
Conservatory
International Exhibition
Riding Sch.
Palace Gate

PHIL SMITH

Curling Up Tight

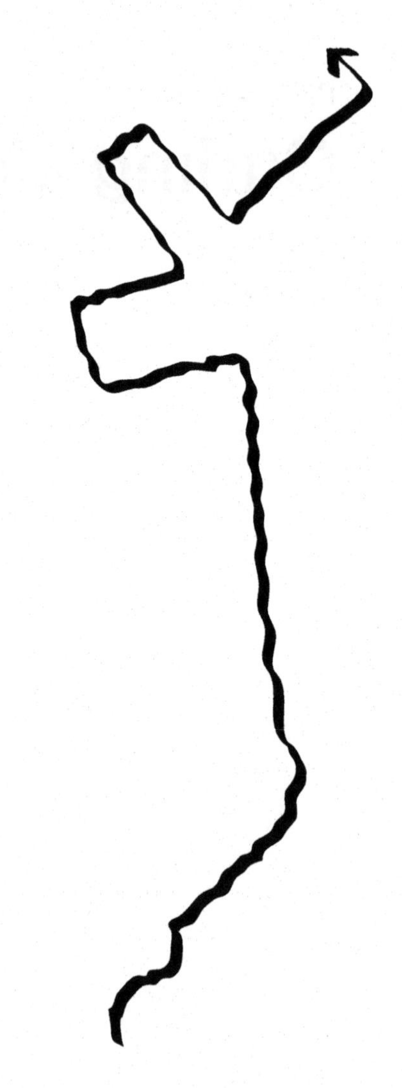

What do we learn? That the city repeats us back to itself? That it repeats itself to us in forms we'd already imagined? Not always. When I think about these moments on our walk, when the city did neither, I lose the beginning of these questions: the unease of the property developer at our taking such a close interest in the shifting fabric of his property (and the inspector, without a ground to be on, even more nervous) its door left just far enough ajar for our curiosity, the possibility that our presence was something worse than accidental, that something was emerging to meet us from that peeling wall with its rectangles of something else that was possibly once art under the attrition of darkness and damp, the pink shirt that could barely contain the developer, the bell labelled "NIGHT", the women behind the embassy asking "Bulgarian?" and with no follow-up but angry disappointment when we had expected an extended script, the residents who hid behind their accents their local knowledge, my failure to make any connection at all with the many mews except for an adolescent late night TV association to games without a ball, as London itself full of obtuse murder, concrete foundations on a round-about garden that taunted my default paranoia with their ordinariness, a church doorway where no one hung about, bricks with nothing scratched into them, 'the village' that I could never quite see despite the bereted men in conversation on a doorstep and the pairs in cafes we elected not to patronise, the lines of pillared porches which even in the afternoon sun are too much lit by the dim and rusty light from a Hammer portmanteau going down on a suburb, tomato juice cinematography, my not grasping all the 272 meanings of 'estate', the big hands and thumping feet of the Holy Spirit.

Blow Up (1966).

Sometimes the city does not bring back the same ball that you throw for it to chase.

There was an overarching and tilted narrative that we were sliding down, leaning to the sinister, a narrative we had partly brought with us of course, isn't it always The Way, but one this unseen village was only too happy to play along with, meeting us halfway, non-committal, getting away with it again, the case taken no further, the files stored among so much other noise it had disappeared into the description of a common sense back then of which you say: "well, that was certainly never acceptable to anyone that I knew at the time" and "what are you talking about 'acceptable'? I don't remember that, at all!"

Almost the first thing we'd paused at, after escaping the labyrinth of the station (foiled at first by the locked door next to the gents, and by my temporary wish to remain inside the stories of other visits, to ease my way into this one through its past) was a metal badge in the pavement marking railway property. I'd remembered, putting away the present, eating pancakes at Garfunkels forty years before, with a remote cousin, a chorus line dancer in a West End show. And, why yes, these very metal badges and the stopcock covers and the drain covers, some of them with their own customised esoteric patterns forged not so far away, unmarked by any name so the patterns speak for themselves to those without the eyes to not see, reminding me of a glinting syrup running over a sentiment, cementing every other thing to property, as if it could not, never be, would be forever held firm in contracts and in dim hearings in chambers. Art and the law had wed in forging these badges. The best impressions with the right to remain nameless; to be like cheap and mad Beta Max movies with those old pre-CGI effects that treat human beings as glove puppets; offerings to a Thing without a final shape, resisting product in a processual way that likes to claim it is Very Old, but is as modern as fundamentalism, a medieval barbarity that was branded only last week. A queasy steel fixes things in place, here; the gloop of fatty streets around the station and the over-polishing by passing feet of markers on the edge of an improbably named 'estate'.

On walks like this one I am taking with Simon there is a remaking of people – "thank you for altering me" a geographer emailed me last week – it takes a while and it doesn't seem to be connected very strongly to ideas or even that much to events or narratives, but rather it comes from something to do with the relationship in and by which each walker begins to move themselves across the terrain with other walkers, then to some 'ideal' walk that we are not walking, absence that somehow participates and partly shapes what we do. Such psychic ornaments get themselves re-forged in the shiftings of our pairing, in some furnace close to where we are, momentary idols as good as the real thing, easily gathered up from roadside trash, constituted, undone and then returned to the gutter, disappearing almost as quickly as they come into being; the dissolution of the group beyond individual, the sudden amalgamations and clusterings, the even pacings and spacings, the recalibrating of participants. It is not so much the shape we're left in, but rather the clinker of the walk, the accumulation of details and impressions that will not fit in pocket or pocketbook, that refuses to be confined to a political line or to prose or to anything else for that, yes that, matter. This is the temptation to poetry, which if resisted can change and gratify at once, petty yet more, plateau places of pleasure across which anyone can slice the ups and downs of a journey, a rare time that you do not have to defer. Possibly it is in the fairy tale of relationships, ideology and hooded identities that the altering takes place; not a chosen one of course, but at least it is run by your own algorithms, almost as if such a thing were still possible.

Hardly have we begun, as we encounter our first significant marker outside the station, than Simon explains that one of his colleagues wishes to be remembered to me, which is slightly odd as the day before I had wondered what we might say to each other if we were ever to meet again after forty years. We'd been partners for a while back then. She will, now, walk with us in the Platonic space that opens up, the ideal route blazed partly by what isn't here and cannot be again, but mostly by hope; on top of all this, there is my forty-year ghost, the person I imagined I was then, a Bulgarian trying to get to my embassy. There's some sentimentality in my walking, I know, holding its

Blochian principle of expectation of better things close to its chest, barely disclosed, but carefully nurtured.

The deflating effects of 'Blow Up' barely contain our obsessive attention to detail; the degree is relative, as usual. We race past 257 elements for every one that we pause to savour. This is the gleaning. Cutting ears from the crop at its edges, taking back a little of the surplus pleasure from property. Yet, I never fetched the tiny magnifying glass from my pocket, nor any of the other small instruments, chalks, and so on, that I had prepared. There was so little need for technique, the terrain was giving us much more than we could cope with; aggression in the key of generosity. You might almost call that 'its plan'. In the church I needed to bring us away from the young priest. The building was an exaggerator, polished by bombs and bent by damp; its smoothed six-sided stars that the young priest tries to pass off as unremarkable, standard provisions. Without persuasion he mimes his administration of the sacrament at the altar, dragged democratically westwards into the centre of the nave.

"You look like the host of a TV game show," Simon says. I propose "a theological question, or perhaps this is just my lack of careful observation, but is it usual to have a representation of the Holy Spirit in the form of a man? I can't recall seeing any other example."

Nor the young priest: "it's not usual, no … but I think there is something feminine in the figure …"

"You subscribe to the idea that the Holy Spirit is the feminine part of the Trinity?"

"Well, the word is female, in the Hebrew …" and, quoting from the palimpsest of scripture, he takes us through the gender reassignment of the Holy Ghost from feminine Hebrew, through neuter New Testament Greek to masculine Latin.

"And there, in a sentence", I say, wanting to punch a line under the whole of this, I know where it's going and it won't get any better than this uneasy encounter of a male trio around a vulgar altar discussing women, "is everything that's wrong with Western culture".

On our way out, we check the window again; there is something, according to the rules of Appearance, feminine in the face of that part of the Venn Diagram of God. Landscapity: imposing ourselves on a simulacrum that is especially protected from blasphemy by violence. In another piece of coloured glass ulterior locomotives are still filling Brunel's station with smoke and ashes.

The church is our polished lens, an angular ear trumpet collecting whispers. It has shifted the quality of our walk. From streetcombers for ornaments, we have become exegetes, beginning now to walk on the ideal of the walk, while on another stratum we are curling up in tight circles between Sussex Gardens and the Bayswater Road. Though we do not discuss it, we attempt to walk the shapes we find in a metal security grille across a door at the backs of tall terraces; two circles, one larger than the other, hanging to different sides of a part of the curve of a much larger circle, which if it could be completed would lead us underground to whatever trick the monger knew was buried there when he played his three cards. After three elements–coffee, croissant and scrambled eggs–in a launderette, we are ready. The code is: 'knee–fight – few'. In the electric cooler, fluorescent pictures of scenes from underwater life have been carefully arranged on their sides; bright fish upended, sea grasses swimming like octopi, sharks spearing pastries. Yes, we are, again, ready.

It is at first sight an unremarkable space, perhaps not often remarked upon; a modern conflation of older monuments, jumbling war dead with the great good in a traffic buffer zone, the whole in alignment with a spire clipped of its fungal nave. At the park end is a thick obelisk with a rounded peak, a naturalistic benben, the egg-like island at the beginning of the world, atop which sits a hollow-eyed young boy, naked, not looking out but down and to the side, his head sunk on his collarbone. This erection celebrates a white supremacist, one of The Souls, founder of the Boy's Drill organisation and the Duty and Discipline Movement for 'combating softness'. But softness has combated him; the acids in the exhausts have etched out other faces from beneath his hard exterior, his hard shell is emptied, its eyes cracked and gone, a monument turned inside out, its stone now like a mould of dispossession forged in beds, trenches and Irish farms. The child's face is a ruin. He sits above representations of a City of God on each of the four sides, only visible to me when I begin to climb the thing, Simon's palm on my lower back, the idea all the more miasmic and noxious for being in grains, EMPIRE broken down into individual fragments of pointillist agency and identity.

To HIM the british empire was a goodly HERITAGE to be fashioned like UNTO a CITY of god.

The naked animal, Kong-like, shot down by acid, clinging to the cities, one shoulder drooped, its eyes hollowed upwards into its brain, in a kind of malevolent despair. I quote to Simon the guiding principle of an agent of an institution from a Žižek video – declare the denial of your own interests and you can do whatever the fuck you like–as we cross the Bayswater Road. He knows it. Half of the idea is left with the monuments.

Inside the park, Speke's obelisk coldly claims the Nile.

We meet a woman looking for the statue of Peter Pan, an ideal child sitting on a heap of brassy excrement from which small animals emerge. The woman shows us a picture of one of these dung creatures. She's on some sort of treasure hunt, printed off from the web, she drags a child. We half follow the signs to Diana's garden and find nothing, while I whittle on, distractedly, about her magical Shakespearian body. In the middle of the park, unexplained and unsigned, is a peculiar arrangement of three steps. For the third time, the rule of three. Two steps, the smallest, are made of stone and appear heavily eroded, no more than broken tooth stumps. The third bears a greening metal plate that declares it constituted of

> GRANO METALLIC STONE
>
> the invention of a Mister J. H. Bryant of London, a composition of blast furnace clinker and granite, crushed up and then chemically treated, dried, mixed with Portland cement and brought to a pasty consistency by the application of an alkaline. Then cast. The atoms of the vitreous slag presenting themselves above the surface of the other more easily eroded materials, the whole giving an impression of rough stone.
>
> PHYSICAL ENERGY
> BY G F WATTS OM-RA

The ground beneath the horse is a coppery sea, two solid square bolts awash in it, holding back the horse from leaping to the sky, binding the green waves to the base. The horse's crazed face, its flaring nostrils eating up into its face, make a reasonable companion to the naked boy lifted out of reach by the Meath-head obelisk; sad loping giants they are that are left to haunt these skylines of Augustine's catastrophic idea.

At the Albert Memorial, Hiram holds up a corner of the ENGINEERING foot; the walk's third script for sacrifice for the purpose of a great other. Simon and I share certain histories here; we've already walked together before this first time, through the chequerboard temples and landing strips of our male lines. Their golden bodies, ideologies made the flesh they can never quite be, ever quite be.

We talk about the stories that we heard back then, in the late 70s, early 80s, the gossip about the establishment rings. Simon has a story about a scandal about to break that doesn't. Brittan. Uncle Mac. This park is full of men's names. But it really is about the whole thing, the war on vulnerability and softness as the unrecognised criminal ritual that underpins the architecture of reality, the asphyxiating of the cowering child in our questions then. The bodies I didn't believe in that have all turned out to be true. But that is still a lie until they are exposed again and again, and then a third time, as a Body of Lies.

In the toilets of the Royal College of Art, Simon notices that his green carnation has gone, leaving only a short stem and a pin. I laugh at a large metal cabinet marked "CLEANERS". Although I barely clock it at the time, we're really breaking the rules by entering a place of work like this, a familiar place, and Simon begins to conduct business outside with a student who gets us back into the hypnosis of the 'drift', responding to Simon as if he'd never met him before. I wonder if Simon has made everything up, all he'd need to do is learn the name of the security guard; the Bulgarian women accost us as if they EXPECT us to speak Bulgarian. As if we might have cut ourselves free of one thing only to be caught up in something quite else.

After a final loop, I begin to fear time, anxious about trains, we march back across the park over-efficiently until it becomes clear how close we are to where we had begun, and slow down as the route becomes recognizable again.

Charlie Cairoli (left) with Paul Freedman, the whiteface clown who scared me.

We talked about clowns. Coco. Charlie Cairoli. That sinister one made of triangles who played straight-faced, part of Cairoli's troupe, white as a corpse, like something escaped from Flatland into the nightmare-geometry of a tent. The patterns on his upturned cone hat are similar to those of the customised drain cover ornaments; grilles over the doors to abjection. They came for you in your sleeping places, these patterns and shapes. What does the recent shift in the Spectacle of clowns signify? From a fear on the edge of the circus ring and the burger ad to a full-blown serial-killing horror myth? Are we getting closer to Uncle admitting what children's 'entertainment' is?

We pass again the giant parts of a dried tree trunk, fossil-like, on the porch of a Home of Masks; another door that opened just enough and at just the right time for us. The broken teapot where I could lay out the principles of the walk; open to the possibility that this wounded artifact might represent some smuggled authenticity from far away, or bought joblot from a shop around the corner. And I had told the McCurdy story: the petty thief killed by cops in 1911 in Oklahoma, his body never claimed, embalmed by the undertaker and displayed, bought by a passing showman for exhibition as 'The Bandit Who Wouldn't Give Up', sold on and sold on, turning up as a model ghoul in a 'Laff-In-The-Dark' Ghost Train, discovered when his 'plaster' arm broke off to reveal a bone inside. Truth in fake and fake in truth. Bone under paint and paint under bone. The Body of Lies, that we'd 'mapped' (another abused idea) across a few streets and one part of a park, is the stitching in the spine of that work.

Coincidences that are not accidental; teased out in dialogues from brassy piles of excrement. Are you ready with that pin?

ST. MATTHEW BETHNAL GREEN
SOUTH WEST DIVISION
MILE END OLD
MILE END NEW TOWN
WHITECHAPEL
MILE END ROAD
WHITECHAPEL ROAD
COMMERCIAL ROAD
WHITECHAPEL HIGH STREET
EAST LONDON COLLEGE
Jews Burial Ground
Mortuary Chap.
Church CEMETERY (Disused)
LONDON HOSPL.
Whitechapel Station
Great Assembly Hall
Brunswick Hall
Brewery
Burial Ground (Disused)
Schools
St. Dunstan's Church
Almshouses
Rowton House
Gas Works

ROSANA ANTOLI

Walkative: A Choreography of Resistance

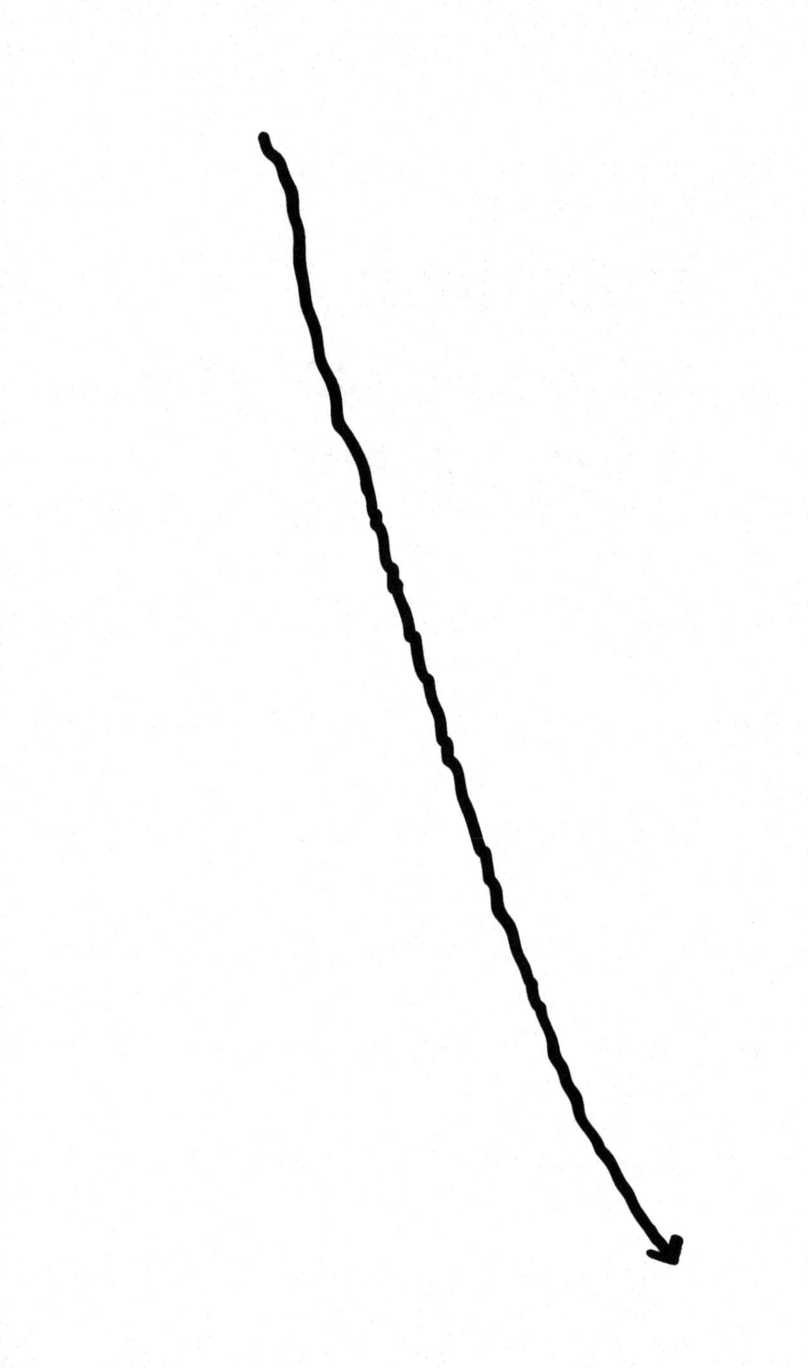

> Virtually all cities across the world are starting to display spaces and zones that are powerfully connected to other 'valued' spaces across the urban landscape as well as across national, international and even global distances. At the same time, though, there is often a palpable and increasing sense of logical disconnection in such places from physically close, but socially and economically distant, places and people.[1]
>
> ...
>
> The surprise, the indefinite, the unexpected intervenes, furthermore the intention of the artist, in the realisation of a work of art – which has been described on many occasions as a 'process', 'experience' or 'event', emphasising their transitory and deliberately perishable nature – [...] Nowadays, we accept this in art and also in our lives – in our world – the only thing of which we can be certain is the uncertain.[2]

As an artist I am interested in how notions of 'group' and 'community' are culturally defined and constructed, and how my work might redefine critically the characteristics and attributes of a certain area through revisiting the existing established representations – maps, relationships... and making visible the relations between subject and object in the city.

On a cold and sunny morning in early January 2015, as a result of research I had been doing at the RCA into the concept of 'resistance' and its relation to the global economic consequences that have transformed some neighbourhoods in East London, I set out from Mile End tube station with the intention of walking towards its Aldgate East counterpart and taking photographs as I went of possible scenarios and landscapes that might unfold in my final performance. In 'Walkative: From Mile End to the City'[3] I address the changes to the social structure, and highlight certain displaced elements of this particular geography. The walk and the sequence of choreographed movements and subtle gestures I incorporated into it took about 30 minutes. I didn't quite expect, however, the bemused reactions of some passers-by – though retrospectively, it is clear how displaced and decontextualized these subtle gestures must have appeared.

I also didn't expect that this project would become a collaboration through a chance encounter with a complete stranger, local to the Mile End Road, called Graham.

Central to the methodology of my performance art practice as exemplified in this walk are the elements of chance, serendipity and coincidence, and how these might serve to modify and improve the original idea. I understand chance as that thing that human beings cannot control. It is only when I explore uncertain paths that I am able to guarantee that something magical or unknown might appear; I embrace absurdity as the impossible use of reason in our daily routines.

My first idea for this performance was to record myself walking and making a sequence of movements that were intended to be a response to the architecture, pedestrians and other elements that I encountered on my way. In the straight line we can trace between both areas, that is, the continuation between Mile End station via Whitechapel Road to Aldgate East, there is a 'palpable and increasing sense of logical disconnection' suggested by Graham and Marvin, quoted in Bauman above. I also had in mind what French urban sociologist Chombart de Lauwe asserted over sixty years ago, that, *'an urban neighbourhood is determined not only by geographical and economic factors, but also by the image that its inhabitants and those of other neighbourhoods have of it'.*[4] The movements and gestures I generated during the walk would therefore be intended to act as a critical mirror, a video image of a newly constructed sensorial city, a reimagined area – a reflection of the dissonant emotions and feelings that these two neighbourhoods produce.

The finished piece, the video performance 'Walkative: From Mile End to the City', is also informed by Debord's theory of the Dérive, where Dériver is to drift; to walk through various ambiences where the walker is aware of psychogeographical effects during the journey.[5] Of course, in the city the walker is presented with numerous obstacles such as the concrete zones and fixed elements that condition our walks through them. This diverges from Debord, however, who, rather, asserted that: *'chance is a less important factor than one might think'.*[6]

I am, however, attracted to the idea[7] that in order to truly drift we need to be like Bas Jan Ader, that is, by getting lost, being brave and encountering the abyss.

This surrender to chance is exemplified by my first encounter with Graham Farrell after a few minutes of exploring that part of the Mile End Road in the immediate vicinity of the tube station. Walking westwards, I begin to slow down, I close my eyes, an act of concentration that is aimed at heightening perception, a way of somehow examining. I hear a male voice. It wants to know why I am moving so strangely (with eyes closed and performing a series of repetitive and displaced gestures). I tell him a little bit about my interest in Mile End as a zone of resistance. This becomes the point of engagement between us.

Graham is in his late 40s, early 50s, and tells me that his parents came over from India in the early 1960s. Though unemployed, he is dressed somewhat ambiguously in the high visibility work-wear of a construction worker. He is an engaging, and for me somewhat charismatic character, who quickly reveals his political outspokenness particularly in his opposition to what he feels is the increasing gentrification / appropriation of his neighbourhood: In the writing of this I look back at the iPhone record of our first conversation. He tells me, '… If you look at these areas, they are famous for Charles Dickens, Karl Marx … you can see a great culture, a great architecture. But now, these capitalist speculators are building these concrete and glass sets (sic) with no architecture or humanitarian value at all …'

We agree on a collaboration that will take place a few days later. One that starts at Mile End and terminates at a symbolic boundary to the City: Aldgate East. He will be a representation of the consequences of }the economic failure within society. And through his movements – Graham is also an amateur dancer, a beautiful coincidence – he will reinterpret the route.

Two days later I am accompanied by Erola Arcalis, a photographer friend who is filming the whole thing, and Graham and I have already established our modus operandi: The itinerary is given by me and he will choose his movements and locations. It is clear that he has strong views about what Simon, in our re-walking of this route a few months later, observed to be 'the zones of capital and community and the liminal spaces in between'. Graham's identification of his class location seems both fatalistic (we may never win) but pugnacious (we mustn't lose). I am reminded of the same impossible chess-like attempts to move forward in Samuel Beckett's *Endgame*,[8] when you are aware that the game might be lost but you mustn't give up. This is the feeling of resistance: this is the gesture I needed to work with.

Graham dances the straight line – it is an exciting connection when in our re-walk Simon sees a parallel with William Kempe's dance from London to Norwich.[9] He chooses where he wants to move, he points out places like the hostel for the homeless opposite the East London Mosque that have a personal significance, because many of his friends are now there. He performs without seeming direction, but rather improvises the movements he feels at each moment. At the outset I feel there is an organic quality to all this; then Graham seems to occupy the whole pavement space around him, and as he dances he engages cheerfully with bystanders and passers-by, some of whom clap, cheer or stop to take in his elegantly awkward dance. He seems relaxed amongst friends and community members in 'his' neighbourhood.

As we approach Osborn Street, leading into Brick Lane on our right and close to the familiar landmark of the Whitechapel Gallery–the demarcation point between zones – we begin to sense a clear difference in the area we are entering now, the pavement space less welcoming, becoming rather, a crossing path (camino de paso) with little space to interact in community. These 'alienating' spaces are translated through Graham's mood and body movements, which communicate as subdued, melancholic even, his movements more mechanical. The traces he leaves in the space more geometrical, robotic and somehow smaller. The participation with the public has also changed. There is little, if any, response.

I revisit this walk with Simon King a few months later. Simon, as part of the 'Walkative' project at the RCA, has inspired me to think about how walking when done consciously as a relational public gesture can be an act charged with political, social and artistic meanings. Thus, re-enacting with him as closely as possible the way I performed and narrated the experience of the original walk, resulted in a mutual referencing of aspects of the politics of space, the particular and charged history of this part of London, and the importance that our gestures have in the everyday. Simon and I exchange emails about this aspect after our re-walking. Zygmunt Bauman's thesis of living in a time of liquid modernity seems particularly apt to the discussion. He sends me the following:

> *The picture emerging ... is one of two segregated and mutually separate life worlds. Only the second of the two is territorially circumscribed and can be caught in the net*

> *sewn of orthodox topographical, mundane and 'down to earth' notions. Those who live in the first of the distinct life worlds may be, like the others, bodily 'in the place', but they are not 'of that place' – certainly not spiritually, but also quite often, whenever they wish, not bodily.*[10]

Bauman's observation indeed seems pertinent to my original collaboration with Graham. A sense that there are invisible frontiers within cities, collisions in the relational models between subjects and the objects, and it thus becomes a complex but necessary task to map an area to reveal the hidden power commands that structure them.

ENDNOTES

1 Stephen Graham and Simon Marvin, *Splintering Urbanism*, Routledge, London, 2001, p.285. Quoted in Zygmunt Bauman, *Liquid Times– Living in an Age of Uncertainty*, Polity Press, 2007, p. 73.

2 Nicola Mariani, N°6 *Black Swan Magazine, NYR Notas y Reflexiones*, 2015. http://notasyreflexiones.com/nicola-mariani-article/.

3 'Walkative: From Mile End to the City' focuses attention on problems that concern local territories to understand the circumstances of the political and economic situation of a country. *Choreographing Resistance* has the intention of just such a mapping that carefully reveals a transformative dance, an ephemeral action as a critical mode of representation that appears after the encounter with these divergent atmospheres.

4 Chombart de Lauwe, *Paris et l'agglomération parisienne*, Bibliothèque de Sociologie Contemporaine, P.U.F., 1952.

5 As '*Psychogeography* could set for itself the study of the precise laws and specific effects of the geographical environment, consciously organized or not, on the emotions and behavior of individuals.' Guy Debord, *Introduction to a Critique of Urban Geography*, 1955.

6 Guy Debord, *Les Lèvres Nues* #9 (November 1956) reprinted in *Internationale Situationniste* #2 (December 1958).

7 Bas Jan Ader, *In Search of the Miraculous*. Last Performance. 1975.

8 Samuel Beckett, *Endgame*, Faber & Faber, London, 2009.

9 William Kempe (died 1603), was an English actor and performer. In his performance 'Nine Days Wonder' he danced from London to Norwich (about a hundred miles), in a journey that took him several days spread in several weeks, often amid cheering crowds– Quoted from Wikipedia. https://en.wikipedia.org/wiki/William_Kempe.

10 Zygmunt Bauman, *Liquid Times –Living in an Age of Uncertainty*, Polity Press, New York, 2007, p. 74.

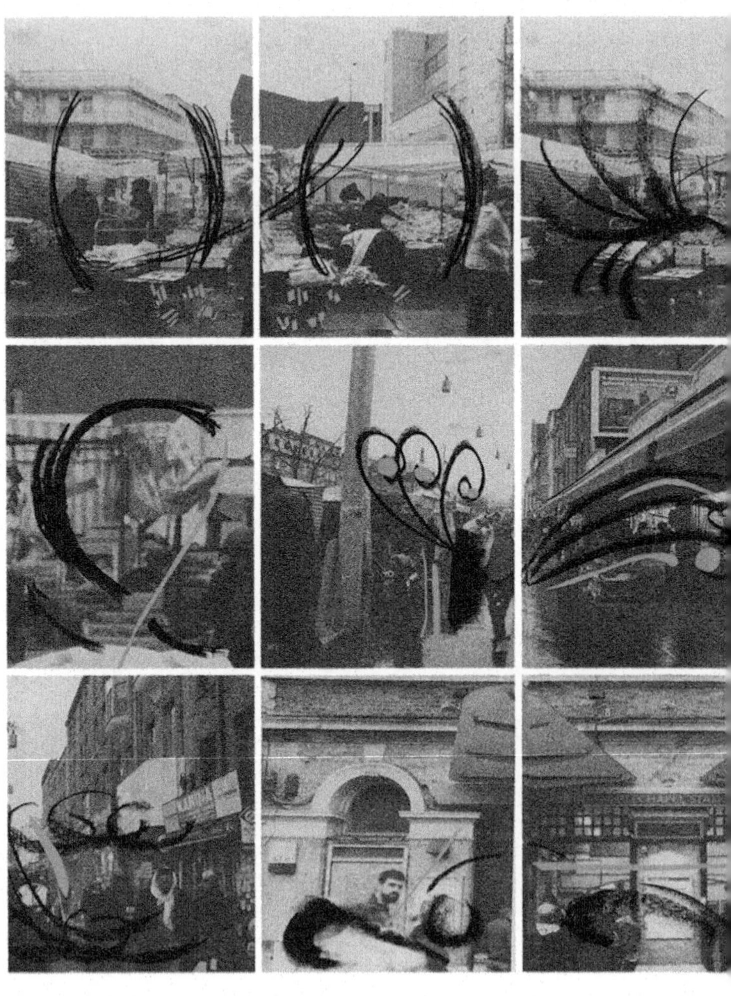

Rosana Antoli, Choreography Of Resistance.
Photography and drawing on paper. 2015.

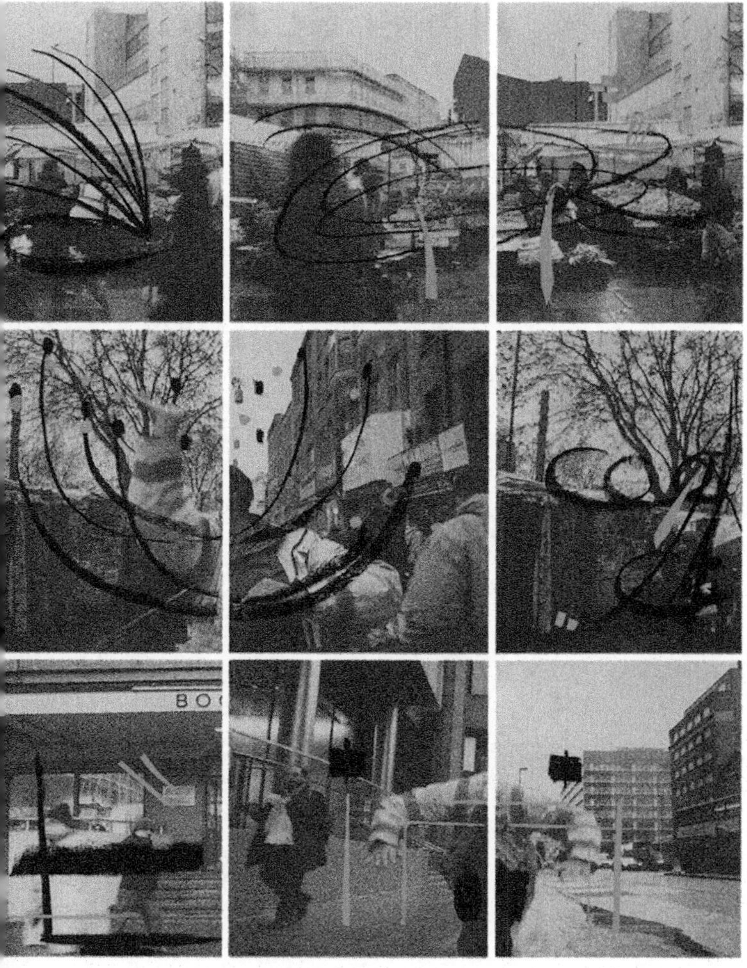

WILLESDEN
U.D.
WILLESDEN
GREENFORD U.D.
WEST TWYFORD
WORMWOOD SCRUBS
HAMMERSMITH
NORTH DIVISION
HAMMERSMITH
PADDINGTON
ST MARY ABBOTTS
KENSINGTON
KENSINGTON
ST MARGARET

TOM SPOONER

The Sound of Sweetness on the Grand Union Canal

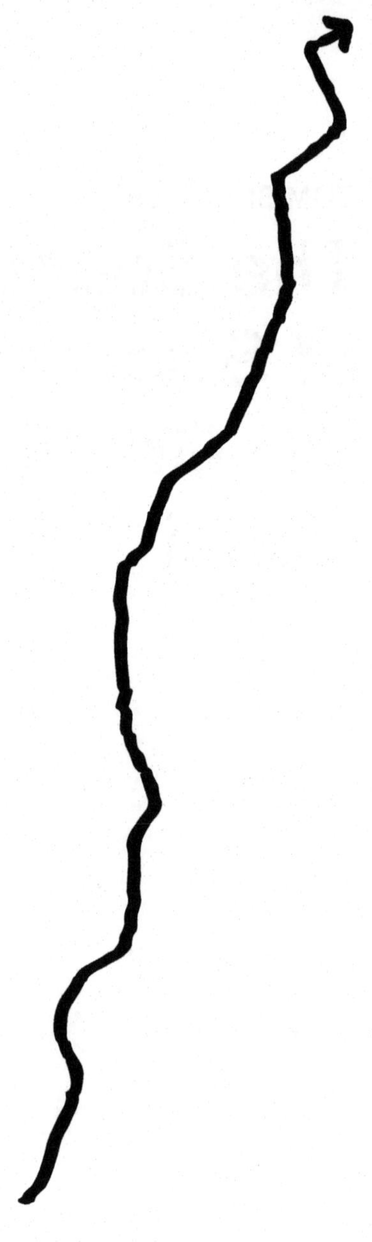

On 11th March 2015, the gallant Tom Spooner and brave Simon King struck a course northwest on the Grand Union Canal, exploiting the terrain and the psycho-social boundaries imposed upon them by the city. They have left this message in the hope that others may come and join them in a great urban gathering at the Twyford aqueduct to celebrate their autonomy.

– Message in a bottle

We met on a post-rush-hour weekday morning on the concourse at Paddington Station. On your recommendation I had been reading up on Phil Smith's walking methodology, Mythogeography. Whilst we ate a hurried breakfast of pastries and coffee outside one of the food kiosks, we read aloud from Phil's published writings some of the highlights of his mytho approach to walking–much of it was reminiscent of Situationist psychogeography. The texts, we agreed, offered compelling, and at times ludic(rous) insights into walking, or drifting, in non-places, as a process of challenging the monuments of commercial tourism, and transforming overlooked areas of the public realm into sites of reverie and wonder. There are accounts in Smith of walkers operating under outlandish pseudonyms, such as "The Crab Man", and "Ninjalicious", defying and walking out on "The Spectacle", an unashamed nod to Guy Debord's 1967 text. However, we agreed it would be foolhardy to blindly follow this dogma, which also stipulates in The Handbook of Drifting: "20/Displace your erotic feelings for each other to the landscape."

Under dull skies and suitably swaddled against an occasionally chilly breeze we set out from Paddington Station in a fairly uneventful start to our walk and where soon the soulless edifices and walkways of the Paddington Basin beyond the Westway begin to be replaced by the more salubrious environs (pristinely detached houses and lush greenery) of Maida Vale and Little Venice which nestle around an opening on to the Grand Union Canal.

I had already decided that we would walk part of the Paddington branch of the canal because much of it as far as I was aware still resisted gentrification and was occupied predominantly by rundown and unremarkable industrial estates. This I had hoped would open up more opportunity for the sense of play and spontaneity, so fetishized in Smith's writing, and indeed, by the Situationists in their hunt for sites of psychogeographical curiosity. Having read Smith, I anticipated the dialectic that might unfold or suggest itself, where the critical would come to merge with the absurd in a new urban awareness.

I had encountered sections of the canal a few years earlier as an impoverished undergraduate based in the Harrow area, commuting to and from the city by bicycle. There was something I had experienced there in its desolate hinterland which drew me back. It was something ineffable, an aesthetic appeal maybe, embedded beneath my consciousness. I might describe my actions now as a neo-romantic ruin lust, a yearning for that clearing in the woods, where the emotionally dulling technological canopy of the city dissipates in a fleeting, and almost revelatory, moment. I wanted to re-summon those spirits, internal or external, that I had felt previously but only in passing, and in isolation.

THE WALK

Following the canal, we head northwest, away from the idyllic sights of Little Venice. Curious cardboard markers, freshly taped to trees and lamp posts along the way, provide some amusement. We speculate whether we are following someone's directions to an illegal squat party, or retracing part of a charity fun run, or whether they simply have something to do with directing the steady flow of barges on the canal beside us.

The boats seem to cruise along at their own pace, as autonomous entities, quite removed from the regulated, sanity-grating, stop-start, traffic systems we are so unnaturally acclimatized to in the city. It's quite soothing, hypnotic almost.

We re-join the Westway briefly and trek past barren stretches and graffiti-covered pillars, rubble, and broken glass, beneath it. Its weather-battered supports, and exposed underside, reverberate with community unrest. Nearby, a considerable walk from anywhere, someone has dumped a pile of old furniture. An England flag tied to a makeshift mast has been dashed, along with this fly-tipper's dreams we presume, into the abandoned heap. A notice is attached, helpfully encouraging passers-by to take whatever they want.

A graffiti culture has evidently been growing for some years all along the canal side. Some of the harder to reach pieces date back to the 1990s, an indication, perhaps, of the street-venerability of their creators. We ponder on the habits and sociability of these enigmatic artists, their empty beer cans and the remnants of their burnt out cardboard crates, strewn in semi-circles around vacant benches beside the canal, telling tales of urban gatherings. These traces summon visions of hard-core taggers and vagrants, convened like nomadic druids, around makeshift bonfires, exchanging their stories and secret knowledge away from prying eyes.

The inner city slips away and the view is replaced with an expanse of freight railway networks, depots, and churned up earth. Mossy railway bridges slink overhead, connecting the lines. Some industry occupies the opposite bank. The graffiti flourishes. The path narrows and we file between the canal and patches of shrubbery, stinging nettles, and high fences topped with razor wire.

On the outskirts of Wembley, where perhaps only the most hardened dog-walker would normally tread, we begin to notice a few shanty-like structures. Blankets and bits of corrugated metal are strapped to rusted girders that support elevated sections of disused, or barely used, factories and warehouses abutting the canal bank, the destitution unlike anything one would expect to see in 21st-century London. As we continue our solitary walking (how many people do we encounter in either direction?) more piles of empty Special Brew and White Lightning cans suggest that things are quite different here at night. I wonder whether these constructions are occupied, and, if so, by whom. Have they been moved on, which is not unlikely, or is there an unseen human presence, sleeping off a hangover and waiting for the next canal-side party?

At the Twyford aqueduct, over the North Circular, we stage a mythogeography-inspired intervention using a glass bottle we find on the tow path and a scrap of paper from my sketchbook to cast an improvised message in a bottle into the canal. In the prank-like spirit of Smith's critical practice, I jot something equally absurdist and I hope, compelling, which in some way reaffirms, for ourselves, and any would-be finders of the message, what we are trying to do there.

The sound of sweetness
Sterio
DOLBY
Digita
Mfg. By Mumbai

Crossing the North Circular, we enter the heart of Metroland and for a while wander through clusters of communities that have formed quite haphazardly around the canal. Unsightly brown council houses are squashed into areas bounded by the canal, pockets of industrial recession, and railway intersections.

Between Stonebridge Park and Alperton, we discover an old cassette tape player cradled in a straggly, wind-blown shrub by the canal side. Inside, is a tape with the artist and title inscribed: By Mumbai, "The Sound of Sweetness". The batteries have long since died and we can only speculate what sounds the tape might play, who it had belonged to, and where it originated (I have since searched unsuccessfully for the tape online). We imagine a poignant story behind this fragment: of one man's plight in the big city. Perhaps a bit down on his luck, and missing home, this unseen character had retreated to the canal bank in order to relax in its relatively scenic terrain, a place where he could listen unmolested to the sounds of his homeland. For me, there was something anarchic, sublime even, in this possibility.

We finish our walk at Alperton, a very average London suburb that I have never visited before, and quite likely, will never visit again. A sign on the canal path informs us the next stops are Bath or Birmingham, both some 111 miles away, so it's an appropriate juncture, we agree, to conclude our drift. At the train station we bid our farewell and part company.

Rattling through London on the Piccadilly and Metropolitan lines and trying to make some sense of the walk and crystallise in my mind some of its high points, I perused the pictures I had taken on my iPhone.

The tube passed through some of the suburbs we had seen on our walk. Elevated railway sections commanded a superior view of those disparate territories, but they commanded nothing of the now invisible people who lived there. The moment reminded me of the famous view described by Michel de Certeau from the top of the New York World Trade Centre, of the streets below, which could tell him nothing of the people who inhabited them.

There was nothing radical, or overtly revolutionary about our walk. It didn't arise from a tactic that we had hoped would lead to tearing down the establishment from the inside out as the Situationists had planned, and failed to do, some sixty years earlier. That was not our intention. Our observations, experiences, and interactions with the physical environment, though, undeniably stimulated and informed our subjective perceptions of it in ways that cannot be conceived of through laboratory experiments, books, computer screens, or the totalising views provided by conventional maps.

The sights and feelings I have described here might be considered poetic images. They were conceived through a culmination of lived experience, reverie, and self-conscious imaginative free play, and they opened up new worlds, of human possibilities and potentialities, beyond their initial encounter, as they impacted on our individual, and collective psyches. The phenomenologist Gaston Bachelard perpetuated this idea that poetic images, found in the everyday, offer not only ephemeral moments of comfort and solidarity, but also extend the horizons of epistemology. They broaden the scope for understanding ourselves as people, and the question of where and how we gather such information.

The mental images we conceived of on our walk, the individual and collective memories we took away, the photographs we took, have become conversational pieces, the focus of critical discussion, and ways of making new connections between the built environment and the people who inhabit it.

CODA

That liberating, almost ethereal sense, I first experienced in those non-spaces some time ago, would never have been enough for me to re-visit them alone. My own rationality, and the pressing nature of the everyday, would not have permitted me to return on the grounds of such an ungrounded motive. Your invitation for a walk, chosen by me, was the catalyst for my return. Our shared experiences, and on-going dialogue, were essential in reifying those ghosts, and reconnecting with them. Self-consciously transforming the metaphysical nature of those territories, collectively, for me, could be the beginnings of a new urban awareness. I psychologically remapped a ghost territory that was situated somewhere between dream and reality on the peripheries of my consciousness. Psychologically remapping one site in a vast, but exhaustive list of many, in a metropolis as big as London, in this light, becomes a way of overlaying an on-going, and very personal, narrative, onto sites which might otherwise be reduced to coordinates on a map. I wonder now, as I did then, about the role that Smith played in directing our thoughts and actions that day. Much of Smith's writing, prior to our walk, had brought to mind the activities of an anarchic movement known as Neoism, which from what I can tell, seemed to fizzle out at the end of the 20th century.

Its proponents, too, based on the rather questionable existing accounts of their accomplishments, used collective pseudonyms, and promoted an ideology based on parody and subterfuge. They engaged in the propagation of such academically taboo subjects as ley lines, and dabbled in performance-based praxis, such as psychogeography. The group notably, and hilariously, through their writings, on a number of separate occasions, tricked journalists, who had failed to do their research, into publishing articles based on entirely fabricated ideas and events.

Naturally (as I'm sure you can understand), I had my reservations about following Smith's writing so rigidly. There was this worrying sense that we were walking, quite literally, deeper and deeper, into the clutches of an old practical joke, designed to ensnare academics and social commentators. Then again, engaging, perhaps loosely, as we did, with something as autonomous and free-floating as Smith's methodology is precisely the open-ended approach urban epistemology requires. Adopting a droll sense of humour, in tandem with an acute critical awareness towards the built environment, and the everyday, recalls that dialectic I had set out in search of. I maintain now, we cannot leave our futures purely in the hands of academics, sociologists, and rather turgid 20th century critical texts, which can bear little, or no relation, to present circumstances. Reality and lived situations are so much more affecting. So long as we come to terms with the fact that the immediate act of walking is not going to physically change the landscape, not remarkably anyway, the possibilities for future change, physical or metaphysical, are limitless.

Mythogeography, urban walking, and drifting, all seem superficially quite egocentric, instantly gratifying, and perhaps self-indulgent, but then I have to ask, how are we as artists, and human beings even, ever going to change the world, except by first experiencing it for ourselves? Changing the world is a gradual process. I also believe it can be both physical, and metaphysical, and I would argue that the latter is actually more significant and meaningful. I would not describe our walk together as an instantly revelatory or life changing experience, and do not think the next one will necessarily be so either. My epiphany has been that walking should be a never-ending process, a critical tool at our constant disposal, for reconnecting disconnected territories, and reconciling ourselves with those territories, giving birth to new ideas about the nature of cities and everyday urban life.

L. B. & S. C.
L. C. & D.
Victoria Bridge
Pier
RIVER
Parly. Co. Union & Parly. Boro. By.
Pier
NINE ELMS
Mud
Dock
Goods Depot
Filtering Beds
Reservoir
Southwark & Vauxhall Water Works
Filtering Beds
Reservoir
Field
Gasholder Station
Battersea Park Rd.
Sta.
Gas Wks.
Ch.
Sch.
School
Nine Elms Wks.
Queen's Rd. Sta.
Longhedge Works
Hall
Mission Room
Goods Depot
Schs.
Chap.
Church
VAUXHALL PARK
St. Peter's House
Baths
School
KENNINGTON
SOUTH LAMBETH
Ch.
Chap.
Hall
Orphanage

DUNCAN JEFFS

The Optimists

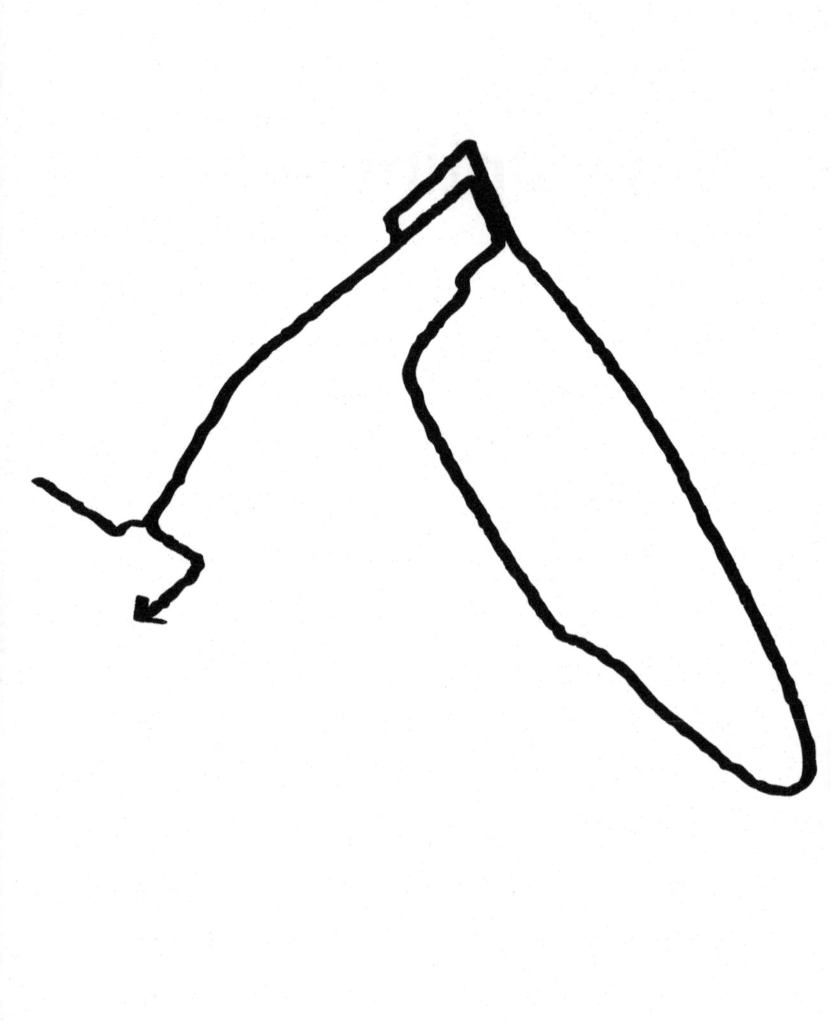

Time present and time past
Are both perhaps present in time future
And time future contained in time past.
If all time is eternally present
All time is unredeemable.[1]

My choice for our walk would be through an area that I was already beginning to navigate in terms of my practice and everyday thinking. From late summer 2014 I spent a year in a flat on the Savona Estate; a small group of low-rise blocks at the western end of Nine Elms Lane. It is inhabited by council tenants in the main, with a few flats shared by students and construction workers. It sits between two areas; a connective between the Patmore Estate to the south and the riverside stretch of de-industrialised space now being developed under the umbrella of 'Nine Elms on the Southbank'[2]: Battersea Power Station, Riverlight Quay, Embassy Gardens, and One: Nine Elms.

The lines from T. S. Eliot above resonate with an idea that a place in time is never completely set, that there are multiplicities and layers of meaning that play out in a non-linear transformation of spaces in time. The development narrative only scratches the surface of this within its advertising hyperbole yet the true nature of such rapid conversion of place is complex, appealing to the critical and explorative practice of art. Living in, walking through, and documenting this space has been woven into my own practice, using art as a tool for traversing and emphasising the multiplicities and veils that contest the reductive line of civil prosperity through private regeneration.

A discussion of these issues set the pretext for our walk, threading into ideas that had come about during the *Walkative* project the previous year, a return to the area in which we had started this dialogue, a continuation using walking as a tool for furthering the discussion and seeing new outcomes developing from our corresponding and independent documentation.

Walking from Wandsworth Road Overground we cut straight into the Patmore between two buildings onto a sub-street running alongside an overgrown park. The high grass is thick with Russian comfrey and nettles; there is a trodden path that winds through the centre leading to the draping curtains of a large willow. It feels strangely suburban, reminiscent of the lost space between new-build streets and cul-de-sacs, a marginal territory of kids getting wasted, rough sleepers and junkies looking for a place to disappear. From outside there is a lulling benevolence amongst the purple flowers and the sunlit golden-green of the leaves.

The warm air and evening light activates the energy of the estate – especially when the fruit trees are in blossom and the air is filled with a mixture of scents: curry, the bread factory and coffee roasting plant along the railway, the sweet smell of skunk lingering in the connecting tunnels – the potent aroma of hazily drifting on summer evenings getting high.

We were drifting too, moving through the estate without a specific route but rather a trail that cut through tunnels and turfed areas, meandering towards the eastern border where a razor wire fence runs alongside the road. We stop at a section of wall wheat-pasted with two screen-printed images. The graffiti is a juxtaposition; a pair of guns forming a strange figure next to a mushroom cloud of spikes, parts of which have been ripped away so that it looks as if it is blending into the bricks where yellowing limescale has built up on the mortar.

There is a sinister feeling about it; they are like waypoints or markers for something yet to happen – a precursor perhaps to some kind of dissent that could spread out of this network of low-rise blocks.

Reaching the north end of Savona we experience an abrupt shift in aural mood, the rumble of heavy traffic and construction noise serving to mark the boundary between these two zones. On the very edge of the estate is the newly refurbished Duchess public house, an English Heritage repackaging that is in line with the gentrified, good life stratagem projected by the place makers. The pub's décor consists of feature displays of ornately framed black-and-white prints of naked women in classical poses and reproduced Brit-Pop artefacts; a piano, a guitar and a Vespa all painted with the Union Jack. It pulls from history a comparably insipid ambience envisioned in the place makers'[3] printed hoardings that surround Battersea Power Station across the road. The wartime slogan: "WHO'S ABSENT? Is it You?" is painted on the wall with the image of John Bull; the pink skin tone matching the starched collar of a thick-set business man smoking a Cuban cigar and leafing through the *F.T.* outside. I think of the graffiti we saw previously, its placement on this invisible border somehow emphasising the tension between two distinctive zones, the growing presence of class cleansing as standard in the process of gentrification.

It is at this point in the walk where our conversation becomes more speculative, reading fragments of text from the billboards and hoardings, and trying to coax out ideas and imagined futures this site could be part of. Looking up at the power station, its red bricks defined against the grey clouds, we think of Alfonso

Cuarón's dystopic vision of London in his film *Children of Men* in which the power station features as the military-protected enclave of a rich Minister for the Arts. There is significance in the themes of infertility as a metaphor for the logical trajectory of late capitalism and a world in conflict over the movement of desperate refugees and rebel uprisings fighting a fascist state. The film's imagery becomes a useful tool for challenging the developer's visual expurgation of possibility and the inherent layers of meaning yet to be revealed through unpredictable and imaginative activity. The demarcation of time from the problems of the present moment is contained in the hyperbole of one statement printed on the hoardings: '2020' the year of completion, an echo of perfect vision and an undisputed success. These plywood walls surrounding the site are a temporary solution before the area is fully composed with the necessary forms of security and control, the invisible borders that are re-working the spacial divisions of the city. Saskia Sassen also notes the shift in the way these urban borders are working:

> Cities have always had walls [...] what is interesting today is that the walls are deeply perforated; the walls are not working. So the next step is all kinds of securitising, the weaponisation of urban space, the weaponising of luxury buildings, the gated community being the most extreme form. I think the real walls (of future urban space) will be invisible, but if you cross them you will know it and they will know it.[3]

Moving east down Nine Elms Lane we reach the Riverlight development, at the mid point of our walk, we sit on a bench within the token gesture of public space in between the still emerging towers; inky glass panels framed by garishly painted steel balconies. Reflecting on the strange nature of this space in its unmistakable confusion of public and exclusive we discuss the newly appointed vitrine gallery occupying one side of a lobby in the Riverlight One tower. The space, Studio RCA, is a temporary venture conjured as part of the place-making scheme for Nine Elms, in this case headed by the company Future City. It is an awkward space and immediately feels much more like a lobby than a functioning art space. Inside, the air is thick with the smell of chlorine from the swimming pool that you can see down to through a patterned glass wall. The clinical smell is at odds with the history of the land: where these luxury dromes now exist was once marshland. In a strange reoccurrence of this, a rising damp is emerging even while the building work is still in progress, two inharmonious expansions again beginning to establish a disturbingly accurate realisation of dystopic visions. Ballard's *High-Rise* fits perfectly; the immediate demise of the architecture being the first stage of a spiral into primal conflict that is in a dark juxtaposition with the residents' attempt to maintain their construct of success and luxury.

From the Riverlight building we continue along Nine Elms Lane. The next enclave we pass is the Embassy Gardens development; a New York apartment block simulacrum boasting a sky pool that connects the two buildings. Alongside it, is the new American Embassy, a giant cube of glass and incendiary-proofed beams

Where London living meets international luxury. There are images of models standing among the grey-scale backdrop of minimal furniture, staring into the middle distance, uninterested, as if avoiding our pointed gaze. As we reach the Vauxhall intersection with its traffic island adorned by strangely architectural billboards, we swing around back onto Wandsworth Road. At the point that these two roads meet, now being prepared for the raising of the Chinese development 'One Nine Elms', two towers bolstering the emergence of this exclusive zone with their hybrid of luxury apartments and hotel service. Only seconds from this plot we leave the road and enter the car park of the flower market, which is part of a large series of warehouses that make up New Covent Garden Market. Walking through while the market is empty we sense that this space is at risk, slowly being circled by developments inherently at odds with the crude functionality of this industrial microcosm. Moving through the market there is a palpable shift of atmosphere; it is a space for recurring bouts of activity, a host to a weekly boot sale and the manic convergence of food traders in the early hours of the morning. This flux is part of a working community, bringing another meaning to the idea of recurrence: Where workers once moved to build and operate the power station there is now a merging of a new workforce, livelihoods and culture existing as a counter-dimension to the regeneration; somehow powerful in its presence despite its transient pattern of emergence.

As we exit the market we walk back over the boundary into the Savona Estate, linking our walk in a circle. We come back to ideas about time scales, how the proximity of embedded activity and place with the rapid development highlights the fascinating multiplicities of this stretch of London. With both of us having lived here at different times, witness to different changes and issues, the ability to thread together our experiences and observations whilst walking lends itself well to the circle we have plotted, as it is at once cyclical and open, new trajectories and ideas splintering off as we continue.

ENDNOTES

1 Eliot, T.S. *Four Quartets*, Faber, London (1943)
2 http://www.nineelmslondon.com
3 Sassen, S. (2006) '*The Possibility of Hope*', *Children of Men*, Directed by Alfonso Cuarón [DVD] Universal Pictures UK

Notes on Contributors

Rosana Antoli, born in Alcoi, Spain, is a London-based artist who studied at Valencia Fine Arts University before finishing her MA in Performance/Sculpture at the RCA in 2015. Her work combines performance, dance, moving image and drawing, and is focused on the intersection of art, society and everyday life.

Sean Ashton writes fiction, criticism and poetry. Recent work includes 'Hello-Goodbye in Gethsemane' (*Poetry London*, 2015), and 'Mr Heggarty Goes Down' (*Collapse VIII*, 2014). He is the author of *Sunsets and Dogshits* (Alma, 2007) and the novel *Living in a Land* (EROS, 2016). He also writes for *Art Review*.

Amy Blier-Carruthers is a lecturer at the Royal Academy of Music and King's College London, where her research and teaching interests revolve around performance style and recording practices. She has most recently been invited to speak at Princeton University, University of Oxford, Wigmore Hall, and the Smithsonian Institution. Her monograph is soon to come out with Routledge, her other work is published by Oxford University Press and Bloomsbury, and she is co-investigator for the AHRC project 'Classical Music Hyper-Production and Practice as Research'.

Rut Blees Luxemburg's photographic works create immersive and vertiginous compositions that challenge established urban perceptions and reveal the overlooked, the dismissed and the unforeseen. Blees Luxemburg's photographs have been exhibited internationally and are in many public collections. She is a Reader in Urban Aesthetics at the RCA, London.

Roberto Bottazzi is an architect, researcher, and educator based in London. He is the Director of the Master in Urban Design at The Bartlett-UCL. Bottazzi's research on the impact of globalisation and digital technology on architecture and urbanism has been widely published both in the UK and internationally.

David Dernie is an architect and Dean of the Faculty of Architecture and Built Environment at the University of Westminster. His published books include *Material Imagination* (2016), *Architectural Drawing* (2010), *Exhibition Design* (2006), *New Stone Architecture* (2003), *Villa d'Este at Tivoli* (1996) and *Victor Horta* (1995).

Duncan Jeffs is a London-based artist. Often collaborative, his practice uses images, noise, video, found materials and appropriated media content to weave together an ongoing montage; layering fact and fiction into objects and temporary installations that mutate as they are assembled in various sites.

Jaspar Joseph-Lester is an artist, Reader in Art & Post-Urbanism and Head of the MA Sculpture Programme at the Royal College of Art. His work explores the conflicting ideological frameworks embodied in representations of modernity, urban renewal, regeneration and social organisation as a means to better understand how art practice can redefine masterplans and regeneration schemes that determine the cultural life of our cities. He has exhibited his work internationally and is author of *Revisiting the Bonaventure Hotel* (Copy Press, 2012).

Adam Kaasa is an interdisciplinary scholar who specialises in the politics of the city, foregrounding the role of architecture and design. He completed his PhD as a SSHRC Scholar at the London School of Economics. He is Director of Theatrum Mundi and Research Fellow in Architecture at the Royal College of Art.

Ahuvia Kahane is Professor of Greek in the Department of Classics at Royal Holloway, University of London. His research is focused on aspects of literature and thought in classical antiquity and its reception. He has recently co-edited a collection of essays on the gods in epic and is completing a book on literary genre and historical time.

Simon King, co-founder of the Walkative project, is a tutor at the RCA. Currently undertaking a practice-led PhD at Birkbeck, University of London, King's research is interested in the dialogic, convivial and performative aspects of group-led walking. As Noble & King he works and walks collaboratively with the artist Corinne Noble towards the creation of public art walks in London.

Sharon Kivland is an artist and writer working in London and France. She is a keen reader, considering what is put at stake at the intersection of art, psychoanalysis, and politics. For some years she has been following Sigmund Freud on holiday. She is Reader in Fine Art at Sheffield Hallam University.

Nayan Kulkarni is a visual artist whose practice engages with contemporary urban experience through exploring issues of light, time and image. His current research seeks to establish new ways of understanding the city as a *dynamic luminal image* in order to help identify what is really at stake when the sun goes down.

Esther Leslie is Professor of Political Aesthetics at Birkbeck. Her books include Hollywood Flatlands: Animation, Critical Theory and the Avant Garde (Verso, 2002); Synthetic Worlds: Nature, Art and the Chemical Industry (Reaktion, 2005); Derelicts: Thought Worms from the Wreckage (Unkant, 2014), Liquid Crystals: The Science and Art of a Fluid Form (Reaktion, 2016) and Deeper in the Pyramid (with Melanie Jackson: Banner Repeater, 2018).

Douglas Murphy is an architect and writer living in London. He is the author of *The Architecture of Failure* (Zero Books, 2012) and the recently published *Last Futures* (Verso, 2016), a study of technology and nature in post-war architectural avant-gardes.

Jean-Luc Nancy is the author of *La communauté désoeuvrée* (translated as *The Inoperative Community*, 1991) and has also published books on Heidegger, Kant, Hegel and Descartes. One of the main themes in his work is the question of our being together in contemporary society.

Laura Oldfield Ford is a London-based artist and writer concerned with issues surrounding contemporary political protest, urbanism, architecture and memory. Since graduating from the RCA in 2007 she has become well known for her politically active and poetic engagement with London as a site of social antagonism. She is the author of *Savage Messiah*.

Steve Pile is Professor of Human Geography with the Open University. His research centres on the relations between places and power. He is author of *Real Cities* (2005) and *The Body and The City* (1996), and editor, with Paul Kingsbury, of *Psychoanalytic Geographies* (2014). He is currently working on early Freudian psychoanalysis and geographies of the body.

Peter Sheppard Skærved is a Grammy-nominated soloist and dedicatee of over 400 works for violin. He performs worldwide, and has recorded over 70 CDs of music from the 17th century to our own time. He is the Viotti Lecturer in Performance Studies at the Royal Academy of Music, and works with museums worldwide.

James Smith is an architectural designer based in London at the Royal College of Art. Previously, he studied at the University of Cambridge before working in Berlin. His interests lie in the role of architectures beyond the physical at the dawn of the anthropocene.

Phil Smith (Crab Man, Mytho) is a performance-maker, writer, ambulatory researcher and a core member of Wrights & Sites. His publications include *The Footbook of Zombie Walking* and *Walking's New Movement* (2015), *On Walking, Enchanted Things*, and the novel *Alice's Dérives in Devonshire* (2014), *Counter-Tourism: The Handbook* (2012) and *Mythogeography* (2010).

Tom Spooner is a London-based illustrator, writer and lecturer. His practice is driven by a fascination with the urban landscape, the socio-political structures of public space, and ideas surrounding place. Walking-based praxis and observational drawing initiatives take the fore in his approach to image making and study of the built environment.

Peter St John is a founding partner at Caruso St John Architects. The practice came to public attention in 1995 with the New Art Gallery Walsall. In 2013 Caruso St John completed the first phase of the masterplan for the restoration, refurbishment and extension of Tate Britain.

Jo Stockham is an artist and Professor of Printmaking at the RCA. She has exhibited widely and undertaken research residencies at Kettle's Yard (1989) The Mead Gallery (1997), Yaddo, New York (2001) and Wimbledon Centre for Drawing (2007).

Richard Wentworth is a chronicler of daily life. His extensive archive of photographs, *Making Do and Getting By* (1974 onwards), captures the provisional ways in which people modify the world they inhabit.

Index

Index of Places

Acknowledgements

We would like to thank our contributors for their involvement in *Walking Cities: London*. We would also like to thank the Research Office and the School of Fine Art at the Royal College of Art, under the stewardship of Dr. Emma Wakelin and Professor Juan Cruz, The Faculty of Architecture and The Built Environment at the University of Westminster, in particular Professor Lindsay Bremner and Professor Harry Charrington and The Royal Academy of Music for their support. Samuel Jones, Flaminia Rossi and Eilis Searson at Camberwell Press have all worked beyond the call of duty to produce a beautifully designed and inspiring publication. Harriet Edwards and Irene Auerbach have provided invaluable support with proof reading and Christine Shuttleworth has helped enormously by providing us with an excellent index which has been extended for this volume. We would also like to thank the National Archive of Scotland for the generous permission to include their maps in our publication and Southwark Sunshine for permission to include images from their archive.

UNIVERSITY OF
HEART
OF LONDON
WESTMINSTER

Walking Cities: **London**

SECOND EDITION

Editors
Jaspar Joseph-Lester
Simon King
Amy Blier-Carruthers
Roberto Bottazzi

Special Adviser
Professor Ahuvia Kahane

Copy Editor
Harriet Edwards

Indexer
Christine Shuttleworth

Design
Camberwell Press
Samuel Jones
Flaminia Rossi
Eilis Searson
James Edgar

Inside Cover
Front: Richard Wentworth, *Barnsbury, London, 2008*
Back: Richard Wentworth, *Bloomsbury, London, 2007*

First edition 2016
Second edition 2020